2009

G O L D R O A D
Arizona

On

Historic Route 66

THE *Golden* YEARS 1937–1942

*Personal Glimpses
and
Insights of Life Lived In The Gold Mining Camps of
Goldroad, Oatman, Katherine & Cyclopic*

REMEMBRANCES

of

NORMA JEAN RICHARDS YOUNT

I

Goldroad
Arizona
On
Historic Route 66
THE *Golden* YEARS 1937-1942

The fragmented sentences and unusual punctuation
and words were intentional. They help tell the story
the way the author wanted it told.

For information or additional copies:
Norma Richards Yount
Phone 1-480-888-1217
Cell 480-688-2754
nryount@cox.net

Published by Aardvark Global Publishing

ISBN 978-1-4276-3852-6

D e d i c a t i o n

Dedicated to my father and my mother who will always be remembered, and who tried so very hard to measure up—and did;

To my daughters, grandchildren, great-grandchildren, and those who come after, I write these memories with the hope that what I have written will show them that imperfect people, who live in an imperfect world, who honor their commitments in their everyday lives by doing the ordinary mundane things required of them, will produce posterity who will also honor their commitments;

Also, to those very special people who shared their lives with me in that never-to-be-forgotten place—Goldroad, Arizona;

****

"This is a story that needs to be told. I am glad you are doing it. I worked with Leo Duriez on a daily basis for four years, and he was a good man. Goldroad was a very happy time in my life—a lot of good people lived there."
----- Morris Bird, Timekeeper/Accountant--1937-1942-----

"Goldroad was the happiest time of my childhood. My father made more money in Goldroad than he had ever made in his life"
-----Joan Bird, My Best Friend-----

"My happiest memories are in Goldroad. I look back and am amazed at the good people who lived there."
-----John Sayer, My First Boyfriend-----

"Have intended to answer your dear letter which I have put in our treasure box. We love all your family. Leo always speaks highly of your father—and how much he helped him around the mine."
----- Mrs.Leo H.Duriez-----
Wife of Goldroad Manager
Letter of 24 March 1974

"We were poor, but we didn't know it".
-----Cloyd Henline-----

And, finally, to my equal partner—Richard Yount—who really made it possible for me to write this book.
III

THE BILL RICHARDS
FAMILY
1942

Bill and Lillian Richards

Billy - Age 8   Norma - Age 11   Vella - Age 13

Contents

Contents

INTRODUCTION

That day in early November, 1942, when our family loaded into our 1937 Nash and filled the gas tank for the last time at the Dunton Standard station in Goldroad, I was excited and anticipating the new experiences awaiting us at the United States Smelting Refining & Mining Company's new operation at the Bullfrog Shaft in Vanadium, New Mexico. We were to live in Silver City, about a fifteen mile drive from the mine, while we and the other transferred supervisors waited for our homes to be built in Vanadium.

I adjusted and fit in quickly with my new home, school, and friends in Silver City, and felt happy, but at intervals the same dream would reoccur. In this dream, I would be sobbing uncontrollably and saying, "I want to go back to Goldroad!" This dream continued over a period of years, but I never dwelt on it nor thought too much about it as I went about my life.

But as the years passed, I found I still carried a deep love for Goldroad—its beautiful mountains I had played on, and the very special, good people who lived there who were so much a part of my life. I carried a longing to go back, but never had the opportunity until 1957 when I was twenty-six, married and had one daughter. When we pulled our car around the mountain on the look-out point at Sitgreaves Pass, and I got out of the car and walked over to the edge of the road and looked down at the part of Goldroad I could see, tears came welling to my eyes, and I cried with the same joy one experiences after having been separated from a loved one for a long period of time. It had been fifteen years—I was home.

This is my reason for writing the book, *Goldroad, Arizona on Historic Route 66*—love and appreciation, and to let those who care enough to read it know what really happened in Goldroad—to put faces and lives on the people who played in the mountains; worked in the mine, mill, and shops; pumped the gas; sold the groceries; taught in the school, and were mothers in the homes—who all did their jobs so very well.

In talking with a few of the people who lived in Goldroad, two common threads have been found in all of their remembrances, whether they were children at the time or adults. These common threads were, it was the happiest time of their lives, and the goodness of the people who lived there.

INTRODUCTION

Morris Bird expressed his feelings by saying, "This is a story that needs to be told. I am glad you are doing it. I worked with Leo Duriez on a daily basis for four years, and he was a good man. It was because of the loyalty the men had to him that kept the CIO from organizing them. Not one out of four hundred miners joined, and that was unbelievable to the men in Oatman who were very strong CIO members.

Leo Duriez, Manager of Goldroad Mine

"Candelario Mendez, who was a small man, and Matias Calderon, who was a large man, were general mine foremen, and they can be given credit for the peaceful atmosphere in Mexican town. Goldroad was a very happy time in my life—a lot of good people lived there."

Joan Bird, my best friend and niece of Morris Bird, said, "Goldroad was the happiest time of my childhood. My father made more money in Goldroad than he had ever made in his life."

My first boyfriend, John Sayer, said, "My happiest memories are in Goldroad. I look back and am amazed at the good people who lived there. One time I went back and cried as I sifted through the dirt where our house had once stood. Because I have decided to be cremated, I have thought seriously about having my urn buried somewhere in Goldroad."

INTRODUCTION

When Cloyd Henline and I discussed our remembrances of Goldroad—the *outside plumbing* of many of the houses, the simple forms of entertainment we enjoyed—his comment was this, "We were poor, but we didn't know it." However, it must be noted we were not alone in this, the entire world was also poor during this time, even the miners in faraway Cornwall, England were feeling the effects of this worldwide depression.

Perhaps, because Cloyd was born and raised on a ranch in Oregon on the eastside of the Cascades where there was no ethnic mixture, he was impressed by the ethnic diversity found in Goldroad.

By living and working there, he felt he gained a better concept of people. One man he still considered a good friend was Augustine Rameriz.

Although the Goldroad mining force was made up almost totally of Mexicans recruited from the Fierro, New Mexico, area where Mr. Duriez had been located in the late 1920s, before the Great Depression closed the mines in that area in 1930, Goldroad had its snowbirds. They were miners who would come rustling a job in the fall and leave in the spring for the mines in Colorado before the weather became extreme. These miners were a mixture of *Cousin Jacks* (Cornish), Russians, and Slavs.

In writing this story, it has not been my intention to portray anyone in an unfavorable light or to hurt, but to present life in Goldroad honestly and accurately as seen through the eyes of a small girl.

The Mexican people who lived in Goldroad, and who were so much a part of my everyday life, were not purposefully omitted from my recollections. But, this omission is due to the social structure of the era in which we lived with regard to Mexicans and Anglos. They were physically segregated from my life except for the experiences we shared at school. Those people in Goldroad who had come from other parts of the country—the mid-west, Oregon, Utah—felt the social structure in Goldroad represented a caste system. But it was not something they openly expressed their opinion on or tried to do anything about. If they had, whether school teacher or company employee, they probably would have been fired.

INTRODUCTION

To those of us who had been born and raised in Arizona and New Mexico, and had grown up with the system of segregation between Mexican and Anglo, it was accepted, not questioned.

Mrs. Sayer, and I do not know who else was involved, created quite a stir in Goldroad when the Girl Scout Troop was first organized and it was opened up to Mexican girls as well as Anglo.

When I spoke with Madeline Plummer about Goldroad a few years ago, she mentioned the caste system in Goldroad. But I had never known anything else. From my earliest memories in Solomonsville, Arizona, there had been a Mexican town. But the system was not as far reaching in Goldroad as it was in the New Mexico mining area where we were transferred in 1942. Separate schools until high school were the norm. Seating in the theaters was segregated by an invisible center line—Mexicans on one side and Anglos on the other. In Santa Rita and Hurley, large company mining towns in the area, not only segregated schools and theaters existed, but there were separate social clubs, complete with swimming pools, tennis courts and bowling alleys, for Mexican and Anglo.

They all—Silver City, Santa Rita, Bayard, Hurley—had their Mexican towns, as did Vanadium where United States Smelting, Refining & Mining Co. (USSR&MCo) built our homes. The Mexican town the company built was down the hill from our Anglo houses.

But by the early 1960s, at the time Vella Richards and Rosie Hernandez were married and lived as neighbors at the USSR&MCo in New Mexico, the mine was no longer operating and company houses were rented to Anglos as well as Mexicans. This was a large step toward desegregation. But Anglos and Mexicans were still not socially mixing, although Vella and Rosie's young daughters played together. And over the years—through the use of education by the Mexican people—Mexicans and Anglos have begun to mix socially more in this area of New Mexico.

Thus, old customs, whether right or wrong, die hard.

Chapter 1

A Safe Harbor In A Terrible Storm

Mr. Duriez told the man to find my father and tell him he had a job for him in Goldroad.

"This is one place I wouldn't want to live!"

These are the words spoken by my mother as she drove through Goldroad in early 1937 with friends on her way to Needles, California.

Why would anyone want to live in such a place as this—an isolated mining camp set on the sides and tops of boulder-strewn mountains, bereft of all green vegetation except greasewood and an array of desert plants which thrived in the hot, dry climate. A place so hot, Phoenix at noonday in mid-summer seemed an oasis in comparison. Why would people huddle together in this seemingly hostile place where most of the houses were relics from a past of openings and closings and were below the normal standard of the people now occupying them.

Goldroad was made up of people like my family. People who had been raised well, and had lived well themselves, until the terror of the Great Depression hit sweeping them helplessly along with it. Leaving them confused as to how they were going to find jobs to feed, clothe, and shelter their families, and feeling, for the first time, the fear of not knowing when, or if, there would be another paycheck, and all the time desperately looking for jobs which were not there.

These are the people who looked beyond the physical appearance of Goldroad and saw in it an opportunity for the first time in five or six years to have a steady job and a place to settle their family, knowing they now had a way to provide for them—Goldroad was that place—a safe harbor in a terrible storm.

All of these feelings were a part of me the spring day, March 10, 1937, when my father took me with him to Goldroad to seek out Leo Duriez, the Manager. He had sent word to my father in Kingman by a Mexican man, who was a mutual friend, that he had a job for him in Goldroad.

My little five-year-old heart just soaked up a feeling of security and well-being as I played contentedly on the office steps while I waited for

A Safe Harbor In A Terrible Storm

Daddy to emerge from the office. I felt safe and secure, and it was almost as if I drew those feelings from the high, protective walls the mountains created around me, the friendly efforts by the Mexican man to engage me in talk as he worked on the rock wall in front of the office; and the genuine feelings of respect and friendship I saw expressed between Daddy and Leo Duriez when they emerged from the office together and greeted me on the steps—I bonded with Goldroad that day. And, these many years later I still return to its safe harbor when life beats me around, and it is there I draw deep on the memories and feelings indelibly stamped in me by the mountains and by the people who lived there.

Goldroad Arizona 1938

A Safe Harbor In A Terrible Storm

This is the story of some of the families who, with us, the Bill Richards family, found this safe harbor. They were: the Bill Sayer family, the Leo H. Duriez family, the Paris V. Brough family, the Cloyd Henline family, the Joe B. Peeples family, the Bert Rindlisbach family, the Don Massey family, the Kirby family, the Tom Redding family, the Lamar Bird family, the Morris Bird family, the Floyd Bird family, the Bill Doolin family, the Gale Cudney family, the Bill Hicks family, the Alice Plummer family, the George Marich family, the Pete Kristich family, the George Phillips family, and the Walt Elgin family. Other families came to Goldroad, but these are the ones who indelibly stamped their life upon my life and from whom I have drawn strength, security and peace.

Daddy graduated from high school at Tempe Normal School in Tempe, Arizona, which is now Arizona State University. Although at this time he could have taught school, he chose not to do this. He never explained this decision to me. Instead, in 1922 he went to work for the Southern Pacific Railroad and worked there until November 8, 1926, when he received word of his father's death. In his grief and haste, everything he could not get into one large, black suitcase was left in his living quarters in a railroad car pulled off on a siding. Included in those items left behind were his tools, which he never returned to get.

It was on this job where he learned about electricity. He had never liked electricity. But he had decided, after losing his job at the USSR&MCo in Fierro, New Mexico, losing the service station-garage in Solomonsville, Arizona, and passing from one short-term-going-nowhere-job to another because of the Depression—if he was going to be able to support his wife and three children, he had to have a job that would do this—and electricity was it. When our family left Safford, Arizona, the Christmas of 1936, and went to Kingman, Arizona, his first job was climbing power poles stringing electric lines with a crew. He received ten dollars a day for ten hours of work. That was good money. The electric company in Kingman had offered him a job after construction of the power lines was completed, but before this could happen, Leo Duriez sent the man to find Daddy in Kingman to offer him the job in Goldroad.

Daddy decided to take the job in Goldroad, because he felt it would be the best thing for his family, and it was. Daddy later had many opportunities to go with other companies that appeared to offer more opportunity, but he stayed with the USSR&MCo, because he felt it provided a more stable life for his children.

Safe Harbor In A Terrible Storm

Our first house in Goldroad was owned by Mrs. Joseph Onetto, Flora. Prior to this we had lived in the *Boulder City* house in Kingman owned by Auntie and Uncle Joe. The man who had directed Daddy to Goldroad and Mr. Duriez, had worked in Fierro, New Mexico, with my father five years previously. He had seen my father on the street in Kingman, and the next day when he went to his job in Goldroad he told Mr. Duriez he had seen Bill Richards. Mr. Duriez told the man to find my father and tell him he had a job for him in Goldroad.

My father had worked for Mr. Duriez in Fierro, New Mexico, for several years until 1931 or 1932, when the operation closed due to the Depression sweeping the country. Joe Peeples had also known Daddy in Fierro. He and his wife Ethel and daughter Shirley were now living in Goldroad, and he was now Cashier.

At this time, Daddy was not hired as Chief Electrician—Charlie Claunch held that position—but Daddy was hired with the understanding he would be given this position when Charlie completed the trailer he was building to haul his household goods out of Goldroad. We would then move into the house on the hill where Charlie lived.

Until that time, Daddy did all types of electrical work for the company, and many nights he would come home from climbing power poles with oversized slivers of wood in his arms and legs. This would happen when his climbing spikes would slip out of the pole, and he would slide down until he either stopped himself by reinserting the hooks into the pole or by hitting the ground. Each evening Mother would patiently dig out the slivers with a needle. But a large one on the inside of his left arm was never retrieved. My parents were a little concerned it would work itself into a blood vessel and eventually find its way to his heart.

Because of the limited experience Daddy had with electricity at the Southern Pacific Railroad, he spent many evenings while we lived at the Onetto house studying the three large red electrical textbooks he had purchased through a mail order company. They were part of an electrical course he had paid for but had never pursued further. The books interested me, and as I looked through them at various times, I found slips of paper where Daddy had drawn circuits for electrical installations he had made in the mill or mine.

The Mexican houses in Goldroad did not have electricity. Some were already built, and others were in the process of being built when Daddy arrived. But he eventually wired all of them for electricity. They were privately owned houses. He would go down to Mexican town after he got off work at 4:00 p.m. and wire these houses. I always went with him.

4.

Safe Harbor In A Terrible Storm

And, sometimes my sister Vella would go. If the family had children, I would play with them in the yard while Daddy worked.

Coming from an environment where only English was spoken, the first time I went to a Mexican home with Daddy, their language confused me. I could not understand the Mexican they spoke, and because I could not understand them, I assumed if I garbled my words, they would be able to understand me. How wrong I was! They giggled and did not know what to think.

After arriving home, I asked Daddy why I could not understand their talk. He told me it was because they were speaking Mexican—a different language than what we spoke. At that time, Daddy could speak Mexican, but he became more proficient as he worked with the Mexican miners. The owners of the houses he wired paid him two or three dollars for his work. Two or three dollars does not sound like much money now, but Daddy was earning about one hundred fifty dollars a month, plus overtime, for eight hours a day, seven days a week. This amount paid for wiring a house was not out of line. And the extra money was welcome in helping him care for his wife and three small children.

MEXICAN TOWN
Fortner's Store White Building Upper Right
Catholic Church White Building Upper Center
(Courtesy of Mohave County Historical Society)

Safe Harbor In A Terrible Storm

While we were still living in Kingman, and after Daddy got the job in Goldroad, Mother purchased a 1937 silver Nash Lafayette.

Mother bought the Nash without Daddy being with her. He had not been able to make a decision about a car but had been hoping they somehow could get a Buick. Mother knew there was no way we could afford a Buick at that time. And, we were in dire need of a car as ours had been left at the ranch in the Hualapai Mountains. After the shock had passed of seeing his wife and children drive up in a new car to pick him up at work, he accepted the purchase of the Nash very well.

However, the car did have one engineering flaw—the fan required a periodic squirt of oil to keep it operating properly. But, Daddy could never seem to remember to give it that one squirt of oil before it refused to run. We were stranded a number of times between Goldroad and Kingman. The simple solution to the problem would have been to keep a can of oil in the trunk for such emergencies, but this never happened. Instead, in one such emergency, Mother's expensive jar of facial oil that had been left in the car was used to lubricate the fan. The choice between the prized oil and being stranded was a difficult one for Mother to make, but in reality she never had a choice. The critical need for the use of her oil did not diminish Mother's annoyance with Daddy because of his failure to oil the fan before we left home.

Lillian and Bill Richards-1937 Nash

6.

Chapter 2

The Onetto House

This was a unique house, even by Goldroad's standard.

Flora Onetto was the wife of Joe Onetto, a former manager of Goldroad during another opening. He had died a short time before we arrived there.

Mrs. Onetto rented out several houses she and her husband had acquired from previous mine operations. Our first house in Goldroad was rented from her. This was a unique house, even by Goldroad's standard.

It had two roofs–both were corrugated tin. The two roofs made the house cooler, but the lizards and other creatures also liked this cool, shaded area. Our parents were annoyed by the sounds they made in the ceiling above us, but Vella, Billy and I were always excited when we heard them scurrying around. The tin roof also made a comforting sound when rain from the infrequent storms hit it.

The house had a full-length screened porch on two sides–south and east– from the roof to the floor. Another cooling feature of the house was the Virginia Creeper vines that grew on chicken wire enclosing the front yard from the ground to the top of the screened porch and over the yard to the edge of the porch.

Mother used a small electric fan during Billy's nap to keep him cool. She moistened a dishtowel, placed it over the front of the fan and the cooled air blew over him. The towel remained moist long enough for Billy to get to sleep. Once he was asleep and the towel had dried, the heat did not seem to bother him.

The fan was rarely used except for this purpose. Most of the time our family was too busy with other projects to sit in one spot to enjoy its breeze.

We constantly played at something while Mother's time was filled with the chores of keeping a family of five fed, bathed and in clean, ironed clothes. She was fortunate to be young, twenty-six at the time, because every job was made more difficult by the old-fashioned equipment she had to use—a tub and scrub board instead of a washing machine; an electric iron without a thermostat; a broom rather than a vacuum cleaner; a cool- box made from burlap and a chicken wire rather than a refrigerator.

The Onetto House

The Onetto house had two cook stoves—one was a wood stove and the other was coal oil or kerosene. Mother used both—the wood stove when Daddy remembered to chop some wood, and the kerosene stove when he had not. When our stove ran low on fuel, Mother sent Vella and me to the Standard Station to buy more. She sent us with a small, metal container that had a spout. In order to keep the kerosene from sloshing out of the spout as we carried it home, Mother would push a small potato over the opening.

Many people in Goldroad went to the Colorado River to get mesquite wood for their stoves. The river was about ten miles away. It was also a good place for a picnic or fishing. All along its banks the area was covered with trees providing a good cover from the sun.

Several families, including the Sayers, had a picnic one evening in the trees by the river after the men got off work at 4:00 P.M. The adults enjoyed talking and also eating the good food brought by the women while the kids filled their time with playing.

Mr. Sayer took a few minutes away from the adults to teach us an Army song. It went like this, "I had a good home but I left, I left, I had a good wife but I left, I left," etc. We sang the words over and over again and added new ones as we marched around. The point of the song was to always be on your left foot when the song said left. When night set in and it was too dark to see, everything was packed up and we went home.

Clothes were washed on a rub board with water heated outside on an open fire in a wash tub filled with a bucket from the kitchen sink.

Mother's red, electric iron without the thermostat had to be watched carefully and unplugged before it reached the point of scorching the clothes. She had mastered this technique. Occasionally though, after much nagging, Mother would allow me to iron the handkerchiefs or the pillowcases. Needless to say, many times after I had ironed they would be put away with the scorched imprint of an iron on them. This was due to my inexperience and my concentration on ironing out the wrinkles while forgetting to check the heat of the iron.

Due to the age of the house, the wooden floors were difficult to sweep with the broom. I know linoleum was on some of the floors, but others were exposed wood. The large screened-porch had bare wooden floors and were difficult to sweep.

Our family slept winter and summer on the screened-porch. This was our bedroom. Sleeping outside year around did not cause any discomfort from the cold because of the mild winters in Goldroad.

The Onetto House

One winter Mother tied a quilt for each of our beds. She laid out the dark blue flannel material on the floor. Over this she unrolled the cotton batting, then placed matching material over the batting. She threaded heavy, red twine through an over-sized needle and with large stitches sewed all of it together over the entire quilt. The twine was then cut in the proper places and tied in square knots. The edges were turned under in a seam and sewed together.

Flora Onetto, wife of Joe Onetto, on steps of the "Onetto house"
(Courtesy of Mohave County Historical Society)

The bed where Vella and I slept had an old-fashioned wrought iron headboard, and a mattress stuffed with straw or something that made it very hard. The mattress was laid on horizontal, not coil, springs. The bed was high off the floor, and I soon learned, after a fall or two, to wake up and catch myself before I fell completely out of bed–it was a long fall to the floor!

The Onetto House

Our parents' bed was placed head-to-head with ours. My younger brother Billy was only two-and-a-half years old when we arrived in Goldroad, so he slept in a small bed at the foot of their bed.

Mrs. Onetto owned the beds, the cot in the living room, and the two stoves. Two oak rocking chairs and two oak library tables, which had belonged to Mother's grandmother, and our large radio with legs furnished our living room. The inside bedroom was not used but held a brass double bed Mother had painted an off-white color. A nightstand made from a wooden orange crate stood on end and was decorated with a dusty rose skirt. The skirt was made from an old curtain she had dyed with Rit, and the bedspread was dyed to match.

Our dining room was a separate room but was open to the living room and had doors leading into both the kitchen and the bathroom. The dining room was where we ate our meals, although the kitchen had a small table.

Every meal we ate in the dining room had a pattern to it. We would all sit down to dinner. Billy would become angry because his bread was not buttered properly. Daddy would take the bread and say, "How does Daddy's little man want his bread buttered? Like this?" No, Daddy's little man did not want his bread buttered like this. Billy would yell and under the table he would go. Daddy would try coaxing him to get him out from under the table by saying, "Well, does Daddy's little man want it buttered this way?" More yells and fussing from under the table and still no little man would emerge. Daddy would then try every possible way a piece of bread could be buttered, and, of course, none pleased Billy. After five or ten minutes of this noise and fussing, Mother would take over and run Billy outside while we finished our dinner in peace. But no sooner would Billy get outside than he would start calling, "Ba Ba (Vella Mae), ask Mama if I can come back in. Tell her I'll be good." Then Vella would coax Mother to let him come back inside to finish his dinner.

After a little coaxing, Mother would always allow him to come back. He would be good for the remainder of the meal, eating his buttered bread the way Daddy had last buttered it before he was sent outside. But every night we had to go through this ritual at the dinner table. Billy finally outgrew it when he was four or five, but I dreaded mealtime because of the disruption we had each night.

The Onetto House

Billy Richards at the Onetto House–2 ½ years old–before haircut

We used the old furniture in the Onetto house and the few family pieces we had, because all of our bedroom sets, upholstered chairs and couch had been left behind in our house in Safford, Arizona, when Daddy and Mother, Vella and Billy left for Kingman the Christmas of 1936. I was already on the Newberry Ranch in the Hualapai Mountains just east of Kingman with Auntie and Uncle Joe. They had brought me back with them on their return from a trip to Safford, Arizona, on business.

Our family had struggled in Safford. Daddy had held several jobs since leaving the USSR&MCo in Fierro. The first was a garage he and his brother, Tom, bought in Solomonsville. Uncle Tom was the mechanic, and Daddy did tire repair, miscellaneous jobs, and the pumping of the gas—and you really did need to pump the gas out of the underground gas tanks into the glass tank at the top of the gas pump to fill the car's gas tank!

They lost the garage because Daddy was too tender-hearted when people needing gas or repairs would ask for credit. Everyone was struggling to make a living, and he felt sorry for the customers when they did not have the money to pay him. And, Uncle Tom could not be depended upon to stay at the station to run it when it was his turn to man the station. I can remember as a two-year-old child driving by the station with Mother and Daddy when he was supposed to have the station open, and hearing their expressions of disbelief, dismay and frustration when they discovered the garage, which appeared to be open for business because the lights were on, and the doors were open. But Uncle Tom was no where to be found.

11.

The Onetto House

After losing the garage, Daddy took whatever job he could find—he worked a short time as a draftsman for the Soil Conservation Corp in Safford, and was selling Watkins products when Auntie and Uncle Joe took me to the Newberry Rarch in the Hualapai Mountains southeast of Kingman.

By this time, Mother had taken a job at the Gila Laundry in Safford where we had moved sometime before Billy was born. Vella, Billy and I were left with a babysitter. Vella was at school most of the day, Billy was a baby in a kiddy-coop, and I was a very curious and busy four-year-old. After some time, my parents discovered the babysitter had not been treating me very well. But they did not know I had seen her boot Vel out the back door when she tried to make a peanut butter sandwich after school.

So, they made plans for me to stay with Auntie and Uncle Joe on the Newberry Ranch until Christmas when they would come to get me. However, shortly after their arrival at the ranch, a huge snowstorm hit the area, and we were snowed in for a month. The snow was up over the eaves of the ranch house, and a path that was over my head was dug to get to the outhouse. Snow was melted in a pan on the wood stove for our water.

When wood for the stoves got low, Daddy and Uncle Joe saddled two horses and found a dead tree. They dynamited the tree and dragged it back to the house for our firewood. At least once when our food supply got low, they rode horseback into Kingman to get a few groceries.

As the snow began to melt a little, huge icicles formed and hung from the roof of the house. An adult would pull one down for me, and I would chew and suck on it until it was gone. Playing in the huge snowdrift by the back door was another fun activity the snow provided.

When the snow was finally melted down a little, and the ground was still firm and the creeks were not yet swollen from the melting snow, we left the ranch and moved into a motel on Route 66 in Kingman. All of us rode in Auntie and Uncle Joe's car. Their car was newer than ours, and it was risky enough getting one car out over the narrow, windy road.

Mother was anxious to get our family moved from the motel and spent many days looking for a house to rent. She felt discouraged by her lack of success. No one wanted to rent to a family with three small children.

This attitude upset Mother. She had never allowed us to be destructive in any homes we had lived in whether our own or rented.

The Onetto House

Norma Jean Richards–5 years old–visiting at ranch of friends of Auntie and Uncle Joe while living on the Newberry Ranch in the Hualapais

About this time Auntie and Uncle Joe decided to buy a lot with three houses on it. One of the houses had been moved in from Boulder City, Nevada, where the Hoover Dam had just been completed. These houses were scattered throughout Mojave County and were easily identified by their box shape and white paint. We moved out of the motel into their Boulder City house, and it would forever be identified in our family as the Boulder City house. It was this house where we were living when his old friend from Fierro spotted Daddy on the street. My parents never returned to Safford to retrieve their furniture or anything they had left there.

The Onetto House

The one celebration we had with Auntie and Uncle Joe in the Boulder City house taught me a lesson I have never forgotten. The lesson involved a special fruit salad Auntie always made at Thanksgiving and Christmas and other special holidays. And even though times were hard, and we were still struggling through the hard economic times of the Depression, the salad was being prepared for this special dinner.

Mother and Auntie were in the kitchen busily preparing our dinner when a knock came at the door. Auntie answered. There stood a little Mexican man with a gunnysack. He was begging food for his own family's dinner. Without a word or any hesitation, my great aunt turned on her heel and went straight to the table where the ingredients for the fruit salad lay. She picked out the choice fruit from the table and gave it to him. The lesson she taught me that day, without saying a word, was this—you always give away the best you have.

Years later I realized she was living what the Savior said, "When ye have done it unto the least of these my brethren, ye have done it unto me." Now, each Thanksgiving and Christmas, our family prepares the same salad. This brings a part of Auntie into our celebration. She had a pure, childlike love of Christmas. Christmas was a special, happy time for her, and she retained this excitement until her last Christmas.

Sometime after we left the Newberry Ranch, Mother and Daddy, Auntie and Uncle Joe, Vella, Billy and I drove out to the Hualapais to get our car, clothes, furniture and dishes that had been left behind. We were unable to drive any closer to the ranch house than a mile or so away. The streams created by the melting snow had washed out the road too badly. The women and children waited in the car while Daddy and Uncle Joe walked the remainder of the way to the ranch house and carried out boxes in their arms with only the necessary items. Because of the gullies and ditches created by the run-off from the melting snow, walking was difficult and some of the dishes were broken as they were jostled about in the makeshift boxes as Daddy and Uncle Joe struggled to carry them to the waiting car. Among the broken dishes was the favorite white plate I always insisted on using at each meal. Because of the impossibility of getting any car over the road from the ranch house, Mother and Daddy left our car at the Newberry Ranch and never returned to get it.

Sometime later after we had moved to Goldroad, Uncle Joe and a partner re-opened a restaurant and dance hall located about five miles east of Kingman on Route 66. It was called The Desert Inn. In his new role as a business owner, Uncle Joe wore a dress shirt and tie–something I had never seen him in before.

The Onetto House

His friends and relatives had a nickname for him—the foxy grandpa!

They hired a band to play at The Desert Inn. Three of those members would remain family friends throughout our lives. When Uncle Joe was diagnosed with terminal cancer of the pancreas ten years later in Tucson, Arizona, where they were all living, those three members of this band—Billy and Betty Burke and Eldora Porter—would be a great support to him and our family.

Opening night our family went to the club. Billy Burke was on the electric guitar; Betty played bull base; Eldora played violin and her husband was on the guitar. The dance hall was an outdoor area. Outdoor dance halls were very common at this time. Air conditioning had not been developed and summer evenings were much cooler outside. Mother and Daddy danced, but there were few other customers.

Billy and Betty Burke Band–Picture taken in dining room of the Biltmore Hotel, Phoenix, Arizona, December 15, 1937–Billy in center–Betty on his right

The Onetto House

Slot machines were in several Kingman businesses at that time and I loved playing them. Mother would not provide the nickels—Auntie always did. She was a slot machine fan. The evening we were at the club, Auntie gave me a nickel. I put it in, pulled the handle and waited—not expecting any nickels to come out was I surprised when they began dropping out in such large numbers some hit the floor and rolled across the room! My excited cry was, "Look at all the nickels!" I excitedly retrieved all that I could find.

But the Desert Inn was a short-lived business venture for Uncle Joe. It closed within a month, and Uncle Joe went back to his normal jobs associated with the cattle business—one exception being a short time he tended bar at Dinty Moore's for Bert Claridge, a friend he had known earlier in Safford. The bar was located on the west side of the street just south of the Central Commercial.

For a time he was cattle inspector on the Hoover Dam. It was called the Boulder Dam until the Republicans regained the White House many years later with President Eisenhower. Auntie and Uncle Joe lived in an apartment the short time I visited with them in Boulder City, Nevada. They later moved into a house and I spent a few days there, also.

Uncle Joe took me to work with him every day. He had no office as cattle inspector, so we hung around all day with the rangers on the dam. They were tour guides for the trips the public took down inside the dam. Anytime I wanted to go they took me with them. It was much cooler inside the dam than standing in the hot sun on top of it. No visitor center or other facilities were available except rest rooms. Uncle Joe's job was to inspect the cattle for diseases when they were transported across the dam out of Nevada into Arizona.

Uncle Joe told me the story of a small dog that attempted to jump a short distance from one wall of the dam to the other. He lost his footing and fell down the face of the dam. The dog's owner ran to the elevator and was immediately taken to the bottom of the dam. She ran out on the platform at the base of the dam erroneously thinking she could retrieve her dog. But all she found was a small ball of fur.

Each evening on our way home from work, Uncle Joe stopped by Lake Mead to let me swim. Actually, I did not know how to swim. I just walked on the bottom and flapped my arms. Lake Mead at that time was the largest man-made lake in the United States. One time I decided to make my way to a wood raft anchored a short distance from me on the boundary of the roped-off swimming area. I literally got in over my head and had a terrible time getting back to shallow water. Uncle Joe had wandered off for a short time, and when he came back to get me for our trip home to Boulder City, I did not mention what had happened to me. But I had learned a lesson. On our next stops at the lake I stayed in shallower water.

During my stay, Auntie was grinding Uncle Joe's meals, because his teeth had all been pulled and he had not yet received his dentures.

One evening I heard Uncle Joe and Auntie discussing their finances. It seems they had a problem—more bills than money—a problem not unusual at this time in our country. They were deciding which bills had to be paid at that time—the butcher, the rent, and so on. After their discussion was over, Uncle Joe and I went to the grocery store where he bought meat and other items for our dinner. Several times he asked me if I wanted candy, but each time I told him "No." From their conversation I knew they were short of money, and it made me uncomfortable knowing they were spending money and had bills that needed to be paid.

At this time, he was also raffling his saddle by selling tickets among the other government dam workers.

Each day on the Arizona side of the canyon several workers performed a dangerous dam maintenance procedure. The workers were individually lowered by rope a distance down the perpendicular face of the canyon where each performed his work while attached to this rope. Because of the hazardous nature of the work, every precaution was taken to assure the maximum safety of the worker. One precaution was to discard the rope after only one use. Being the good cowboy that he was, it hurt Uncle Joe to see all that good lariat rope being thrown away, and he retrieved all he felt he could use.

While they lived in Boulder City, he and a friend visited Indian ruins in a canyon along the Colorado River. The hike was long and strenuous. Because many others had visited these ruins, what they found at the site was not worth the pain experienced in getting there.

At the Onetto house, the screen by my bed had a small opening near the bottom, and one night a kitten that had adopted me found the opening. Each night thereafter I would go quietly to the opening, gather the kitten in my arms, and carefully climb into bed hoping not to draw Mother's attention to what I was doing. The kitten became my bed partner for a time until Mother discovered small bumps on my neck and chest. When I told her I had been sleeping with the kitten each night, she assumed fleas from it had made the bumps. But I knew they were caused by the needle-sharp claws of the contented kitten as it purred in my arms each night and licked the salt from my neck.

17.

The Onetto House

I could sense a lack of conviction in Mother's tone of voice when she told me I was not to sleep with the kitten anymore, so I quietly continued retrieving her through the hole in the screen each night at bedtime.

Mother must have sensed the need I had for the company of the kitten, because she never said anything more about my sleeping with it. She knew of my love for animals, especially cats. My first purchase at age three in Safford had been buying a kitten from a small neighbor friend for a penny. Mother made me return it. I was heart broken.

The small bumps on my neck and chest made by the kitten were nothing compared to the huge welts on my arms and legs when I awoke. They were the work of Hualapai Tigers. We had never heard of Hualapai Tigers before moving to Goldroad. I might add we never encountered them after leaving the Onetto house. They must have been indigenous to Goldroad, but specifically to the Onetto houses, because when we moved on the hill, I was never bothered with them again. No one in our family ever saw a Hualapai Tiger while we were in the Onetto house and could not have identified one if we had seen one running around during the day.

But I was always grateful when I awoke in the morning and found I had been bitten by mosquitoes and not by Hualapi Tigers. Their bites not only itched, but they also hurt and remained for a much longer time than a mosquito bite. Frank Onetto, Flora Onetto's brother-in-law who shared the house next door, was an expert on Hualapai Tigers.   He told us we could keep them from biting us by placing newspaper on the floor by our bed each night. He never told us what the next step was after placing the newspaper on the floor, but I suppose it was to get up during the night, raise the newspaper and kill the Hualapai Tigers gathered there. No one in our family ever did this—maybe because I was the one who got most of the bites.

To cool down our drinking water in the summer, we placed it in a large clay ouija covered with burlap and hung under the eaves of the screened porch shaded by the Virginia Creeper vines. We used the ouija until we purchased our Sears Roebuck Cold Spot refrigerator. The refrigerator was sent in by truck from California and arrived in a wooden box.

There had been no ice to speak of for me since leaving the Newberry Ranch in the Hualapai Mountains, and I was eagerly anticipating the arrival of our new refrigerator. It conjured up visions of my own personal cache of icicles, but Mother popped my bubble when she set the rule regarding unnecessary openings and closings of the refrigerator door. We were not to get into the refrigerator to get ice—this would put a strain on the cooling unit and wear it out.

The Onetto House

Even with this rule and other precautions that were taken to help prolong the life of the refrigerator, our first refrigerator turned out to be a lemon.

After a short time of use, a new cooling unit had to be purchased to replace the defective one. This was an additional financial burden our family did not need. For many years, the name Cold Spot was associated in our minds with inferior products. Although my visions of all the ice I could eat did not materialize, the enjoyment Vella, Billy and I received from the refrigerator box more than made up for it. The box at times was a temporary home for orphaned chipmunks, a fort, a play house, and a hide out—depending on the need.

Before we purchased the refrigerator, our food was kept cool in a tall, rectangular-shaped box made by stretching chicken wire over four two-by-fours stood on end with burlap bags hung over the wire and kept wet with a running hose. It had a door and shelves inside and stood outside by the kitchen door.

The kitchen sink was also homemade and was metal welded together with the seams exposed. To wash our long hair, Mother would lay us on the drain board of the sink. We always complained loudly, because she did not wash our hair, she scrubbed our head. One time Babe Cudney, the wife of Gale Cudney, the mine foreman, washed our hair, and I was amazed at the difference in the two washings—Mother's hard scrub, and Babe's soft wash.

Although we bragged on Babe's soft wash and hoped Mother would adopt it, she was not swayed, and we continued to have our head scrubbed.

Because the water in Goldroad was very soft, Mother used 100% Spanish Castile soap on our hair, which made our hair shine beautifully. Putting the bar of soap into a pan of water and cooking it until the bar melted made the shampoo. A few of our friends' mothers commented on the shine of our hair and asked how Mother did it. We were always eager to share the formula.

The clear 100% Spanish Castile soap was purchased at the Oatman Drug Store. I looked forward to our trips there, because we always sat at the fountain on the high stools and had a cherry coke. The ice in the cherry coke and the overhead-ceiling fan made for a very refreshing and cooling experience—a short respite from the heavy heat. Mother and her friends would linger at the fountain talking and drinking their cokes. We didn't mind because the stools swiveled around, and, if we were very quiet and turned very slowly, Mother would allow us this diversion. On very rare occasions Mother would buy an ice cream cone for us to eat in the car. But, getting it eaten in the 110+ degree heat before it melted was a very big challenge.

The Onetto House

That is probably why the ice cream cones were rare occasions—Mother did not like the mess they created. And, to make matters worse, I always bit the bottom out of my cone, and the melting ice cream ran not only from the top of the cone, but from the bottom as well!

The Oatman Drug Store also served as the telephone office. It was on the second floor of the building. During high school, June Henline, who later became Cloyd Henline's wife, was the night operator for the town of Oatman. She slept in the office and took all night calls coming through the switchboard.

The Onetto house had a bathroom. It really was a *bath* room, because all it had was a bathtub and a sink and medicine chest. There was no water heater in the house. During the summertime, the water coming out of the faucet was warm enough for us to bathe comfortably. In winter a small electrical device ordered by Mother from a magazine ad heated our bath water. The heater was placed in the water and then plugged into the electrical outlet. Of course we never got into the tub with the heater, but I often wonder how we escaped electrocution from just standing near the metal tub while the water was warmed. We had been cautioned by Mother never to get into the tub with the heater or to touch the tub when it was on. What amazes me is that we never did either of these things.

The electrical outlets in the house were open sockets where the plug was screwed in, not pushed. When young children of crawling and toddler age were in the house, there was a temptation to put fingers or toys into these open sockets. The electrical wires were strung outside the baseboards and wall to the ceiling where the light sockets were attached. A wood stove in the living room was the only source of heat for the house—no central heating there.

Due to the absence of a toilet in the bathroom, we used an outhouse located up the hill from the kitchen door. Our outhouse had the standard toilet paper of the day–a discarded Sears Roebuck or Monkey Ward catalog. Our family had come from homes with inside plumbing, so this outhouse was a new experience for us. My parents had used them as children, because nothing else was available at the time, but since their marriage, indoor plumbing had been in their homes until the Onetto house experience.

But my parents accepted all of these inconveniences without complaint. They were grateful for the good job Daddy had and knew the inconveniences were temporary until our move to the house on the hill.

The Onetto House

One fun thing about the outhouse, though, was being allowed to take a lighted candle to see our way when we used it after dark. Sometimes I would let the wax drip into my hand and roll it into a small ball. Then I would run a threaded needle through the balls and make either a bracelet or necklace for play. I even made an attempt at painting them with my bright red fingernail polish.

Our chicken coop was attached to one side of the outhouse. During the day when I could not coax Vella or Billy to make the trip to the outhouse with me, the clucking of the hens as they scratched in the dirt by the half-open door comforted and bolstered my courage as I sat there. Just as long as I could hear something alive I was not afraid. The chickens really became my friends because of the comfort they gave me.

One of the chickens scratching outside the outhouse door was a large, magnificent white rooster I had received at Easter when he was just a small green chick. Even though the rooster's feathers had become a brilliant white, his ears still carried traces of the green used to dye him while he was a chick.

The rooster had been played with like a doll all of his life. I dressed him in doll clothes, wrapped him in a blanket, and carried him like a baby. One time I nagged my mother until she allowed him to spend the night in the house perched on the legs of the radio. Needless to say, this was a one-time experience for the rooster. In the morning when Mother saw the droppings he had left during the night, he spent the remainder of his nights with the other chickens in the hen house.

One day when I was bent over by the kitchen door petting another chicken, the pain of the rooster's sharp claws on my back surprised me. Because it was summer, I was wearing a backless sunsuit. There was no serious injury, just a few scratch marks, but my feelings were badly hurt. My beloved rooster had hurt me! My parents thought it wise at this time to find another home for him, and he was given to a family in Mexican town who had chickens.

Two other special chickens scratched around in the dirt by the outhouse. They were a Bandy rooster and a Bandy hen—Mickey and Minnie Mouse. Mr. and Mrs. Willis, rancher friends of Auntie and Uncle Joe, had given them to me when they sold their Scar Face Ranch east of Kingman. I had spent some time on their ranch with Auntie and Uncle Joe before Mother and Daddy arrived in Kingman. They had wanted to buy the Scar Face Ranch but had been unable to come to an agreement with Mr. and Mrs. Willis.

The Onetto House

The little rooster and his hen had caught my eye on my first visit to Scar Face Ranch, and Mr. and Mrs. Willis knew how much I liked them. Mrs. Willis smoked, not a common thing for a woman at that time to do. She used a cigarette holder. When time came to light her cigarette, she would say, "Norma Jean, come light my pipe." I loved lighting her pipe. They brought Mickey and Minnie to me at the Boulder City house in Kingman sometime later. They had sold their ranch and were leaving the area for good and wanted me to have the two small chickens. The last thing Mrs. Willis had me do was light her pipe. I never saw them again.

The Scar Face Ranch was located north of Highway 66 on the way to Hackberry and Peach Springs. The rock formation that formed the scar face, was a short distance up the south side of the mountain range facing the large valley east of Kingman. The ranch house was located below the rock formation. The front yard was on a slight incline and held a large garden area where watermelons and other vegetables were grown.

On one of our visits to the ranch, I was allowed to pick a large watermelon from the garden for our evening meal. Of course I wanted to eat it immediately. Because of my stubborn insistence that it be eaten at that time, Auntie took it and hid it from me.

Later while Auntie and I were taking our afternoon rest, I discovered the watermelon under her pillow. I think she was playing a game and intended I find it at that time, because the large size of the watermelon could not have been hidden all that time with the small pillow.

Toward evening Uncle Joe joined Mr. Willis and other cowboys in butchering a steer. As Uncle Joe made the first cut with his knife to skin the steer, his blade went too deeply and cut a small hole in the intestine. He immediately stuffed a clean piece of rag into the hole to protect the meat from contamination.

They skinned and gutted the steer, and hung him high off the ground with a rope from a pole by his hind legs. The intestines were carried out of the area to keep the wild animals away from the carcass. It was left over night to cool out, and the next morning the part not reserved for steak was cut with the grain into narrow strips eight to ten inches long for jerky. Salt and pepper were added, and it was hung over wire lines (clotheslines) to dry in the sun. Uncle Joe would joke that the pepper was added to hide the flyspecks.

When the jerky was completely dried, it was placed in clean white cotton sacks and hung by a rope from the rafters of a shed. The meat reserved for steaks was wrapped in heavy canvas tarp each morning after the breakfast steaks were cut.

The Onetto House

Then the wrapped meat was placed in a cooler area out of the sun. At night the tarp was removed and the meat was again hung high outside to cool out.

Each morning and evening the cowboys and other hands were served steaks, milk-gravy and biscuits. Jerky was taken on their all-day horseback rides over the ranch to check the cattle. They had no ATVs or four-wheel drive vehicles to use. In the summer the heat was intense, and the winter brought numbing cold. Unlike the cowboys I tried to imitate, I disliked steak and ate biscuits and gravy instead. However, I did love jerky and would grab a handful whenever the opportunity presented itself.

Periodically, the day would come when Mother would tell us we could not use the outhouse for a while. The reason was, Mrs. Onetto needed to clean out the hole under it. Our outhouse was different from others in camp. The hole under the building extended beyond the back wall leaving it open in the back so it could be cleaned out from behind. What Mrs. Onetto did with what she took from the hole, I do not know, but when she was finished, everything smelled much better.

Mrs. Onetto was not a young woman. She was sixty-one at the time we moved into her house. A short time before we arrived in Goldroad she had been widowed. This left the responsibility on her for maintaining the rentals she used for her livelihood. But after she laid a new floor in our kitchen, Mother refused to let her do anything else on the house, although Mrs. Onetto mentioned frequently her desire to calcimine the house. Mother threatened Daddy with bodily harm if he sent Mrs. Onetto to the house again to do anymore repair work. Of course, Mother did not let Mrs. Onetto know she did not like her repairs. She did not want to hurt her feelings. Mrs. Onetto was a kind, thoughtful woman, but was certainly not able to do the repair work needed on this old house.

Our house was not the only house she owned and maintained. My uncle Don (Son) Massey and his family lived in two of her houses while they were in Goldroad. The first house had one large room, which served as kitchen, bedroom, and living room. While living there, one night his wife Henny put bacon rinds in the oven with the thought of later making cracklins. Unaware of the bacon rinds in the oven, Uncle Son got up the next morning and built a very hot fire in the wood stove. The bacon rinds got too hot and caught fire and almost burned the house down.

23.

The Onetto House

This house was a short distance below the schoolhouse on the road to the wash where the Mexican swimming pool was located. Their house was also equipped with an outhouse that Mrs. Onetto had to maintain.

The Katherine Mine

Prior to coming to Goldroad, Uncle Son and Henny had lived at the Katherine Mine. It is located approximately two miles north of Bullhead City. At the time they lived at the Katherine, there was no Bullhead City nor Davis Dam. Their construction began after the war started and we left Goldroad.

The Katherine Mine was very isolated and the narrow winding dirt road over high mountains west out of Kingman made it difficult to reach. Our family made the trip one time, and the memory of the long, hot drive still remains in my mind.

Uncle Son and Henny were a very young couple still in their teens with a baby daughter, Bobby Kay. Because of the extreme heat, the baby did not move constantly like a normal baby but lay listless with very little movement. An older and much wiser woman living in camp saw the condition of the baby and encouraged Henny to frequently put her in a tub of water. Wisely, Henny took the woman's advice, and this probably saved the baby's life. When we arrived for our visit, Henny had her outside in a tub of water.

The Onetto House

Like Goldroad, the Katherine had no trees or air conditioning. But Henny and Uncle Son's house also had no running water. Their water was kept in an uncovered barrel by the house. One day when Henny went to the barrel to get water, she discovered a dead rat in it. After this experience, they put a cover over the barrel, but for Bobby Kay's use, they got piped water from a neighbor's house. But even the piped water was always boiled before it was given to the baby.

Henny's only means of cooking was a two-burner gas hot plate, and every time it was turned on it caught fire. One pot was all she had for cooking; their table was two boards placed on two supports side by side with large cracks in between; their chairs were wooden dynamite boxes turned on end that Uncle Son had brought from the mine. The one purchase they made was a Kelvinator refrigerator.

The living room held a cot and old, worn out overstuffed chair given to them by Auntie. It had a spring poking through the fabric. In order to make the chair more comfortable to sit in, Henny placed a pillow over the protruding spring.

Uncle Son (Donald Reid Massey) & his wife Henny (Henrietta)
25.

The Onetto House

Their bedroom was an open porch with no screen, and the scorpions found at the Katherine were so large they would not fit into a glass milk bottle. When Henny found a small scorpion, which are far more poisonous than the large ones, in Bobby Kay's bed, her mother, who lived in California, gave her a baby bed completely enclosed with screen. These beds were called a kiddy-coop, and nothing got inside one of them.

Henny's mother, on her way back to her home in California after her visit with Henny and Uncle Son, wanted to turn around and go back to the Katherine to get Henny and the baby and take them home with them. But her husband told her it would not be a wise thing to do. He believed she would be going back to California with them on her own if she were not happy where she was. She accepted his logic and knew he was right, but she still cried all the way home.

When the baby was not in a tub of water, Henny put her in the kiddy-coop with a wet towel over a small fan Auntie had given her to let the cooled breeze blow over her.

Someone had left some chickens behind when they moved from the camp. They looked strange and unusual. And at first glance it was difficult to recognize them as chickens. Due to the constant and intense heat, they had lost all of their feathers and were in a continuous state of molting. Their exposed skin quickly tanned into a deep, brown color.

Henny and Uncle Son's house was built off the ground on stilts, and at a certain time of the day the sun was just right for Henny to sit by the house in a small patch of shade. The air coming from under the house was slightly cooler than the surrounding air. In order to take advantage of the limited shaded area created by the house and the cooler air from under the house, she had to carefully place Bobby Kay on her blanket in a specific spot. She then assumed a cramped position herself, and the chickens found whatever shaded spots left. What a sight they must have made all huddled together — baby, mother and tanned featherless chickens.

The Colorado River was only a short distance from their camp. Uncle Son and Henny spent many evenings after work with friends picnicing along the river. Because the Davis Dam had not yet been built, the river flowed fast, wide and muddy. It was not a river to play in. However, one night being young and foolish, Uncle Son decided to prove he could swim across the river and back. His decision might have been foolish, but he had his youth and strength as a strong swimmer in his favor.

The Onetto House

Swimming across the river would have been difficult enough, but he had to swim back as well. There was nothing on the Nevada side except trees and desert and Needles, California, thirty miles south.

He dived in and successfully completed the swim across. This swim drastically drained his energy. But the swim back took every ounce of remaining strength he had and left him exhausted and spent when he again reached the Arizona side of the river. Although he recognized within himself how fortunate he was to have survived such a dangerous swim, he never admitted to anyone he ever doubted, while fighting the strong currents and the fatigue, his ability to make it back to his own side of the river safely. However, he never repeated the swim.

Uncle Son-Don Massey

Outside entertainment was not available at the Katherine. It was isolated in an area far from any other camp or town. Being young and in need of something to do after work, they frequently joined others in camp playing softball. Their ball field was the large, low, flat area between the two rows of houses. At this time the Katherine was a small operation with few employees, but they managed to get enough people together to get a game going.

The Onetto House

All men worked hard at their jobs. And you felt lucky to have one. The only time Uncle Son was allowed to take a break on his job was to roll and smoke a cigarette. And those times were limited. But being very young, he was an optimist—many evenings after work he roamed the hills around the Katherine placing, under rocks, empty Prince Albert tobacco cans containing his claim to the mineral rights on the land. This was a futile activity, but to him it was his only chance to become a millionaire.

But the Katherine Mine closed in late 1938. This left Henny and Uncle Son without a job again. Goldroad at that time was one of the largest producers of gold in Arizona. There were other mines: Copper Queen, United Verde, and New Cornelia. But because we were in Goldroad and a job was available there, Uncle Son and Henny lived with our family in the Onetto house until they rented their own Onetto house.

Uncle Son and Henny slept on the north side of the screened porch. It seemed every night Henny would wait until they were in bed to say, "Son, would you get me a glass of water?" He would grumble a little, climb out of bed and make the dark walk to the kitchen in the back to get the water.

Billy and Bobby Kay were three years apart in age and spent a lot of time fighting with each other. One time, Bobby Kay hit Billy over the head with his metal *Bob Burns Bazooka* horn and brought blood. But they were well matched in aggravating each other.

Any water used in the kitchen or bathroom of our Onetto house did not go into a septic tank. It was carried by a pipe fifteen or twenty feet in front of the house where it ran across the road and made puddles for the cars to splash through on their way to our house or Flora and Frank Onetto's house. Even though Mother was constantly after him to stay out of the water, Billy thought of those puddles as his private play area.

He wore blue and white-stripped coveralls, which snapped up the front and had a snapped drop-seat in the back. Because he had shoulder-length blonde, curly hair, his actions and these overalls were the only two things from a distance that identified him as a boy. One day as he approached the house, he was heard to repeatedly to himself, "I'm justa pettin'(sweating) and a pootin (tooting)." He definitely was all boy.

The Onetto House

The day Daddy took Billy to Oatman for his first haircut was quite an occasion. He was four years old. Mother had not been willing to give up his beautiful blonde curly hair, and Daddy also was not in any hurry. His parents had not cut his long curly hair until he was at least four, either. Everyone was satisfied with Billy's long hair but Billy. He was beginning to notice the short haircuts of his friends and was nagging for his own.

Arizona Hotel, Oatman Barber Shop, Drug Store and Honolulu Club
(Courtesy of the descendants of Flora Onetto)

When we returned to Goldroad after his haircut, all of the kids in camp gathered around commenting on the change in his appearance. He enjoyed all of the attention and put his hands over his ears and said in a typical show-off boy voice, "Oh, my ears, my ears! Oh, my ears are cold!" He got a lot of mileage out of the haircut before the evening was over.

The Onetto House

Jimmy Bird, Billy Richards (in his blue stripped overalls before his trip to the barber), Vella Richards, Mamie Kirby

Mac McConnell and his wife Sue lived in a small house not far from our home and the Onettos'. They were a young couple with no children but seemed to enjoy them. Sue was half Cherokee Indian and wore beautiful Indian jewelry. Her hair was long and black. Their small front porch held two cages with running wheels for his squirrels to exercise.

From the Hualapais, before our move to Goldroad, tough times followed us to the Kingman Boulder City house. But Vel had it the hardest. When the weather cooled and the first flutterings of snow fell at the Newberry Ranch in the Haualapais, Auntie got out the Sears, Roebuck catalog and asked me to choose a coat. The coat with a separate fur-trimmed hood caught my eye and I would not settle for less. It was the nicest and most expensive. In Kingman, at first, Vella had to walk to her school located on the side of the hill at least a mile away across the railroad tracks and Highway 66 in her lightweight coat. She was a second grader. But it was soon decided, in order for her to stay warmer, she would need to wear my heavy coat with the fur-trimmed hood. And I did not mind sharing the coat with Vella, but I was upset when someone at school promptly stole the hood. Also, Mother used an undershirt of Daddy's as a slip to help keep Vella warm. Chicken pox kept her out of school the last month of school. It had been a very difficult year for her.

Chapter 3

Oatman — A Place We Passed Through On Our Way To Needles

I felt sorry for the little old man.

Oatman was a two-barbershop-town. One was located on the curve of the highway as it left town toward Topock, and the other was under the high boardwalk which ended at the drug store. This is the barbershop where Billy had his first hair cut, and the one Daddy used most of the time. The shop on the curve next to the service station-dance hall had pictures of scantily dressed women on its walls. These pictures appeared each month in the Esquire men's magazine and were considered very risque`. The shop owner had enterprisingly taken a few of the pictures from past issues and thumb tacked them to his shop's walls.

Not many women frequented barbershops. They were mostly a man's domain. But mothers occasionally took their sons or daughters for a haircut. I was in the shop with the risque` pictures one time to get Daddy. He noticed my attention had been drawn to the pictures of the women on the walls. And, maybe, that is why he always used the other barbershop—it was a family shop with no Esquire pin-ups.

Honolulu Jim's was a two-story bar and dance hall. In front of the building was a service station with a tall flagpole located farther out in the street. This is where U-turns were made. Dances and basketball games were held on the second floor of the building. On occasion Mother and Daddy, with some of their friends, attended dances there. But they decided not to go back after feeling the floor giveaway as they danced.

A younger group of men in Goldroad got together and formed a basketball team. The team was made up of Bill Parra, the forward and best player on the team; Morris Bird; Mac McConnell; Cloyd Henline; and Don Johnson. Uncle Son substituted in a couple of the games. One of the regular players was unable to play, and our family went to watch him.

But the games were later stopped when it became apparent to the players the room had begun to sway more and the floor had begun to bend more.

Uncle Son enjoyed the two games he played. He had been a basketball star at Safford High School a few years earlier, and he missed the fun of playing.

To fill some of their time after work, Mac McConnell, Cloyd Henline, Don Johnson, and Morris Bird decided a tennis court would be a nice addition to the camp. However, no available level area large enough for a tennis court could be found in Goldroad. Little Meadows was a beautiful green, level area beside a creek where Goldroad got its drinking water. It was located east over Sitgreaves Pass about three miles as the crow flies, but about five minutes on the winding Route 66. Permission was given by Leo Duriez to use the land. And a bulldozer tore up the land a little, but the court was never completed. A lack of time on the part of the men involved was probably the biggest reason.

During the time we lived in Goldroad, Kingman was the largest unincorporated town in the United States. Being unincorporated was a decision made by the business people in Kingman. And it was a well-organized plan carried out by local merchants that included the Central Commercial Company and Babbitt's Grocery.

Large chain stores such as Penney's and Safeway had a policy against opening stores in unincorporated towns because of the laws governing such towns. Kingman's business leaders were aware of this policy.

And with no competition from chain stores with lower prices, the local merchants controlled prices keeping them higher. But because of the higher prices in Kingman, Mother did all of her important shopping in Needles, although the drive was ten or fifteen miles farther.

Our grocery shopping was done at Safeway, and the clothing shopping at Penney's. When an emergency would arise, Mother would shop in Oatman.

One day she was making blouses and full skirts for Vella and me and had come to the point in her sewing where she needed buttons for the blouse. Rather than waiting for our monthly visit to Needles, she decided to try the small shop in Oatman owned by a little, old, foreign man. Mother found the perfect buttons for the blouses in the shop. They were a little more expensive than she would have paid at Penney's in Needles, but she bought them anyway. Vella and I had not gone to the shop with her but were doing our own shopping in another store. Later when we all met at the car, she was pleased with the buttons she had found but was annoyed by the odor in the store.

Oatman—A Place We Passed Through On Our Way To Needles

After much discussion and thought, Mother decided the odor must have come from the old man using a corner inside his store for a restroom rather than making the effort to use the outhouse behind. She had a very well trained sense of smell and never went back to the little store to do anymore shopping. I felt sorry for the little, old man.

In the fall of 1941 when I was ten, we passed through Oatman on our way to Needles to shop. Vella and I spied two beautiful dolls in one of the store windows. At the age of twelve, I do not know how excited Vella was about the dolls, but I wanted one of them for Christmas!

One of the dolls had golden blonde curls, blue eyes and was dressed in a pink silk bonnet and coat. The other doll had dark brown curls, brown eyes and was dressed in a light blue silk bonnet and coat. They were Horsman dolls; they cried Mama when tilted; and their glass eyes moved from side to side and closed when the doll was laid down.

As we examined them closely, immediately I knew which doll I wanted— the doll with the brown hair and brown eyes like mine. Vella was pleased with the blonde, who had blue eyes like hers. The dolls were expensive--$5 – but Mother agreed to buy them for our Christmas. This was my last Christmas doll.

Vella and I still have these dolls. I took the brown curly wig off many years ago and lost the blue silk bonnet and coat, but she sits on my china closet dressed in my granddaughter Kelsea Elwood's blessing dress. The last time I saw Vella's doll, it still had the blonde curls and pink silk bonnet and coat and sat in a small rocker in her bedroom.

The Oatman Theatre where our family attended the movie every Sunday night had only one visible attempt at beautifying the interior— star-shaped shades on the ceiling lights. I appreciated this one attempt and admired them on each of our visits.

The advertising billboard for the theatre was on the curve of Route 66 in Goldroad at the bottom of our hill. It was made of wood and large enough to display two theatre-sized posters. Chicken wire over the front held the posters in place and protected them from the wind.

Oatman—A Place We Passed Through On Our Way To Needles

*The Oatman Theater on left as seen
coming into Oatman from the east from Goldroad*

The hard-earned money of the husbands during the time of this Great Depression was used for the necessities of life for their families. But once in a while his wife would decide she needed a touch of something special in her life and would make an appointment at the Oatman Beauty Shop.

On occasion Mother did this. Other women in Goldroad—Mrs. Duriez, Mrs. Brough, Mrs. Peeples, and Mrs. Sayer—also used the beauty shop.

The owner of the shop was the daughter of a well-known and respected man in Oatman. But she became dissatisfied with the sameness of her routine and lack of excitement in small-town living and left Oatman to live in a larger town out of the area. She thought the move would add the excitement and adventure to her life she thought was missing. But after a time, she returned to her Oatman shop and made this observation to a few of her patrons: It's better to be a large duck in a small pond than to be a small duck in a large pond. That thought has come into my mind many times over the years as I have thought upon my own life and where I have been. But I have not yet come to any conclusion as to the validity of the statement.

Although our family did not know Otis Willoughby or his family at the time we lived in Goldroad and his family lived in Oatman, we have made contact through the wonderful media of the internet and e-mail. Our living in San Tan Valley Arizona, and he living in Cedaredge Colorado, was bridged when his brother-in-law saw our book at the Olive Mill, and purchased it, and sent it to Otis. The Olive Mill is a popular tourist destination located about five miles from our home, which is part of the Greater Phoenix area.

34.

Oatman—A Place We Passed Through On Our Way To Needles

As our lives ran parallel—his in Oatman and mine in Goldroad—Otis's memories of his life in Oatman add much to understanding life lived in these two isolated mining camps, only a mile apart, during the years of the Great Depression. Rather than trying to re-write his story, I have decided the best way to do this is to let him tell his own story in his own words—who can tell your story better than you? When our stories touch, I will add my thoughts and feelings. So—here is Otis Willoughby's story:

My father went to Mohave County soon after his graduation from Manual Arts High in southern California. He was employed by his uncle Nathan Tarr in Kingman, Chloride, White Hills, Goldroad, Oatman, and other mining camps. Mr. Tarr was a partner in Tarr-McComb, the main hardware and mining supply firm in Kingman. Dad delivered supplies to the various mines using a Model-T Ford truck.

Prior to his marriage, my father worked in the mill in Goldroad; that must have been in the late 1920s or early 1930s. In fact, he nearly lost his life there when he was making some adjustments on the trough system that distributed the mill tailings into the evaporation pool. Evidently he slipped into the liquid tailings and began to sink. A fellow worker threw him a rope, but the men were afraid that they would pull Dad in two, because the suction of the muck was so great. It must have been much like quicksand. They were able to pull him out of the tailings safely. I don't know how long after that he continued to work in Goldroad.

My great-uncle Samuel Gilmore worked in Oatman at the Tom Reed mill. He had a single niece, Agnes McClashan, who lived and worked as a secretary in Los Angeles. Uncle decided to play cupid and brought Agnes out to Oatman where she met Sam's co-worker, my dad. In due course they were married. My brother, sister, and I were all born in Los Angeles, where there was family support and better medical facilities than were available in Mohave County. My brother and I were delivered to Oatman, along with our parents in Dad's Model-A Ford. My sister arrived in their brand new 1940 forest green Ford Delux sedan.

My memories of Oatman and Goldroad are just as precious as yours. The hospital in Goldroad must have become operational about 1942. I fell off the slide in the playground of the Oatman School and broke my arm. I was taken to the hospital in Goldroad, but the doctor there sent us on to Kingman. Once there, my arm was set, and the doctor decided that it would be a good time to have my tonsils removed, since I was going to be incapacitated anyway. The only good thing that I remember about the incident was that my grandmother read " The Swiss Family Robinson" to me while I was recuperating.

Oatman—A Place We Passed Through On Our Way To Needles

I don't remember the water in the Oatman pool being as murky as you describe it. It was probably good clean water pumped out of the Tom Reed. Compared to the heat of the Oatman day, the pool represented a welcome oasis. A teen-age girl (Doreen Dunton?) frequently took me out to the deep water and kept me afloat. My mother was sure that I would drown.

I had my first Coca Cola at Roy Dunton's station in Goldroad. We had stopped there to have a blown tire replaced before going to Kingman. On another occasion I spent the day there with my dad while he worked with someone to construct a trailer out of spare parts salvaged from worn out vehicles found in the desert.

I know that my dad was acquainted with yours. Dad had the responsibility for the Oatman water supply. I believe that your father must have had the same part in running electricity to the pump booster station located on the road between Oatman and Silver Creek. The water pipeline was run along the surface of the ground. Whenever a dip in the terrain was encountered, the pipe was supported by X-shaped wooden supports. Sometimes the pipeline would freeze and split. Dad would have to repair by wrapping the pipe with red rubber innertubing and wire. No portable welder was available to properly repair the pipe.

When the mines closed, we remained in Oatman until 1945. Dad worked first at the gunnery school at the Kingman Army Aircorps base. Later he worked on the construction of the new railway bridge at Topock, and still later on the construction of Davis Dam. Finally the dam construction was halted because of the scarcity of materials, because of the war effort. We moved to Boulder City in the summer of 1945. I have gone back to Oatman several times. I am always amazed that the houses were such little cracker boxes. Most of the landmarks are now gone, but at least there are a few recognizable structures left in place, e.g., the school and the hotel where I took violin lessons from Joe Brandenburg.

Perhaps we had a little too much freedom. One time there was a grease fire in a small cafe adjacent to the Standard service station. While the owners were making repairs many of the perishables were stored in a small shed. The owner's son stole a carton of cigarettes and we hid them in an abandoned mine tunnel near our home. Naturally we had to try them.

When we returned home from our experiment, my sister (age 4) had a couple of small holes in her doll's blanket. Our mother asked if we had been playing with matches, to which Margaret responded, "No, we were smoking." Wrong answer, as you can well imagine.

Picture taken around 1944 of Otis with his dog Stubby; " Stubby because of his short tail. Regretably my dad had to shoot Stubby before we moved to Boulder City. Stubby had been trained to protect our chickens, rabbits, fuel oil drum, and other property that could easily have been taken by the hoards of Depression era refugees that were passing through Arizona on Route 66 on their way to California. He was too territorial to make the adjustment to city living. Certainly this was the saddest day of my youth."

(Courtesy Otis Willoughby)

37.

Oatman—A Place We Passed Through On Our Way To Needles

Picture taken October 13, 1939 on the front steps of the Willoughby house in Oatman. Agnes-Otis-Otis Sr.-Richard
(Courtesy Otis Willoughby)

When we lived in Oatman I never heard the term "Snob Hill" being used to describe our neighborhood. Some of the homes were a little nicer than many in town. When I have returned to Oatman in recent years, I have been surprised to see that all of the homes in the neighborhood were a little more than tiny cracker boxes. We did have indoor plumbing and a water heater which was rarely used because the banging noise when it was in operation convinced my mother that it was going to explode. Water for baths was usually heated in a large tub on our wood-burning range on the back porch.

Waste water from our house and our neighbor's went into a cesspool in a gully between the two homes. The pool was roofed over with old pipes, mine rails and sheets of galvanized tin plus a layer of dirt. My brother and I played a game of chicken to see who was brave enough to walk across the rather flimsy covering. Since it was quite springy, we were sure that we would fall in.

Oatman—A Place We Passed Through On Our Way To Needles

Our neighbors were the LeBeau family. Fred LeBeau, the father, was the butcher at Bill Ridenour's general store. Their children were much older than we were. Dudley (b. 1924), the youngest was much like an older brother to me. He made all kinds of clever wooden toys for me including a gun that fired strips of rubber cut from an old inner tube. Dudley joined the Air Corps and became a pilot. Later he enjoyed a career with United Air Lines. He died just more than a year ago.

Fred had a pet chipmunk Shorty who pretty much enjoyed the run of the house. Shorty met an untimely death when he ran under the tip of a rocking chair at just the wrong moment.

One of my best friends was a boy named Jack Lee. Perhaps this was the son of the Ivan Lee that you mentioned. Jack may have been a year older than me, but we were in the same grade in school. I know that he had siblings including a younger sister whose name I have forgotten.

Picture taken April 19th, 1939
Otis age 4 and Richard age 17 ½ months
(Courtesy Otis Willoughby)
39.

Oatman—A Place We Passed Through On Our Way To Needles

There was a little community church in Oatman. It was located about ¼ mile north and a little east of the Alamo building, the one with the weak floors where most of the community activities were held. It even had a steeple and a bell.

I remember that fateful day of December 7th, 1941. I was walking home from church with my mother, my brother, and my baby sister who was being carried by our mother. Johnny Carerra called out to us from the door of the Ice House to tell us of the Japanese attack on Pearl Harbor.

Clyde Babb often conducted Community Sings during the war. Janie LeBeau played the piano. Chairs had been carried out of the Church into the gravel area in front of the Church. The piano was rolled up to the double doors at the front of the Church so that it could be heard without actually bringing it outside. Mr. Babb stood on the little porch so that he could be seen. A single light above the door was the only illumination. This arrangement allowed us to sit outside where it was much cooler in the desert evenings than it would have been inside the Church.

We sang patriotic songs and inspirational and sentimental songs from both the First and Second World Wars, songs like "Over There," "How're We Going to Keep Them Down on the Farm," "Coming In On a Wing and a Prayer," I'll Fly Over the White Cliffs of Dover," etc. Everyone seemed to know the words. There were no song books or sheet music. Those were memorable times for a young boy.

The Ice House was located on the south side of US 66 in the middle of Oatman. That would have put it almost directly across the street from the Oatman Hotel. In the pre-refrigeration days, ice was used for prolonging the shelf life of meat, milk, and other perishables. Ice was also used in trucks to preserve shipments of perishables. Whenever the grocery store—at one time a Central Commercial—would receive a shipment of perishables, the left-over ice was just dumped at the edge of the road. It was great fun to make snow balls out of it. Obviously it didn't last long in Oatman.

We were lucky in that we had a refrigerator. It was smaller than the one in our 5th-wheel travel trailer. Several of our neighbors still used ice boxes, as did my maternal grandparents in southern California. Their ice was still delivered by a horse-drawn wagon as late as 1940. The ice man wore a special leather apron over one shoulder to protect himself from the cold and melting ice as he carried the ice from the wagon using a huge set of tongs.
---Otis Willoughby

Chapter 4

Our Good Friends—Frank and Flora Onetto

He always called her the little woman.

Frank Onetto owned an old coupe with wide running boards. Billy thought Frank was special. Everyday he stood at the bottom of the incline leading up into the driveway where Frank parked his car. Frank stopped and picked him up as he came home from work, and they rode up the short incline together. They did this for a long time, but when Billy finally tired of it, Frank was a little hurt and disappointed that he had lost his riding partner.

When Frank returned from a vacation, he brought gifts for our family. Billy received a white suit with short pants; Mother a beautiful, red, velvet dressing gown lined with light blue satin. Frank knew what made pretty women look even prettier. In his younger days he had been known as quite a lady's man. Vella and I received Indian-made beaded figures made from a rabbit's foot. They were considered a good luck charm by many. And I still have this rabbit's foot. I do not remember my father receiving anything.

At one time Frank had been married to a lady in Oatman who owned the Nigro Grocery Store. She was known as Mrs. Nigro when we came to Goldroad. Obviously she had remarried after her divorce from Frank. And nothing more than this was known or discussed in our family about Frank's marital status.

We did not trade at the Nigro Grocery, but before Christmas saw a beautifully decorated, light-blue Christmas tree displayed in the window. Every time we went by the store, I would admire the tree. After the holidays, we drove by the store and discovered the tree had been taken out of the window and thrown beside the door. We begged Mother to stop and ask for the tree. She did, and we happily loaded it into our trunk and took it home with us. The other kids in camp envied us, because we had the blue Christmas tree from Nigro's. The tree was put in our front yard, and all of the kids played with it until it was battered and broken and finally discarded. Before it was thrown into the trash can, I took a small piece of the glittered, blue branch and saved it in a small box with my other treasures.

Our Good Friends—Frank and Flora Onetto

Sophie Port—1900--Frank's fiance
who died of pneumonia before
they could marry

Frank Onetto
(Both Pictures Courtesy of the Descendants of Flora and Joe Onetto)

Frank and my father were good friends and talked many evenings after work. They sat on the running board of Frank's old car, which was parked between the two houses. One evening as they were sitting and talking with Gale Cudney, they noticed a kitten playing with something under the car behind their feet. They did not think too much about it and continued talking. But a short time later when they looked closer, they were surprised to discover the kitten was playing with a rattlesnake.

Our Good Friends—Frank and Flora Onetto

After the snake was killed, they spent time looking for a mate, because they believed snakes were always found in pairs. But we never found another snake around the area, nor any other place in camp for that matter.

Sometime during our first holiday season in Goldroad in 1937, before Christmas day, the Elks in Kingman held a special Christmas party for all children. There were carols, reindeer and Santa Claus, who handed each child a mesh bag filled with candy and an orange. But the excitement generated by the crowds in and around the Elks Hall created almost a fantasy world taking me to a high level of excitement and feelings of pure joy. Anticipation of Christmas, with its expectation of new toys from Santa Claus, when mixed with the beauty of the Christmas carols, brightly lighted Christmas trees and the thoughts of a bag of candy, came together for me and made a memorable night of happiness.

But Santa Claus frightened Billy—he was only three. And Daddy accepted the bag of candy for him.

Our family tradition of having Santa Claus come on Christmas Eve rather than Christmas morning was begun on this Christmas. The reason for the change was that it made it possible for Mother to relax and enjoy Santa and the gift giving. Christmas morning was left free for her to prepare the large Christmas dinner that was served at noon.

This first Christmas Eve in Goldroad Vella, Billy and I were taken next door to stay with the Onettos while Santa delivered our toys. He was to honk our car horn when he left. And it was very difficult for us to contain our excitement while we waited for him to do this.

But after what seemed like an eternity, the horn did finally honk, and we quickly ran the short distance between our houses.

All lighted up by its own small lamp, Vella and I found a table and chairs set with small china dishes; a small electric stove that really heated; and the scene was completed with two baby dolls in a cradle-bed. I do not remember anything else, but I am sure there were other toys as well. What we received was not important. Because I can still visualize this Christmas scene and remember the warm, contented feelings I experienced as I entered the room.

Perhaps the reasons why this Christmas was so special to me were the circumstances our family had experienced the previous Christmas at the Newberry Ranch in the Hualapais. Extreme hard times were a part of our family's economic situation at that time. Daddy had no job and no assurance he would get one when we left the ranch after the snow melted and we could leave.

Our Good Friends—Frank and Flora Onetto

Mother had brought Vel's and my doll bed from the previous Christmas with her from Safford and painted it light lavender. The paint had been brought with her as well. We received this bed and a doll for each of us. I had asked many times before Christmas for a live horse of my own and was hoping against hope I would receive one Christmas morning. But there was no horse in the corral when I looked. But by the time the Christmas of 1937 rolled around, Daddy did have a good secure, steady job with the Company among men who were his friends. And we had our own house and a new car. But most of all, we had the feeling of security—something our family had not felt since the Depression started and Daddy lost his job in Fierro, New Mexico, approximately five years earlier.

The following year the company held its own Christmas party at the school. Carols were sung by the students. At the end of the program, and the most important part of the evening, Santa Claus handed brown bags filled with candy and an orange to the older children in camp. But each pre-school child could sit on Santa's lap to receive theirs. Our neighbor and friend, Mr. Johnson, was Santa Claus. And our family's hope was that Billy would not be frightened by him, because he knew and liked Mr. Johnson—but he did not know Santa was his friend Mr. Johnson, and he was frightened and cried and refused to go near him.

My grandparents and Dorothy, my aunt who was three years older than I, were with us the Christmas of 1938.

Because my mother had only the wood stove and the kerosene burners for cooking, Mrs. Onetto offered to let my grandmother cook our turkey in her oven. I do not know how she fixed Christmas dinner for herself and Frank. Perhaps they spent the day in Needles with Mrs. Onetto's daughters and family.

Only after Mother and Mama Bessie were assured by the men there would be no liquor added to it later, they prepared eggnog. Both hated drinking and were upset when it was done around them. Johnny Grogan was a friend of Frank Onetto as well as Daddy. He had no family around so he and Frank Onetto were invited to come over. One of the men, probably Papa Guy, later did add liquor to it. And Mother and Mama Bessie were upset. Johnny Grogan was normally a nice, quiet man, but he and Papa Guy got a little loud after drinking the liquored eggnog. Frank was not part of this disruption. He was a gentleman in our home and around our family. This part of our Christmas leaves a bad memory.

44.

Our Good Friends—Frank and Flora Onetto

In July, 1937, Morris Bird, newly graduated from college, arrived in Goldroad as the company Timekeeper/Cost Accountant under Joe Peeples. This was his first job. Because there was no place for a man alone to stay, Joe Peeples made arrangements for him to sleep on Frank Onetto's front porch. The porch had a heavy covering of Virginia Creeper vines. These vines helped to cool the area as well as provide an area of privacy for him. He slept on the porch for a month.

Margaret, his wife, had remained in Utah. She was to let him know by telegram when she would be arriving at the train station in Kingman. But when she arrived late one evening and Morris was not there to meet her, she called one of the two telephones in camp and got a man in the hoist house, because the other telephone was locked up in the office for the night. A man was speedily dispatched to find Morris at the Onetto's to tell him he had a call from his wife. Morris, in his haste to climb up to the hoist house, bumped his head on a timber. He was not knocked out, but it hurt him for many years afterward.

He was shocked to learn his wife was waiting for him in Kingman. He did not own a car, so Frank lent him his old coupe—a Star Durrant roadster with a canvas top. The top was not only down on the car when he picked up Margaret, but through time and use, the floorboards had worn away and the road could be seen below their feet. The telegram Margaret sent to Morris arrived a week later.

Morris had been able to find an apartment owned by Mrs. Henline. Later, when Margaret was pregnant with their first child, Jimmy, Madeline Plummer, a school teacher's daughter who also lived in the Henline Apartments, and I were upset because she used the sand in front of the apartments to change her kitty litter box. I am certain she never realized we had been playing in the sand pile before she started using it.

The reason for the litter box was Margaret and Morris had adopted two kittens Mrs. Henline had found under the woodpile. Their mother was a Manx and their father was an ordinary cat. The male kitten was a Manx. The female was an ordinary cat like its father, except she had an extra long tail. They were extremely wild when found. Margaret spent many hours trying to get them used to her presence before she was able to get close enough to them to grab the Manx behind the front legs and bring him inside. Over a period of days, the female could see the male behind the screen door and would come out of her hiding place and come up to him. This made it possible for Margaret to grab her. Keeping them in the house made it possible for Margaret and Morris to tame the kittens.

Our Good Friends—Frank and Flora Onetto

When we did catch sight of Margaret on her fast, infrequent trips out of her apartment, we thought she was pretty in her brightly colored kimono but felt she was a little overweight. We did not realize she was pregnant.

When the kittens were older and tame, Margaret and Morris took them in their car down a dirt road and out of camp. When they all got out of the car, Tike, the female, stayed close to them, but Manx, the male, ran as fast as he could. Morris started running after him but stopped short when he discovered Manx had fallen onto a ledge a few feet down in an abandoned mine shaft. They did not know how they would be able to get the cat out of the shaft. But they did decide it would be too risky for either of them to hold the other and reach down to get the cat. Searching around they found an old discarded piece of tin. They slid it down to the cat. Luckily, he understood what they wanted him to do, and he got on it. And they lifted him to safety. After retrieving Manx, they found his paws were covered with thorns from the cactus he had carelessly run through in his haste to get away.

They took him back to their apartment where Morris pulled each thorn from Manx' paws. Because of the intense pain, the cat would nip Morris on the hand each time a thorn was pulled out. But he then quickly licked the spot to show Morris he had not intended to hurt him. One thorn was deeply embedded between the toes. And when it was extracted, Manx bit deeply into Morris' hand but, again, very quickly licked him.

The company built a small house for them next to the Kirby's, and they moved in before their baby was born. The company doctor was J.L. Barritt. But he lived in Oatman because the Duriez family lived in the Goldroad hospital. On March 29, 1938, Dr. Barritt delivered Jimmy Bird in their new house. The birth was difficult. During the delivery the doctor gave Morris a choice between saving Margaret or the baby—Morris told him to save his wife—but he was blessed in being able to save both. Other men who worked in Goldroad but lived in Oatman were Newt Lanier the Postmaster, and two company assayers, Ivan Lee and Ray Sutton.

My friends and I thought Jimmy was the cutest baby we had ever seen. He had dark hair and a little button nose. When he was a little older, Mamie Kirby baby sat him and I sometimes helped her.

Our Good Friends — Frank and Flora Onetto

Joe Peeples was the Cashier and was Morris' supervisor. Mr. Peeples was a very precise and meticulous accountant. He required Morris to figure the company payroll by hand his first year as Timekeeper. Although the Marchant calculator was available in the office for this purpose, he told Morris he had been required to learn that way, and Morris must do it also.

Joe Peeples, Cashier, Paris V. Brough, Mill Superintendent, Gayle Cudney, Mine Foreman

The mystery of how a ten-inch grasshopper got under the porch of the office was never solved. When Morris saw it, he could not believe his eyes. He even ran home to get Margaret to verify to himself that he was not seeing things that were not there. But she also saw the over-sized grasshopper, which had every part of its body proportionately sized. Later they regretted they had not taken a picture of the insect, because grasshoppers of that size were not found in this country.

After Frank Onetto retired from his job at the mine, he sold his old coupe to Philip Duriez, one of Mr. Duriez' sons. He promptly painted it a jazzy maroon color and proudly drove it around camp. And he probably also drove it to Kingman on occasion. Frank had replaced his old car with a new, more modern car. A garage was built to protect the new car from the hot Goldroad sun.

Our Good Friends—Frank and Flora Onetto

One night when a strong windstorm hit Goldroad, the garage blew over onto our car leaving a dent on the top. Frank felt badly about the damage caused to our new car and promptly paid to have it repaired.

But before Frank sold his old coupe, one day Billy and JoAnn Sayer had been playing with a pointed piece of iron. It was not sharp but was great for two busy four-year-old children to use for poking things.

But they got into trouble when they decided to use it to punch holes in the radiator of Frank's car. When my parents found out what Billy had done, they told him they were going to take the money out of his piggy bank to pay for the damage done to the car. Even at his young age Billy had a very high regard for money, and this was a very effective punishment. Of course my parents did not really take his money to pay for the damage to the radiator, but Billy believed they had, and so the lesson was learned.

Our family was introduced to Italian cooking by Mrs. Onetto. We had never eaten Italian squash (zucchini) but enjoyed it baked and topped with melted cheese as Mrs. Onetto had taught Mother to prepare it. She also brought over a cutting from her Italian herb plant (oregano?), which Mother planted outside in a five-gallon lard can. It added a flavor to Mother's soups and stews we all liked. Vella always included it in the stew she cooked on the bonfire for the Sayers and us in the evenings as we brewed our desert tea.

The backside of Mrs. Onetto's house stood high off the ground on stilts. Old trunks were stored in this area as well as old packaged newspapers and magazines, and old bottles—many had turned purple from many years of exposure to the sun. All of this looked very interesting to me. And one day I decided to take a closer look. As I walked along the row of trunks and papers, and before I had a chance to look more closely, Mrs. Onetto came out of her house and asked me to leave. I never went close to the back or front of her house again. The few times I was in her house I was with one of my parents. And it left a visual picture in my mind of darkness and gloom.

Because Frank had been a hard-rock miner all of his life, his lungs were destroyed by the disease that eventually killed all of the men in his occupation if they were fortunate enough to escape the other hazards of underground mining—falling rocks, faulty blasting procedures, or a fall down the shaft. Black lung—silicosis, *rock-in-the-box*--- these were the names used to describe the disease that killed Frank and thousands of other men who chose to make their living in mines where the gold was infused in silica rock.

Our Good Friends—Frank and Flora Onetto

Not only were the men working in these gold mines in danger of contracting this deadly disease, but also the men who worked in the crusher. My Uncle Son's first job with the company in Goldroad was in the crusher. The workers were required to wear masks over their noses and mouths. But this precaution certainly did not eliminate entirely the risk involved working in this potentially dangerous dust.

Billy (wearing a crusher mask) BobbyKay, Vella, KennyGuy

I remember Frank as a large man, but maybe to a child of five or six, anyone seems large. As his illness progressed, we saw less and less of him. And he experienced terrible coughing seizures that caused him to spit up blood.

Mrs. Onetto kept my parents informed of his condition, and my father was especially concerned. She had the complete care of Frank without help from a doctor or nurse. He spent many nights walking the floor without sleep. I marvel now how such a small woman, no longer young—sixty four at the time—could have done all required to take care of the total physical needs of a dying man who was twice her size. A genuine bond of love and caring existed between them. I have no way of knowing why this bond existed, but I do know it did. He always called her *the little woman*, and it was always said with deep respect and admiration. Her willingness to nurse him through his terrible illness and final death was certainly an indication of her deep commitment of caring.

Our Good Friends—Frank and Flora Onetto

Flora and Joe--Why Flora was called the "Little Woman" by Joe.
(Courtesy of descendents of Flora and Joe Onetto)

Even though Vella was only two years older than I was, she was not as active or busy. Frank spotted this difference in us and on occasion, as a compliment to her, referred to her as *the little woman.*

During the final stages of Frank's illness, Mrs. Onetto brought a *Life* magazine to our house. She was very upset by an article in it that had graphic, colored pictures showing the progressive stages of silicosis. Although she had tried to keep it out of his sight, Frank had read the article and had seen the pictures. This caused her great sadness. It had been her hope to spare him the added worry and concern over what lay ahead for him.

As it became more and more difficult for Frank to breath, Mrs. Onetto would come out on her porch each evening and ask us children to put out the bonfire we had made to brew our desert tea. Being young, we did not understand fully the gravity of the situation or the importance of just this small amount of help we could give him by keeping the air free from smoke. We obeyed, but I regret now it was not done with a concern for him and his problem.

In 1940 a few evenings after we had been asked by Mrs. Onetto to extinguish our fires, the word came to our home that Frank had died. He was sixty-five years old. We watched as the hearse drove up the small incline to their house. He was carried out of the house in a large, basket-like conveyance covered over with a white sheet—no outline of a body could be seen. He was taken to Needles, California, where he was buried beside his brother Joe. Mother and Daddy attended the Catholic funeral.

Our Good Friends—Frank and Flora Onetto

Mrs. Onetto continued to live in the house by herself, and when we left Goldroad in November 1942, she was still there.

Mother continued writing to her for a time after we left. When the company required all structures removed, she went to Needles to live with her daughter Rita. She remained there until her death in 1963 at the age of eighty-seven.

She had experienced the death of her husband Joe just three years previously in 1937—a short time before we came to Goldroad. He was sixty-seven. He had been manager of the mining operation in Goldroad in the early part of the 1920s, but it was not operating in the late 1920's. He and Mrs. Onetto continued to live in their Goldroad home until his death. Joe Onetto lived long enough to see Goldroad being prepared to be re-opened by the USSR&MCo in 1937.

Mrs. Onetto was an excellent Italian cook, and while Joe was alive prepared huge platters of spaghetti for Sunday dinner to serve to her family and guests on the vine-covered front porch of their home. Joe required everyone remain at the table until he had finished his meal—which could run to an hour-and-a-half. If you forgot, his large hand very quickly found a shoulder or leg and pulled you back down.

Joe was a large man—over six feet in height. By the time of his death he had ballooned to over four hundred pounds. A special casket had to be ordered to hold his body, and the casket required ten pallbearers to carry it. He was buried in the Needles Cemetery.

The Onettos were a highly respected family whose children were successful in their business ventures. Irene and her husband Si Simon at one time owned the theater in Oatman but sold it and bought the theater in Needles, California. Joe Byers worked for them when he was in high school and was one of the dinner guests at the Onetto table on the porch in Goldroad.

Rita Onetto Connors and her husband owned the bakery in Needles. Joe Byers also worked for them delivering bread. Another sister Lena Sullivan was large like her father and worked in the Needles city government. On one of her visits to Joe's home after his marriage, Lena sat down too hard on their new couch and broke it. She wanted to pay him for the couch, but he refused and later had it rebuilt.

51.

Our Good Friends — Frank and Flora Onetto

Joe Onetto & daughter Irene—Gold Road Mine
(Courtesy of Mohave County Historical Society)

Goldroad December 1936 before the opening 10 March 1937 under snow
that snowed our family in the Hualapai Mountains on the Newberry Ranch.
(Courtesy of Mohave County Historical Society)
52.

Chapter 5

The Goldroad Heat

Phoenix at noon ... was an oasis—a sheer delight ...

It was so hot in Goldroad the residents joked about how the lizards carried sticks around with them to hop on when the ground got too hot for them to run. Our yearly summertime trip to our grandparent's home in Solomonsville, Arizona, took us through Phoenix at noon. But to us coming from Goldroad, it was an oasis—a sheer delight—with trees, grass, and especially the coolers in the stores.

We always stopped and spent time in Newberry's and Woolworth's. I had never seen so many things to buy—and it was so cool inside the stores with the newly developed evaporative coolers! We ate our lunch at the counter in one of the stores, made a few purchases, and were soon on our way over the Superior Mountains to Solomonsville.

When we arrived in Goldroad in the spring of 1937, there was no cooling in any of the homes, offices, or businesses. However, by late 1938 or 1939, most of the homes had homemade evaporative coolers. Our family was fortunate when we later moved to the house on the hill, because Daddy had the carpenter shop make a box for our living room window. This box had three sides with a double thickness of chicken wire stretched over it. Excelsior was stuffed between the wire. Water from a hose ran down over the excelsior. A fan, which looked much like the fan on a car radiator, was placed in the box with the blades facing the open side of the box. This provided cooling for the entire house. For some reason our fan was turned off at night. It was needed during the night as much as it was during the day, because Goldroad's nights were as hot as its days. The large boulders retained the heat absorbed the day, and when the infrequent rains came, the air became steamy rather than cool.

The Goldroad Heat

A home made cooler on Joan Bird's house
In our swimsuits: A friend, Joan Bird, and Norma Jean Richards.
Fern Bird behind us

Because the heat continued through the night, Uncle Son and Henny put their bed outside the house. The legs of the bed were placed in tin cans a little larger than the legs and were filled with water. This kept insects, especially scorpions, out of their bed. They got up before daylight so the entire camp would not see them in their shorts and nightgown.

While Charlie Claunch and his wife lived in the house on the hill, their bed was outside in the summertime. One night a famous Goldroad windstorm hit and blew their mattress off the hill.

Mother never allowed us to go without our shoes until school was out the last of May. When our shoes were first taken off, our feet were tender to the sharp rocks, heat, and stickers. But after a few weeks, they had developed a thick, tough, layer of skin on the bottoms. This made it possible for us to walk over the sharp rocks, through the bullhead sticker patch, and on the hot ground.

The Goldroad Heat

Because of the extremely hot weather a dispenser of salt tablets was available for the miners and surface workers on the outside wall of the lamp room by the shaft. Every time we were there, usually with Daddy, we took a few of these salt tablets. Always after one swipe across our tongue they were quickly thrown away. But each time we had to try them. Perhaps, in the hope they might somehow have changed flavor and become tastier. Maybe even— turned into candy? Children are great optimists and great believers in fantasies.

Oatman was just a mile away, but parents at that time had not yet been programmed to jump in their cars to take their children wherever they wanted to go. Normally the only time our car was driven was when we went as a family to either Needles for shopping once a month; to Kingman to visit relatives; to Oatman for Daddy's and Billy's hair cuts, or to the Sunday night movie.

So the fact that Oatman had a swimming pool and was a short distance away did not help much in getting us there. Mother did give in and took us two or three times during the years we lived in Goldroad. It is probably good she did not take us more often. The possibility of catching hepatitis or typhoid was very high. The water was so thick with impurities it was impossible to see the bottom even in the shallow end.

This was a one-of-a-kind swimming pool. One side of a water tank had been cut away and then welded together with other tanks cut away in like manner—the pool resembled a huge shamrock.

The only available toilet facilities were either the closest large bush, which were not too plentiful in the area, or the old eroded tailings a few hundred feet down the wash. If you chose the tailings, you would quickly discover you were not original in your choice. Most of the time it was just easier to *hold it*.

Goldroad had a new concrete swimming pool complete with dressing rooms—no toilet facilities that I know of because I only saw it from a distance. The only drawback was it had been built for the Mexican people of the camp and was off-limits to the Anglos. Mr. Duriez reasoned the Anglos could use the Oatman pool.

The new pool for the Mexican people indicated the deep love he had for the Mexican people in camp. He had brought them en masse from their homes in Fierro, New Mexico, when Goldroad opened. They or their fathers had worked for him at the Fierro operation five years earlier.

The Goldroad Heat

No one, adults or children, ever questioned the new pool for the Mexicans. It was never discussed in our family and was not discussed by us among our friends. The acceptance by the Anglos of the fact this pool was for the Mexicans, without complaint or discussion, shows the respect the men, their wives and children had for Mr. Duriez.

Leo Duriez, Manager of Goldroad Mine

The love and concern Leo Duriez showed for the Mexican men who worked for him was repaid with an unbelievable loyalty showed by them when the CIO, which was very strongly entrenched in Oatman, tried to organize the miners in Goldroad. When the leaders of the union left Goldroad after their attempt to organize the workers, they had not been able to sign up one Mexican miner or surface worker. An unheard of happening in union organizing among a group of four hundred Mexican workers with only fifty white workers, which included salaried supervisors. This could all be attributed to the respect and admiration the men had for one man—Leo H. Duriez. My dad, Bill Richards, loved him.

The Goldroad Heat

Although the pool was located in the canyon in the Anglo part of town, and we had to pass by it on our way to the areas where we played in the mountains, we never went near the swimming pool. I was never closer than fifty feet to it. As we followed the paths past the pool on our hikes to the mountains beyond, there was never any verbal or physical exchange with the Mexican kids who were swimming there.

Mrs. Bert Rindlisbach was greatly admired and envied by all the other women in camp because of the beautiful flowers and rose bushes she grew. It was gossiped her secret to success was a new product called *Vigoro*.

Even if it were the secret to her success, *Vigoro* was too expensive for most family budgets, even for the extra flowers it might produce. The prettiest rose bushes in town were those raised by Mrs. Rindlisbach. A rose bush grew on each side of the steps leading to her front porch. The yellow rose bush was for her living daughter, Jane Wright, and the white rose bush was for her daughter who had died before the Rindlisbachs came to Goldroad. Jane and her husband and baby also lived in Goldroad.

The one flowerbed we had at the house on the hill was by the back steps. Daddy made it by placing one-by-twelve boards on top of the hard, rocky ground to hold the soil hauled from Silver Creek in a box in the trunk of our car. The only fertilizer the plants in this flowerbed received were the tea leaves from Daddy's nightly pot of tea.

There was only one patch of grass in the entire camp, and it belonged to Walter and Effie Elgin. He was the Engineer. They had no children, but he and my father were good friends. Effie and Mother visited each other, so I was at their house a few times. Their grass was a miniature putting green— miniature, meaning an area about ten feet by ten feet. They put tin cans in the ground for golf cups. Vella, Billy and I were allowed to play *golf* there one time. This was quite a privilege, but I could not understand why anyone would prefer golf to softball.

The Elgins owned the rock house they lived in. They had put a wood addition on to the house and fixed it up inside and out. Although the rock part was old, it was a very attractive home.

The Goldroad Heat

Three rock walls of their home stood for over fifty years until Addwest Minerals covered them over with its dump in the 1990s.

The reason given by the Elgins for not having children was Effie's small size. She stood about five feet tall and was slender. One time they were in a group of people where Mrs. Duriez and Daddy were present. Walter Elgin made the comment that Effie was too small to have children. Mrs. Duriez pointed to a Chihuahua dog with a litter of six or eight puppies and said, "If she can do it so can you, Effie."

Mrs. Duriez was like her husband Leo. There was nothing pretentious about either of them. They were down-to-earth in all aspects of their life. Mrs. Duriez' house was no larger or better than the other company houses built in camp. While other families were comfortably settled in their new company houses, the Duriez lived in the old hospital. Their house was one of, if not, the last to be built. No one really cared if the Elgins had children, but Mrs. Duriez' comment was a logical reply to the reason given by Walt.

The only tree in camp that was not one of the pathetic pygmy-sized castor bean trees was a salt cedar planted by the Johnsons, who were originally from Joplin, Missouri. They went down to the Colorado River, dug up a small tree, brought it back to camp, and planted it on the north side of the house they rented from Frank Onetto. When I went to Goldroad in 1989, this tree was magnificent. It towered fifteen or twenty feet in the air. When we returned in early 1991, the only growth on it was two small twigs on its trunk. The lack of rain during those two years must have brought the tree to this point. But the New Mexico gas company totally destroyed what was left of the tree when it brought its second gas line through Goldroad in the summer of 1991.

Mother and Daddy liked the Johnsons, and we spent time together in each of the homes. Trips were made to Kingman together to visit with their relatives. I especially liked Mr. Johnson. He held me on his lap and pulled his front teeth down. For a long time I tried to do the same thing with mine, but never succeeded. Not long before they left Goldroad to go back to Joplin, he revealed the secret of how he was able to do this—he had false teeth!

On my birthday, Mrs. Johnson gave me a wide, black, taffeta ribbon. I promptly took it home and tied it around the neck of my now-grown cat. Mom kept warning me the ribbon would snag on a bush, and the cat would be caught and die. But she looked so pretty in the ribbon, and I was willing to take the chance. This one time Mother was wrong. The ribbon did snag on the bushes and was soon split and tattered, but my cat always returned home safely. As long as I could make a bow, I used it.

The Goldroad Heat

Mrs. Johnson had nagged her husband for a long time to return to Joplin. We were hoping they would remain in Goldroad, because we had become such good friends with them. But whether he became tired of her nagging, or whether they came to the point financially they could afford to return, I do not know, but it was a sad day for our family when they pulled away from their home to return to Joplin, and we never saw them again.

Jack was Uncle Joe and Auntie's dog. He had been with them on the ranch east of Solomonsville, the Newberry Ranch in the Hualapais and their house in Kingman. Jack was a large dog with long brown hair tipped in black, and he was now getting too old to meet the challenges of younger male dogs in his neighborhood. But, sadly, he did not realize this fact and continued trying to maintain his dominance, although he was badly beaten in fights a number of times.

Finally the suggestion was made by someone in our extended family that the solution to Jack's problem would be to have him stay at our house in Goldroad. Although not many families in Goldroad had dogs, especially large dogs, several did live in Mexican town. When they got wind of Jack's presence in camp, they came by our house and issued a challenge. Jack accepted, although he was physically unable to protect himself. It became increasingly apparent to us eventually Jack would be killed or terribly mangled by the younger dogs if something was not done to prevent it. The only remaining merciful option was to have a family member kill Jack.

For Daddy to kill him was totally out of the question—he refused to even kill a chicken for dinner. Because Uncle Joe was so emotionally tied to Jack, it would be like killing a close friend. Thus, the lot of killing Jack fell on Uncle Son's shoulders. Not a good choice either because he loved animals, especially dogs. His favorite song was *Old Shep*—a song about love between a dog and his master. He carried to his grave a small scar on his lip caused when he unsuccessfully tried to break up a dogfight in Solomonsville when he was a child.

Frequently men and women are called upon to do things that hurt them deeply. But some things simply must be done. This is what happened when Uncle Son took Jack down to the tailings pond one evening and put a bullet through his head. It had to be done—for Jack's sake, to save him from further injury, pain and eventual death in another dogfight he could not win. It would have been cruel to allow him to continue to pull his tired, old body up off the ground one more time to meet the challenge of a younger, stronger dog.

The Goldroad Heat

Doing things that have to be done—almost a lost character trait in the world today. Because the American people had this character trait, the United States was able to beat the Japanese and Germans in World War II, even though the task looked impossible at the time. Today I question whether we have enough people remaining in this country who have this trait to defeat an attacking enemy.

The lack of this vital character trait in people is a factor in the high divorce rate not only in our country but also the world. Fathers and mothers choose what makes them feel good rather than what is best and right for their children.

Chapter 6

My First, Best Friend In Goldroad

…we never fell on the large outcropping of rock below us.

One afternoon in early 1938, Vella, William, Johnny and I were playing on a water pipe not far from our house. We noticed a man busily working a short distance away. He was not a man we recognized. But he came regularly to work on the site. In a very short time the skeleton of a house began to emerge, and on completion of it a family moved in. This was Marie Kirby's family. She was my first, best friend. The man we had seen building the house was her father.

Before Marie came to Goldroad, I had played with different girls in camp. Helen Kristich, who was Vella's age, was one. We held *catholic* funerals for any dead bugs we found and spent hours singing and marching like soldiers in their room-size shower. No one ever knew how much precious water we wasted.

Helen and I also explored the rock rooms under her house that had bars on the windows just like jail cells. Her mother was the first person I had ever seen who thought it more sanitary to let dishes drain dry than use a towel to dry them. Vella and I were the dish washers in our house, and I thought the drain drying was a very good idea, but when I approached Mother about using this method of drying dishes in our home, she was not convinced Helen's mother's way was best. And Vella and I continued with our regular schedule of trading places washing and drying the dishes.

Marie's house had a front porch, a living room, several bedrooms, a kitchen, and an open back porch. The back porch was high off the ground and had about ten steps leading to it. They were on the south side of the house, but the porch was on the west. Facing east, the front porch sat on the ground a few feet from the dirt road in front of the house.

The pipe from the kitchen sink was under the high back porch. And Marie and I spent many hours playing on this large pipe. Because it was high off the ground, we were able to hang from it by our knees. Directly under the pipe where we played was a large boulder. But practice had made us skilled in the gymnastics we performed on the pipe, and we never fell on the large outcropping of rock below us.

My First, Best Friend In Goldroad

Mr. Kirby was a tall, handsome man with dark hair. He always wore a black, cowboy hat. The family had originally come from Oklahoma, but their goal was to get to California. Although Mr. Kirby was always friendly to me, I was afraid of him. He ruled his family with an iron hand.

He did all the punishing of the children. One day Marie had to wait all day for him to come home from work, because he had told her before he left that morning he would spank her when he got home. Her mother felt sorry for her and told the other children to be kind to Marie, because she would be spanked when her father got home—and they all knew what that meant. I think his spankings were more than the few swats my mother gave us when we disobeyed.

Mrs. Kirby was a small, pretty woman with light hair and eyes. She was very timid and submissive to Mr. Kirby. He did all of the grocery shopping. One week he told her she would be allowed to do the shopping that week. When the time came for her to do it, he did it instead. I do not know why. Maybe he was punishing her for something. She was so disappointed she cried.

She had a medical condition that required daily medication. One time when she accidentally spilled her medicine, she was afraid for Mr. Kirby to learn about it. And she did not tell him immediately but hid it from him as long as possible. I do not know how he reacted. I was not there.

Mamie Kirby was Vella's age, Marie was my age, Jessie was Billy's age, and they had a baby about a year old.

Mamie and Vella became friends. Both were quiet and liked to play indoors. Marie and I became best friends and spent everyday together. When we were not hanging by our knees on the pipe under the porch, we were standing on our heads with our feet resting on the wall of their living room. Literally hours were spent in these activities.

When we tired of doing these things, we sang and made playhouses up under the floor of their house. Our favorite spot was under the front of the house where the floor was only a few feet off the ground. There was not much space for movement. But it was a cozy and cool place in the summertime, and we enjoyed it.

Even though I was uncomfortable around Mr. Kirby, I still accepted invitations to eat with them. But before my first meal at their house, because of their unusual table manners, Marie took time to seriously and carefully coach me on what I was to say at their dinner table. And I took seriously what she told me and did what she said.

My First, Best Friend In Goldroad

Rather than saying the usual, "Please pass the beans," as I had been taught, Marie told me I must say, "Thank you for the beans," when I asked for them. As young as I was I could feel the tension at their dinner table. They were all fearful, including Mrs. Kirby, of doing or saying something that would anger Mr. Kirby—but Jessie was the exception. She not only looked like Mr. Kirby—dark hair, dark eyes—but she had his temperament as well. She did not walk submissively before him as did Mrs. Kirby, Mamie and Marie. And the amazing thing was, I never saw him do anything about it. The first time I saw Jessie rebel, I was certain Mr. Kirby would explode, grab her up, and do something terrible to her. He did not, and I do not know why.

At my home the feeling at our dinner table was different from the one at the Kirby dinner table. Ours was a relaxed setting where each person, adult or child, felt comfortable contributing to the conversation. I believe Mr. Kirby loved Mrs. Kirby and his children, but their lives were totally controlled by him, and they lived in a cloud of fear.

He owned a black pickup truck and built a wooden cover, the forerunner of the present-day truck camper, over the bed of the truck so the children could ride in the back. In the middle of the week, after the movie was over, the Oatman Theater held a jackpot drawing for money. In anticipation of winning this money, Mr. Kirby loaded his wife and baby in the cab with him, his other kids, and sometimes me, in the back of the truck and off to the movies we would go.

On one of the jackpot nights, Daddy's name was drawn as the winner. If he had been there, he would have received twenty-five dollars—almost a week's pay. Our family's movie night was Sunday, but, because the movie showing the night his name was drawn starred Jeanette McDonald and Nelson Eddy, we would not have been there anyway. My father disliked their movies, especially Jeanette McDonald's singing. If he happened to be in one of their movies, when she began singing, he would get up and walk out and stay in the lobby.

My feeling toward Jeanette McDonald and Nelson Eddy was totally opposite from Daddy's. I idolized and loved them. After attending one of their movies, I would spend weeks and months singing the songs they sang and acting out the parts they played. The beautiful dresses she wore made me long to have lived when women dressed in such lovely gowns. As I played, I visualized myself as Jeanette McDonald and the handsome Nelson Eddy as my boyfriend. I would sing the *Indian Love Call* to him.

My First, Best Friend In Goldroad

Another movie that gave me many months of pleasure after our family saw it was *Snow White and the Seven Dwarfs*. To be able to see a movie in color with so much beauty and action was a delight in my life. With Vel and my friends, we would sing the songs from the movie and act out the parts. Especially still vivid in my mind are the words of "Hi Ho! Hi Ho! It's off to work we go, with a shovel and a pick and a dynamite stick, Hi Ho! Hi Ho! Hi Ho!" While singing this song, we would line up like the Seven Dwarfs and pretend to march off to work in the gem mine.

We did not have the opportunity to see a movie over and over again as the children do today. One time was all our family could afford, and if you did not catch the movie the first time, you were out of luck.

The Central Commercial sold small, individual ceramic Dwarfs tied on the top of a small amount of candy wrapped in cellophane. The Motz boys whose father was manager of the store collected all seven, but I knew it was impossible for me to have them—they were far too expensive. Our toys were limited to Christmas and our birthday. However, I never felt deprived— that's just the way it was.

Tarzan movies were also remembered and re-enacted by Vel and me. One part of a movie we liked very much was when Jane, Tarzan's wife, was puzzled by the size of the ostrich egg she was to prepare for the breakfast of Tarzan, Boy and herself. We re-enacted the scene over and over again.

Mr. Kirby must have liked baseball, although he did not play on the team, because he took his family to the games in Oatman. He never seemed to care if I came along. The games were good, and an intense rivalry existed between the Goldroad and Oatman teams. During one of the games, a fly ball made a hole in the top of his wooden pickup cover. It surprised me when he did not get mad.

One day as I was leaving the Kirby house and stepped off the front porch to go up the short incline to the road, I looked down and saw a small snake with red stripes lying directly under my feet. I was so frightened I hopped over the snake and started to run. The snake ran right behind me. When I realized the snake was chasing me and was almost touching my heels, I was even more terrified. I ran quite a distance before I was willing to stop to check to see if the snake was still behind me.

When I told Mother about the incident, she said the snake was probably as frightened as I was and was just trying to get away from me. But I was never convinced that was true. Years later I was vindicated when I read that the red racer snake did chase people.

My First, Best Friend In Goldroad

Mother had some dresses she could no longer wear, and she gave them to Mrs. Kirby. Among them was a red dress—red was Mother's favorite color at the time. Marie confided to me later that her dad had not allowed her mother to wear the red dress because "only bad women wear red." Mother was a little disgusted with that remark.

Mr. Kirby began coming to our house in the evenings to visit Daddy. He never brought Mrs. Kirby, and did not include Mother in the conversation. Over and over again he would tell the story about the time he had ptomaine poisoning and was given enough strychnine to kill a horse. When Daddy tired of the conversation, he would turn the conversation to World War I. He was a history buff and could talk for hours on the subject. Mr. Kirby knew nothing about history and he would soon leave.

Our normal family routine was to sit around the radio in the evening and listen to *Amos n' Andy*, *Fibber McGee & Molly*, and *Jack Benny & Rochester*. Mr. Kirby's visits intruded on our family time. Even though radio reception in Goldroad was very poor, we enjoyed our evenings together listening to these programs.

While our family listened to these programs, the Kirbys listened to the *Carter Family*--June Carter Cash's family. Mr. Kirby sent for the Carter family picture. I believe it was a calendar and was offered free for a donation. The calendar hung proudly on their living room wall and was the only picture in the room. Our family felt the Carter family was a little too country for our taste, but that did not affect Marie's and my friendship in any way.

Mamie had a talent for drawing. Occasionally, Mrs. Kirby's parents would come and bring art supplies for her. But Mamie and Marie had told me many times with a great deal of pride that their father had chosen their Mother over all the other girls in the orphanage to be his wife. Once I was in their home when the grandparents came and I could feel their discomfort in being there. But I also could see their resolve to be a part of the children's lives. And I have never understood the situation and am certain there must have been much more to the story than what I was told.

The Kirby family did not stay long in Goldroad, about a year. Goldroad was just a stopping-off place on their way to California. They left sometime after our return from our stay with our grandparents in Solomonsville during Mother's recuperation from tuberculosis. Marie had told me several times they would be moving to California when her dad had the money to buy a *banjo* steering wheel for his truck. This was an over-sized steering wheel with lots of chrome.

My First, Best Friend In Goldroad

Deep inside I was hoping he would never have the money to buy it, but the day did come, and he did load his family and their belongings into the truck and they left. We learned later Mrs. Kirby did not go with them, or if she did, she returned to Kingman sometime later. Henny told us she had seen her working at the five-and-ten cent store, and she was wearing make-up— something Mr. Kirby had not allowed her to do. Later Henny saw her on the street in Kingman, and she was wearing a fur coat.

For a time Vella wrote to Mamie in California, and I wrote to Marie. In the last letter I received from Marie, she mentioned her father had remarried.

A short time after the Kirby's left Goldroad, a new family moved into their house. One morning as we were playing with the Sayers, we became very excited when we noticed a boy about our age on the south side of the house playing in the dirt with a large toy truck. He had dark hair and was a very good looking boy. We learned his name was Colby Phelps, and he had an older sister Agnes who was in high school. His father worked for the company but there was no mother in the home.

But our early hopes for a new playmate did not materialize. Although Agnes was friendly and fit in with her group in camp, Colby was a loner. Perhaps it was because of his physical disability, a cleft palate that had never been corrected that caused his speech to be different. Or maybe it was because he had no mother living in his home. But he never relaxed with us or allowed us to accept him as a friend. And we tried.

The one time I remember playing with Colby was after we moved to the house on the hill. He was larger than Johnny, or even William. And while we were playing, he became angry over something. Because we did not know him very well and did not know what he would do, and we were also a little afraid of him, we decided to leave before he decided to start hitting us. Why he did not follow us at the time we left, I do not know. But this gave us time to climb our hill and hide in the unused coal box behind our house. We had not been in the coal box very long when we heard Colby go to our back door, knock and ask Mother if we were there. Upon learning we were not in the house, he then asked if she knew where we were. She told him she did not know. This was not a lie because she was unaware we had come home and had quietly hidden in the coal box.

During Mother's conversation with Colby, while his back was to us, we carefully lifted the lid and hurriedly peeked out. But we quickly put it down when their conversation was over. Then Colby left and went to his home.

My First, Best Friend In Goldroad

Then we climbed out of the coal box and told Mother where we had been while she talked with him. She was amused Colby had chased all of us into the coal box to hide. But the remainder of the day we stayed out of Colby's way, because we did not know what his intentions had been when he came to our house looking for us. Maybe he had wanted to apologize—something we had not thought of at the time. But that was the last attempt we made to play with him.

I liked Agnes even though she was a lot older than I. When a woman—their mother—came to stay for a time in the house next door to the Kirby-Phelps house, I went there several times with Agnes to visit. The four or five girls who came with the mother were either full or half-sisters to Agnes and Colby, because Agnes referred to them as her sisters. When we went into the bathroom, I was impressed by the many hair brushes neatly hung on the wall, each a different color, one for each girl.

The girls were all very pretty and very feminine. In looks and behavior Agnes stood apart—she had pretty dark hair, but appeared plain when compared to her sisters. And where they were light-hearted and frivolous in their conversation, she was serious and mature. This difference did not seem to affect her relationship with them, but she was like oil in water. The woman and her daughters stayed for a time, but left as mysteriously and quietly as they had come. No one else in camp seemed to be aware that they had even been there and left, except me. I do not know why she and her daughters did not stay in the house with Mr. Phelps, Agnes and Colby, or why they had even come.

Chapter 7

The Sayers And The Richards Kids

There was a special bond that existed between the Sayer's and Richards' kids.

The Sayer family lived one house over from us. The Johnsons lived between. They lived in one of the company houses that had all been painted dark green with white trim. Bill Sayer was the assistant mill superintendent under Paris V. Brough. The Sayer family was in Goldroad because Mr. Brough had recruited Bill Sayer when he worked at the Bingham Canyon operation in Utah.

Members of the Bill Sayer family included his wife Monty, sons William and John, and daughter JoAnn. Their children's ages matched the ages of our family, which in 1937 were 8, 6, and 3. We also shared a strong English background—Bill Sayer came from England as a child; my grandfather came from England as a young boy of fourteen. There was a special bond that existed between the Sayer's and Richards' kids.

My first boyfriend, Johnny Sayer

The Sayers And The Richards Kids

Johnny and I entered first grade together the fall of 1937. Our first grade class met in the new building completed just before school started. Our teacher was a blonde, unmarried woman by the name of Miss Templeton. She lived in Kingman and drove each morning the twenty-five miles to Goldroad.

At the time phonics was not taught in most Arizona schools. But Johnny and I were having difficulty with the new sight-reading method of teaching. And Mrs. Sayer thought it might be helpful for Johnny and me if I would go to their house each morning before school. There she reviewed the reading words with us. But this extra effort did not help our reading. And when the school year was over, the Sayers decided to hold Johnny back in the first grade and not allow him to go to second grade.

Perhaps, because Mrs. Sayer was a trained teacher, she felt her background gave her a better understanding of Johnny's readiness for second grade. But my parents had faith in my ability to succeed and never considered holding me back. And I am grateful they felt this way, because as things turned out, later that summer my mother became very ill with tuberculosis.

My grandmother took Vella and me to her home in Solomonsville where we attended school until Christmas. There I had a tremendous second grade teacher — Mrs. Brimhall — who taught phonics and drilled us on the sounds. When I returned to my class in Goldroad at Christmas time, I could read circles around everyone in the class. I was even sent into the third grade class to read to them. From that time on, I was an A student. But I am getting ahead of my story — more about Miss Templeton. Everyday an incident occurred in our class that still puzzles me. Oscar Armaro was a member of our class. And as Miss Templeton was teaching in front of the class, Oscar would run up behind her, drop to his knees, put his head on the floor and look up her dress. This would also happen if she bent over to do something with her back to the class. Oscar would run up very quickly behind her and do the same thing. Every time he did this, I died a thousand deaths! I was *so* embarrassed. My fear was that he would get caught, and all of us in the class would have to witness his punishment and humiliation. Even as a six-year-old child, I could not understand why Miss Templeton did not see or hear him. And if she did know, and I do not know how she could not have known, why did she allow this behavior to continue throughout the school year.

The Sayers And The Richards Kids

Oscar was a lecherous little six-year-old kid. He not only looked up the teacher's dress, but he also brought a small hand-sized mirror onto the playground each recess to drop on the ground at the feet of any girl he could find standing still for a moment. He would look at the reflection of the girl's pants in the mirror if she did not move away quickly. Why he bothered to go to these lengths is a mystery to me. Most of the girls wore their dresses quite short anyway, and all he had to do to see our pants was to be patient and follow us around for a while. We were very active in our play, and our dresses flew up quite often in dodge ball, flipping over the bars, playing hopscotch or hanging by our knees from the bars. I often wonder what happened to him after a start in life like that!

Miss Templeton was pretty and she was always kind to me. I liked her, but the parents felt she did not put enough time or interest, and effort into her teaching. On one of our trips to Kingman, our family saw her coming out of the cocktail lounge next to the Beale Hotel. That was probably the final straw on Miss Templeton's teaching career in Goldroad. She was not there the next year—Bill Sayer was president of the School Board and my father was on the Board.

During this same period of time, one day as I came home from school for lunch, I was startled by what I saw. As I approached the kitchen door there was blood on the ground and on the door. Frightened, I quickly ran into the house and saw Mother patting the top of Billy's head with a wet cloth. A deep crease about an inch long had been made in his head. Billy and JoAnn had been using a piece of pointed scrap iron to dig a hole in the dirt by the side of the house. They had devised a system—one would dig and the other would pull the dugged dirt to their side of the hole. And the system worked great for a while—until Billy dug before JoAnn finished pulling the dirt out of the hole! The metal point struck JoAnn on her finger. What did she do? Did she run home crying to her mother for comfort? No! She took care of the situation herself—she grabbed the piece of iron and hit him over the head with it!

When I got back to school, I was so upset I started to cry as I was telling Johnny about it. He knew nothing about it. JoAnn had not told her mother why she had abruptly come home and was no longer playing with Billy. If Johnny did not tell his parents what JoAnn had done, they never knew, because my parents never approached them about it.

JoAnn usually wore a little green beanie William had worn when he was her age. Her hair was cut short just below her ears. And Billy liked to tease her by getting behind her, pushing the beanie forward over her eyes, and then giving her hair a little tug. This really made her angry.

The Sayers And The Richards Kids

Although we were good friends, this was not the first time a Richards had been hurt by a Sayer, or a Sayer hurt by a Richards. Rocks were a novelty to us when we moved to Goldroad, and they were everywhere. We used them as entertainment, and we would compete with each other to see who could throw the farthest. But, they were also readily available when we became angry, and it was during one of those times I was hit in the forehead with one.

During our play, William and Johnny, and Vella and I had become angry with each other. They had gone up the hill from our house and were throwing rocks at us, and we were throwing them back. Not long into the fight, I felt a terrible pain on my left forehead, and then the blood began to run. The fight stopped, and William and Johnny ran for home.

Mr. and Mrs. Sayer found out about my injury some way. Our family never told them, because my parents believed parents should not become involved in their kids' fights. They felt we should be allowed to work out the problems by ourselves. Because kids soon make up and are friends again, but parents remain angry. Anyway, their parents found out about it some way, and Mr. Sayer came over to ask me who had thrown the rock. Why ask the question if you are not willing to believe the answer. When I told him William had done it, he did not believe me. He reasoned because Johnny was my boyfriend, I was trying to protect him. Both of them got spanked.

The tables were turned a short time later when I threw a rock at William's homemade, wooden scooter. We would pull it to the top of a hill, get on, and someone would give us a push. And down the hill we would go, steering with our feet, to the bottom. I do not remember the reason William became angry that day and took his scooter and started home with it. But I was upset because I could see no reason for him to be angry and to ruin our fun. And I still wanted to play. Just to show my displeasure with him and what he was doing, I threw a rock at his scooter. It hit the scooter at just the proper angle to bounce up and break one of his upper side teeth. But I had not thrown the rock at him. I had thrown it at his scooter.

Mr. Sayer came over again to talk over what had happened, but my parents never said anything to me about the broken tooth. They knew it had been an accident, and I had not intended to hit William. But I decided on my own at that time never to throw another rock—and I did not.

The Sayers And The Richards Kids

While I still had the knot on my forehead from the rock William had thrown, and by the way I still carry the scar, our school presented a Christmas program for our parents. Because Johnny and I were in first grade, we were members of the rhythm band. Our mothers had been given a pattern to make our band uniform tops. They were made from bright blue material with a cape lined in bright red. White round-like-a-ball buttons were sewed onto red strips of cloth placed horizontally down the front of the top. We wore white trousers. Each top was a little different from the other in the length of the strips of red cloth on the front and the placement of the round white buttons. Each mother had interpreted the directions on the pattern differently. But these differences were minor and only added to the uniqueness of the band.

How grand we looked when we stood to play our sticks, triangles, cymbals, bells and drums! The other classes participated by singing the Christmas carols, but they did not have uniforms. After the program, Daddy made the comment, "Norma Jean always has a bandaged knee, a bump on her head, or a front tooth out when programs are held." I started to dispute what he had said, but realized, after thinking back, he was right.

Mother had given a few of her old ball gowns to us to play *dress-up*. I thought one was more beautiful than the others. It was pale green with a form-fitting bodice and rows of ruffles on the bottom of the skirt. One afternoon my parents drove off for a short time and left Vella and me home. We had the dresses out and were playing with them when Johnny and William came over. They put on the ball gowns. I cannot remember whether Johnny or William had on the green dress with the ruffles, but one of them did. But when they saw my parents driving toward the house, they were so embarrassed at the thought of being caught in a dress, they almost tore the dresses apart getting out of them. They threw them on the ground where they had taken them off and ran for home before Mother and Daddy could get out of the car.

Vella and I stood perplexed and surprised at their sudden change in behavior. We had not seen the car with Mother and Daddy approaching. But when we did, we still could not understand why they were embarrassed to be seen by our parents in a play dress. Mother and Daddy just smiled to themselves and went on into the house without comment. Vella and I retrieved our damaged dresses from the ground and vowed never to let Johnny and William ever wear them again!

The Sayers And The Richards Kids

When we had nothing else to do and we were bored, softball would come into our minds. Johnny and William owned the equipment—balls and bats. Then off to the school playground we would go. It was the only large flat space in camp. After much bargaining for our favorite position, the game would then begin. But the first pitch and ball hit always brought the game to a halt. I do not remember our ever getting past the first pitch before a disagreement over the *rules* started.

No one listened as each person tried to out-yell and out-argue the others. Everyone tried to add credibility to his own argument by adding this phrase, "the rules say." Johnny and William claimed they had a rulebook, but I never saw it, and none of us seemed to care. Because I argued and yelled as loudly as the others and tried to make my arguments more credible by adding, "the rules say" in an attempt to get the game played the way I wanted. I doubt anyone, even Johnny and William, had read a softball rulebook. When we reached the point where we finally realized no one was willing to give in, although we had all shouted "the rule says", William would get angry and red in the face, gather up the equipment and go home. This scenario was repeated over and over again during our years in Goldroad. Obviously, we found this activity entertaining and a normal part of our play, because we never tired of trying to play ball together.

On an incline not far from the road in front of the hospital and not far from the Sayer's house, stood a firebox. Because it was a firebox, it was painted a brilliant red. For us it had many more important uses than being available for fires. First, it was home base for our nighttime hide-n-seek games. During the day, we sat on it, we stood on it, we hung on it, and we played around it with small cars run on roads smoothed out in the dirt.

After the cars and hide-n-seek had passed from our lives, Johnny and William carved their romantic feelings on its lid—WS+VMR and JS+NJR. In 1957 when I returned to Goldroad for the first time since leaving in November 1942, the red firebox was still sitting there just as bright red as it had been fifteen years earlier when I had left. The hearts and initials were as new as the day they had been carved there by William and Johnny.

The hospital across the street from the Sayer house had a large front porch three or four feet high enclosed with boards. Johnny and William enticed Bobby Brough, who was Johnny's age and the mill superintendent's son, to go under the porch through a hole made by pulling one of the boards loose. When Bobby was inside, Johnny and William quickly nailed the loose board back onto the porch. Upon finding himself nailed in and with no way to escape, Bobby began howling and yelling for help.

The Sayers And The Richards Kids

He was eventually heard and freed, but Mr. Sayer, with tongue in cheek, always made the comment he really thought he was going to lose his job over that episode.

One evening Johnny and William placed a *Detour* sign with an arrow on Route 66 diverting all of its traffic past their house, the Peeples, the Rindlisbachs, the Onettos, and on down the hill and around the curve to a dead end at the mill. As far as I know, no adult ever found out who had placed the sign on the highway. But I feel certain if Paris Brough had found out who had directed all of the cars to dead end at his mill, this time he *would* have fired Mr. Sayer.

The Sayer family drove a black Ford sedan. I do not know the year. They decided to replace it and made plans to drive to the factory back east to buy a new Plymouth. By doing that, their family would have a nice trip and also save the shipping charges for the car. Mrs. Sayer made special pillows from drapery samples from the Steinfeld department store in Tucson where Mr. Sayer's father worked. The pillows were to be used as back rests for the driver on the long trip and as pillows for the tired and sleepy children.

About this same time, they acquired an English Bulldog. She was white, and her name was *Suzie*. She was large and ugly—a true, purebred English Bulldog. I remember she had one batch of puppies, but I do not know how they disposed of them. Although I was a dog lover, I never had the desire to pet Suzie. She drooled a lot from her mashed nose and mouth, but the Sayer kids did not mind and were very fond of her.

In summer when Johnny and William were younger and the afternoon heat was extreme, they were not allowed outside to play. Because we had the large screened porch and the vine-covered yard, our play was not as restricted. During these afternoons indoors, we could hear Johnny and William on their beds playing recorders to wile away the time.

When Mrs. Onetto visited her daughter who owned the theater in Needles, she would bring balloons home to us from the theater. We spent many summer afternoons keeping the inflated balloons high in the air away from the rough, splintery floor of the screened porch. Many times Mrs. Onetto brought the unsold popcorn and items left behind in the theater. She was most thoughtful in this way, and we appreciated what she gave us.

Located in the center of the camp on a hill was the big, silver water tank. A siren was mounted on its top, and each day at 11:30 A.M. it would sound letting the workmen and the school children know it was lunchtime. Most of the surface workers and all of the school children walked home for lunch. When we were not in school, the siren let us know when we were to run for home as fast as possible.

The Sayers And The Richards Kids

Daddy always walked home for dinner, as lunch was called then, and Mother always prepared a full meal for us. We were expected to be there and on time. Supper, as it was called then, was a few minutes after the whistle blew at 4:00 P.M. when Daddy got off work and we were out of school. The evening meal was not as large as dinner, but we knew to get home quickly when we heard it blow.

At the base of the large silver water tank, a concrete lip extended out twelve or fourteen inches. It was a good place to play. But sometimes when we became bored with our play, Johnny and William would suggest another more exciting activity—throwing rocks on Cloyd Henline's tin roof just down the hill.   After the rocks hit, it did not take Cloyd long to come running out of his house. But by that time we had run down over the side of the hill onto the road by the conveyor belt into Mexican town.

Cloyd Henline, Goldroad Mine Purchasing Agent

One time, Cloyd had had enough of our rock-throwing game, and he not only came running out of his house, he chased us to the edge of the hill. He stood and looked down on us as we walked along the road by the conveyer belt where we always ran. Because we had been caught, we tried to fool him into thinking we were Mexican kids by using the few Mexican words we knew as we talked to each other. Of course he knew who we were and was not fooled by our attempted disguise. But he probably knew he had succeeded in getting his point across about his seriousness in not tolerating anymore rocks on his roof.

The Sayers And The Richards Kids

The Henlines were a young, married couple. Cloyd had come to Goldroad via school in Southern California and a family friendship with N.R. Dunton. He lived with them when he first arrived in Goldroad. He not only worked in the warehouse as the warehouseman, but he also helped Joe Peeples in the office.

When Don and Yvonne Johnson arrived in Goldroad in the spring of 1938, they became friends with Cloyd and June. The men played basketball on the same team, but the families also spent time at the Colorado River together. Don owned a kayak. They would load it on the car, the women would pack a picnic lunch, and they would head for the river, which at that time was swift and muddy. A sheet would be thrown over a mesquite tree for shade, and they would spend the day eating and talking.

Don built a tent house where he and Yvonne camped out while he built a small, four-room, 20' by 22' house. Construction was 2x4 frame with corrugated iron roofing and siding, and 1/2" celotex inside lining. The floor was clear 1x4 vertical grain T&G Douglas Fir and cost $20 per mbm; framing lumber, studs-joists-rafters, and miscellaneous items ran about $35 per mbm. All building materials were dirt-cheap. And they had to be because, as Don said, they were poor as church mice. After a down payment, he signed a note with the Central Commercial Co. in the amount of $350 to cover the cost of most of the materials.

One evening Mike Romney, an engineer from the Salt Lake office, and his wife went to the Hilltop Restaurant in Kingman with Cloyd and June. This was a very nice place—the elite eatery in the Kingman area. The women excused themselves to go to the ladies room. When coming out, they noticed a man coming in—they had gone into the men's restroom! Now they really felt like two hicks from the sticks.

Cloyd Henline's house was on the hill behind the conveyer belt.
(Courtesy of Mohave County Historical Society)
77.

Chapter 8

Goldroad Grammar School

I never had a teacher I did not like, but George Marich has to be my favorite of them all.

Many dedicated, well-trained teachers were in the Goldroad Grammar School. They were the ones who came and stayed. The others left when their teaching contracts were not renewed.

Looking east up the hill (left): Kirby house, Uncle Son & Henny's 1ˢᵗ Onetto house, Redding house, older school building, newer school building, Morris Bird house, Joan Bird's tent house behind Morris Bird house, Gray house. Looking east up the hill (right): Wright house, Anderson house.
(Courtesy of the Descendants of Flora and Joe Onetto)

Goldroad Grammar School

Alice Plummer, a widow, and her daughter Madeline, who was a year older than I, was hired in the fall of 1938. Although Madeline and I played together at different times, and I spent the night on occasion during the years we were in Goldroad, Mrs. Plummer was always *my teacher* and not *Madeline's mother*. When I returned at Christmas from Solomonsville, I was in her second grade class. She was also my third and fourth grade teacher and the two months of my sixth grade before we left for New Mexico. My friendship with Madeline never affected in anyway the student-teacher relationship with Mrs. Plummer. We never had any personal exchange outside of the classroom.

She was a serious, dedicated teacher who was exact and precise in her teaching. Strict discipline also applied in her classes. If a student broke the silence during study time, they would very quickly be reminded by the loud sound of her long, wooden map pointer as it hit the side of her desk.

She also had a rule about chewing gum. Anyone caught chewing gum during class had to spit it in the trash can. And the wrapped gum in our desk had to be placed in a small box kept in her desk. When enough gum had been accumulated for the entire class to have a piece, she would get out the box, and everyone would be allowed to chew gum for the remainder of the afternoon. To show how serious it was to lose your gum to the trash can, gum was *saved* on headboards, drain boards, or any safe place for later chewing. Rarely was it ever voluntarily thrown away.

The knowledge still remaining with me about this country's history and the geography of the world, I owe to the in-depth teaching Mrs. Plummer did in those areas. And this also applies to English and Math as well. The day-after-day drilling she did with us provided a good foundation for my future learning.

When we arrived in Silver City, New Mexico, in early November of 1942 and I enrolled in the much larger and more sophisticated school system, the report card I brought from Goldroad with all "1s" was not taken seriously by my teacher Miss Williamson. She put me on the 6B side of the classroom rather than the 6A where my report card indicated I belonged.

However, it did not take her long to move me over to the 6A side of the room when it became embarrassingly evident she had made an error in assuming the teaching I had received in Goldroad had not been of high quality.

Goldroad Grammar School

As I proved my ability to be the top student in each succeeding class I entered, inside I always was aware of a feeling of a private victory for the Goldroad School. Because Mrs. Plummer was my teacher three-and-a-half years of my five years-plus-two-months of school there, the credit must be given to her.

Mrs. Plummer's interest was not only with the student who had the ability to learn and who had the opportunity to go forward with it. But she was also concerned about the students who had abilities but were in danger of not having the opportunity to develop them.

One such incident happened on an afternoon when I dropped by Madeline's house to play with her. When I went into the kitchen, Joaquin Garcia (I always thought his name was Holguin) was working with paper and paints. He was a Mexican student known at school and admired for his artistic talent. But to find him in an Anglo home was not only unusual, but it just never happened.

Earlier, when Mrs. Plummer had approached Joaquin's father about his son's talent and about encouraging and developing this talent, he acknowledged the artistic ability of his son, but shared with her his logic and reasons for not encouraging him. He believed Joaquin would never be able to make a living from painting and needed to look to something more realistic—such as mining—for his livelihood.

This explanation did not satisfy Mrs. Plummer, and she determined she would encourage him within the limits of her role as his teacher. He was in their home that day at the invitation of Mrs. Plummer using paints Madeline had received as a gift. These paints were highly prized by her, but Mrs. Plummer had convinced Madeline to share them with Joaquin.

I sensed my appearance had created an uncomfortable situation for the three of them, and without a word Joaquin quickly put away the art supplies and quietly left. I was disappointed, because I enjoyed drawing very much and had always found Joaquin's art work at school fascinating. To have been given the opportunity to see him create, would have made an interesting afternoon for me.

Being Mexican was not the reason Joaquin's dad felt as he did about encouraging him to be an artist. If an Anglo child had displayed the same artistic talent as Joaquin, the Anglo father's response would probably have been the same as Joaquin's dad.

But the Mexican children did labor under an added obstacle to learning that the Anglo did not have—that obstacle was language. Goldroad Grammar School had three first grades—1A, 1B, and 1C. Some Mexican children went through all three before they came into second grade.

Goldroad Grammar School

Not because they were less intelligent than the Anglo child, but because of the language barrier—they had to learn English at school.

When Goldroad closed and the people were transferred to New Mexico, many of the Mexicans returned to their former home in Fierro. It was a very small town approximately five miles north of the main mine where the mill, offices, and houses were built and my family lived. These families were originally from Fierro and had worked under Leo Duriez there before the operation closed a short time after the Depression began. Joaquin's family was one of the families returning to Fierro.

While living at the Bullfrog property, the few times I saw Joaquin, and this was high school age, were when he rode by in a car on his way to the mill area. Maybe he settled for being a mill worker rather than a miner, or maybe he was picking up his dad from work.

One morning the school was abuzz with the news that Mrs. Joe Gallegos had died during the night giving birth to a baby boy.

Her death left a newborn baby boy, four older sons and a daughter. All of the Gallegos children attended Goldroad School except Cecilia, the one girl. At the time of her mother's death she was too young to be in school. Juan was the oldest and was in Vella's class, Joe Jr. was Vella's age but was not in her class, Francisco was in my class, and Severo was Billy's age.

Joe Gallegos was respected and loved by Daddy. His children were always well cared for and well behaved, except young Joe. Perhaps his mother's death was more difficult for him than it was for the others, and he showed his loss in a negative way. Sometime after his mother's death, Joe Jr. had a confrontation at school with the principal, Mr. Sundgren. Mr. Sundgren hit him in the face and bloodied his nose. Young Joe left the school and returned a short time later with his father.

Joe Sr. demanded to know why Mr. Sundgren had hit his son so hard he had bloodied his nose. He expressed his willingness to have Joe Jr. disciplined when he needed it but was angered by the excessive force used in this instance. I did not see the initial conflict between Joe Jr. and Mr. Sundgren, but I was in the classroom after school when Joe Sr. found Mr. Sundgren. Joe Sr. was embarrassed when he saw me in the background and knew I had seen and heard what had happened with Joe Jr.

Each day on his way to the mill to check on the ball mills, Daddy would stop at the Gallegos home just below the conveyor belt to make sure the new baby was doing well. He would take a few minutes to talk and play with him, and when he was satisfied the baby was all right, he would be on his way.

Goldroad Grammar School

When Cecilia entered first grade, her teacher braided her hair each morning when she arrived at school and tied brightly-colored scraps of silk cloth on the ends. The silk cloth had been brought to school to make a stained-glass window for a school play. Joe Gallegos never remarried and was in the group who moved to New Mexico.

Because Anglo and Mexican did not play together, only at school in organized games, the ratio of approximately two hundred Mexican children with approximately twenty Anglos enrolled in the school, made it difficult to find friends to play with. I have listed all Anglo children in camp. Those with asterisks are children either my age or within a two-year range: *William Sayer; *Johnny Sayer; JoAnn Sayer; *Arthur Motz; *Bobby Brough; *Marvin Motz; Helen Brough-high school; *Motz-child; Janet Brough-toddler; *G.W. Phelps; Linda Henline-toddler; Dale Wright; *Vella Richards; Jimmy Bird-child; *Norma Richards; Terry Bird-baby; Billy Richards; *Joan Bird; Margie Duriez-high school; *Alma Dean Doolin; Philip Duriez-high school; Freddy Doolin; George Duriez-high school; Jimmy Doolin; *Helen Kristich; Tommy Cudney; Nicky Kristich-high school; Sharon Cudney-baby; Shirley Peeples-high school; *Colby Phelps; Billy Dell Hicks; Agnes Phelps-high school; *Roger Williamson; *Mamie Kirby; Janet Hicks-baby; *Marie Kirby; Jessie Kirby; *Madeline Plummer; Baby Kirby; *Duane Bird; Bobby Kay Massey; Bird-girl; Kenny Guy Massey-baby; Bird-girl; *Georgina Phillips; *Rosie Redding; Elsie Redding-high school; *Arlene Phillips;Mike Gillespie; Phillips-girl; *Howard Deming; Marich-baby; Fitzpatrick-child; Fitzpatrick-child.

The only fight I know of between an Anglo and a Mexican child was between Vella and Rosie Hernandez. Although Vella was two years older than I, she was no taller. Mother always dressed us alike, and from the back, even Daddy could not tell us apart. Rosie was at least a head taller than Vella, but Vella was feisty and would take on anyone no matter her size.

During lunchtime before school took up, Vella was at the Central Commercial buying candy. Rosie was eating a chocolate cupcake. Rosie said something and Vella lunged at her. Rosie grabbed Vella's long hair with her sticky, chocolate-covered hands, and they fought. One of Daddy's friends at work told him he had just seen his daughter down at the Central Commercial "clean a bigger girl's plow." Daddy was pleased, but Mother was upset with Vella because she came home from school with chocolate cupcake in her clean hair. The fight must have happened on a Monday, because our hair was always washed and curled each Saturday.

Goldroad Grammar School

The happy ending to this story is, when Vella and Rosie were both mothers and had daughters who were the same age and lived as neighbors at the USSR&MCo Mine in New Mexico, their daughters played together.

There were two Mexican families in Goldroad that were different from the other families. In one family, although they were Mexican, the children had bright, red hair. They were older and did not attend school. However, the other unusual Mexican family had a son a few years older than I was. He had blonde hair, white skin, and blue eyes and did attend Goldroad Grammar School. While we were on the playground, I was always startled when he spoke in Mexican—it seemed to be so inconsistent with his coloring.

My father and mother had known this family in Fierro, when the boy was a toddler. His father, who was a very dark Mexican, was especially proud of his son and would take him with him everywhere in the car to show him off.

Softball was an important activity in our lives. It was played during recess at school, and Goldroad's team competed against Oatman's on a regular basis. Mother and Daddy were out of town, and Vella, Billy and I were staying with Gale and Babe Cudney until their return. We had a big game with Oatman, and Babe loaded a group of us into her black, Ford coupe and headed for the game. On the long hill that ends in a right angle at the top, before it winds over to the Silver Creek road, our little Ford reached an alarming speed for such a dangerous hill. Almost before we realized it was happening, Babe reached down and thrust Carmen Mendez' foot off the accelerator. In the cramped quarters, Carmen had unknowingly put her foot on the gas pedal.

Although the swings on the school grounds had been taken down because of misuse by some of the children, we filled our recess time with many interesting activities. Dodge ball was a game everyone seemed to enjoy until the boys joined in, and then the sting on our bare legs from their swiftly thrown balls ruined our fun.

Hopscoch was played with special taws on outlines dug deep into the ground when the dirt was wet. Red glass from old, shattered taillights was the choicest of all taws. Games of jump rope were scattered around the playground. The high, bare bars left from the swings were great for swinging by our hands. And the low bars left from the previous teeter-totters were perfect for doing flips.

When the school playground was enlarged, and a high fence was placed on the side away from the mountain, we no longer had to chase the red, rubber balls down the hill that were used for dodge ball. And the softballs no longer had to be retrieved, either.

Goldroad Grammar School

But when the blasting was done to loosen the rock to enlarge the school playground, although a cover had been placed over the blasting area, a large rock was thrown high into the air. It hit a distance away and came through the Rindlisbach's roof and kitchen ceiling hitting Mrs. Rindlisbach on the head. She was hurt badly, and her head remained bandaged for a long time. Although she recovered from the wound, she never seemed to be quite the same after the experience.

To have an accident with blasting was unusual. Controlled blasting was done all of the time in the mine. And it had even been done previously at a site only ten feet below the rock wall where the lower school building stood— while school was in session.

The company paid for all of Mrs. Rindlisbach's medical expenses, and they never considered suing the company.

I never had a teacher I did not like, but George Marich has to be my favorite of them all. He was my first male teacher. In my opinion, children come in two categories: those who gravitate toward men, and those who gravitate toward women—I was a *man* person, and I thoroughly enjoyed Mr. Marich my fifth grade. He lived on the opposite side of the canyon on the hill near the mine, and I lived in the house on the hill in the middle of the camp.

Because I enjoyed school, I accidentally arrived one morning before Mr. Marich. He teased me and said he would beat me to school the next morning, and he did. But he did not have a chance. I soon realized the advantage I had of being able to see him as he left his house. All I had to do to beat him was to run down our hill to the school when I saw him leave his house. One morning he tried to outrun me when he came around the hill onto the school ground and saw me coming down the hill. But I still beat him. We played the game for awhile, but he soon gave up.

My desk was next to his. One time when I had finished my work before the rest of the class, I took the papers as they were put in his basket and corrected them. He had not asked me to do this. But when I did it, he allowed me to continue throughout the remainder of the school year.

Maybe he was happy to have some help, or perhaps he thought I needed something to occupy my time while he worked with some of the other students.

There were a few mornings when the following happened. After the pledge of allegiance had been said outside around the flagpole, and we had come into our classroom and had settled down for the morning, Mr. Marich would take a small piece of red construction paper from his desk and thumbtack it to the end of the heavy piece of wood he used as a paddle. He kept it sandwiched between the books on his desk.

85.

Goldroad Grammar School

Then he would warn us the flag meant he was in a bad mood, and we had better be on our good behavior. On one of the red flag days, Jose Gonzalez forgot the warning and felt the sting of the heavy paddle.

George Marich was a large man who had lettered in baseball at Arizona State University. Goldroad was his first teaching position after graduation. I believe he had other offers, but the school board, Daddy especially, wanted him because he was Sam Marich's son. Sam was very much liked and respected by the company-men, and they were happy to have his son teach their children. Of course, I knew none of this when I was in Goldroad, other than he had a father in camp, but I just liked Mr. Marich because he was a good teacher and I enjoyed him.

Sam Marich was a Yugoslavian, as were the Pete Kristich and the George Phillips families. Sam Marich's family lived in Globe, Arizona, and we did not know George Marich until he came to teach in Goldroad. When the mine closed, Sam Marich was transferred with us to the operation in New Mexico where he lived in a small one-room house across the street behind us. On a number of occasions he took us to the drug store in nearby Bayard and treated us to ice cream sundaes. After his retirement, he would arrive by bus, stay with us a few days, get back on the bus and return home to Globe.

Fifth through eighth grades were in the older, smaller building which sat a few feet lower than the larger, new building where first through fourth met. A teacher in each building rang a hand bell when recess or lunchtime was over. Then the children all returned to their classrooms.

However, one recess our fourth grade class had already returned to our room when we saw Georgina Phillips run past our windows ringing the bell as hard she could—with Mr. Marich in hot pursuit. We later learned she had grabbed the bell from him when it was time to go back into class and had started running with it. That looked like great fun to me, and I could hardly wait to be in his class the next year and run with the bell.

One of the first grade teachers who had arrived in Goldroad in 1939, a year before Mr. Marich, was Miss Ella Watkins. All of the girls in school thought she was pretty and admired her beautiful clothes and long, painted fingernails. Alma Dean Doolin's two older sisters just knew the fingernails had to be fake. They refused to give Miss Watkins credit for growing them herself. She taught one of the first grades as well as art to the other classes. She was Billy's first grade teacher. The first year she taught in Goldroad John White, a teacher who drove from Kingman each morning in his roadster, tried to date her. But she rejected his overtures, and we, her admirers, agreed with her evaluation of him.

Goldroad Grammar School

But when George Marich arrived at the school for his first year of teaching, we were rooting for him, because we felt it was a marriage made in heaven—he was tall, dark and handsome. But more important than that, he was extremely nice. We felt he was a perfect match for our petite, pretty Miss Watkins. She must have felt the same way, because, instead of rejecting his efforts to begin a relationship like she had with Mr. White, she responded to them.

In October, just one month into the school year, Mr. Marich invited Miss Watkins to attend the college football game his brother was playing in at Flagstaff. And she accepted. They had never dated before. The trip had to be made by bus from Goldroad to Kingman, where the train was boarded for Flagstaff. It was on this first date he asked her to marry him—and she said "yes". He always attributed the swiftness of the proposal to the high, rarified air of Flagstaff.

We were not aware of the marriage proposal but did notice them talking together during recess. We would smile knowingly to each other and express our approval. And it was not long before they were walking around camp together in the evenings.

One evening a few of us, including the Sayers, saw them walking down the highway in front of Dunton's garage. The girls hurriedly got up on the porch of the office, and the boys stayed on the ground, and we started reciting *Romeo, Romeo, wherefore art thou, O Romeo?* They just smiled and walked on down the highway knowing that if they were to be alone, they would have to walk to Oatman, which was a couple of miles. They did not know this, but they were safe from us when they got beyond the conveyor belt that crossed over the highway, because we were not allowed to go beyond that point at night. Neither of them had a car to go into Kingman or Needles for entertainment. But they were probably saving their money to get married.

Ella lived in the Henline Apartments where Mrs. Plummer and Madeline lived, and they had become friends. When she discussed her decision to marry Mr. Marich with Mrs. Plummer, she gave Miss Watkins some good, practical, womanly advice—buy all of the clothes you can before you get married, because after you get married, there will be no money for them.

Goldroad Grammar School

The Henline Apartments

When school was out for summer vacation, they were married in a Catholic Church, but not in Goldroad. And they returned in the fall for Mr. Marich to teach. They moved into the tent house that was owned by Sam Marich. He had shared this house with his dad the previous school year. Sam moved into the dugout behind them. In the proper amount of time, a little baby boy—George—was born. Madeline and I enjoyed visiting him. His bassinet was by the window, and he was fascinated by the movement of a small tree outside, and spent hours talking to it.

Ella made the tent house very comfortable and pleasant. Folded across their bed was Mr. Marich's letterman blanket from Arizona State University and his letterman jacket hung on a nail on the wall. This was a happy family.

Married women with children at home were not hired as teachers in Goldroad. Mrs. Reid, whose husband worked at the mill, either never had children, or, if she had, they were all grown, because she taught in first or second grade. And her students loved her.

One day a Mexican girl who was in her class wore a brightly colored sunbonnet to school her mother had made. It was not long before Mrs. Reid appeared at recess wearing her own sunbonnet she had paid the girl's mother to make for her. Each week at recess, Mrs. Reid would appear wearing a different bonnet.

Goldroad Grammar School

The twenty-five cents she paid the mother for each bonnet helped the family financially, but it was also an opportunity to build the self-esteem of the little girl. I always wanted one of the sunbonnets but could never save the twenty-five cents to buy one. Large candy bars like *Butterfinger,* Baby Ruth, and *Hershey* were only five cents, and a sunbonnet would have cost five of them—a difficult choice.

The first grade teacher who braided Cecilia Gallegos' hair each morning on her arrival at school was the teacher who directed the school's production of the operetta, *HMS Pinafore.* The brightly colored pieces of silk she used on Cecilia's braids had been brought to school by her to be used in making part of the operetta set.

The night of the HMS Pinafore presentation. From left: Norma Jean Richards, Vella Mae Richards, Madeline Plummer

Goldroad Grammar School

There were two female lead parts in the production. One sang the solo, *Sorry Her Lot*, which I was chosen to fill, and the other was *Buttercup*. Everyone thought Helen Kristich was perfect for the role, and she agreed to do it, but felt inadequate about her ability to sing her song alone.

A compromise was reached when it was decided a group of girls would sing her song, "I'm called little buttercup, poor little buttercup, although I could never tell why..." while Helen acted out the part.

The first grade classroom on the north end of the building had a large stage built across one end. We worked long and hard on the production making sets and practicing the songs. I was out of class many afternoons doing this. After months of preparation, the night finally arrived to present the operetta to the camp. All of the partitions in the building dividing the classrooms had been pulled back making a very large seating area for families and guests.

On the night of the operetta, groups had sung all of the songs, and I had been a part of these groups. But I had not noticed how full the building was until I stepped from behind the set into the opening facing the audience and placed my hands on the bench that had been made to look like the railing of the HMS Pinafore and began to sing my solo—alone. The room was full—all of the chairs were filled as well as people standing in the back. My first feeling was shock and my second was fear, a new feeling for me. But the fear quickly passed as I gazed over the heads of the audience and concentrated on singing my song.

After the operetta was over, and I went to stand on the front steps of the school to wait for my family, I was again surprised at the number of people who had attended, not only from Goldroad, but also from Oatman. Ivan Lee, who worked in the assay office in Goldroad but lived in Oatman with his wife Lois and children, came up to me and complimented me on the quality of the entire operetta and specifically on my role. They were impressed with my ability to sing in front of such a large group of people. Mrs. Lee later became my piano teacher when all of us were moved to New Mexico.

Other school productions were presented on that stage and at the school over the years, but none drew the crowd or were as successful as *HMS Pinafore*. However, the teacher who directed it was not as diligent in the classroom in teaching the first graders as she was in presenting operettas. Her contract was not renewed the next year.

Chapter 9

A Well-Rounded Life

Did we miss anything by living in Goldroad?

Although Goldroad was twenty-five miles from Kingman and thirty from Needles, and had no theater or other entertainment, we lived a well-rounded life. Radio reception improved at night, and most families had their favorite radio programs. Time was spent in the early evening talking with neighbors as their children played night hide-n-seek or drank desert tea brewed on a campfire.

Mrs. Duriez and Mrs. Brough attended the Eastern Star meetings held in Oatman. Joe Peeples belonged to the Goldroad-Oatman Chamber of Commerce that met frequently.

The Girl Scouts and Brownies were organized in Goldroad. Vella was a Girl Scout and Joan Bird and I were Brownies. Each week we met at the schoolhouse. We learned the *Virginia Reel, Picking Up Papaws,* and other fun dances. The Girl Scouts worked on badges, and Vella spent much time learning the Morris code and how to use signal flags. When the girls were ready to receive their badges, a bonfire meeting would be held on the school playground where they would be presented to the girls.

One of the hikes and cookouts was held behind Saddleback Mountain in the wash. We learned how to cook *Bisquick* on a stick held over the fire. On the way home, the Mexican girls decided to climb over the mountain rather than going around it and passing by the mill as we did.

Several important activities were held with the Kingman troops where competitive games were held. On one of the activities, I rode to Kingman with the George Phillips family. In the car with us was a deaf Mexican girl. She was a twin and very pretty. Our only way to communicate with her was to make the Girl Scout sign and then nod our heads indicating she was a Girl Scout. She would answer by making the same sign and nodding her head. The deaf sister did not attend school, but her twin did. She told us her sister's hearing had been destroyed by an illness when she was very young. I never saw the deaf girl again.

A Well-Rounded Life

The Phillips family had owned their car only a short time when we rode with them to Kingman for this activity. On the way home, we were eating candy, and I wanted to dispose of my wrapper in the ashtray. But when I pulled the knob the entire ashtray came out of the side of the car. Believing I had broken their car, I was frightened. But they assured me it had been broken before I pulled on it. I then learned their car was new to them but was a used vehicle. It was a dark blue Ford.

The largest and most involved activity we had was a combined May Pole dance with the Oatman troop. All dresses were to be long and all white. Red, white and blue bunting was to be tied bathing-beauty-style across our chest. A Queen of May was to be chosen to reign over the festivities. A few of the women scout leaders thought Margie Duriez, who was in high school, should be the queen, because her father was the manager. But, if she was approached about it, her answer must have been no, because a pretty, grammar-school-age Mexican girl was the May Queen, and Vella and I were the attendants.

Many months of Saturdays were spent at the school practicing the *Minuet*, which was to be danced before the braiding of the May Pole. The braiding itself was practiced as well. The school piano was moved outside onto the playground, and we learned the music and dance to the Minuet.

One Saturday practice was spent with the Oatman girls. Over the months of practice, we had been given one rule that was never to be broken—you must never go over or under a girl two times in succession. Obviously someone had, because when Julie Ames from Oatman and I met, we both were supposed to go under. I knew I was right and had not made an error going around, but she was equally certain she had not either, so we were at an impasse. Contrary to my normal nature, I allowed her to go under, and I must admit I have always regretted it.

The red, white, and blue cheese cloth bunting we were to wear tied across our chests had proven to be impossible to find in the Kingman or Needles area. Mrs. Sayer approached Fern Bird, Joan's mother, and asked if she would buy the bunting on the trip they would soon be taking to California. I was on the trip with them when Mrs. Bird bought the bunting at a large department store.

Mother made our dresses from white, dotted swiss, but she put beading around the neck through which she pulled turquoise ribbon. Although the dresses were to be all white, Mother did not like the looks of them without the ribbon. And she planned to cut them off so we could wear them later.

A Well-Rounded Life

Entry of Queen of May with Vella Mae Richards & Norma Jean Richards (not shown)

Each springtime the hills of Goldroad were ablaze with color from the fields of gold poppies and blue lupines that grew there. Some Saturdays we would carry a wash tub with water up the side of Saddleback Mountain and fill it with poppies and lupines and bring them back home.   Early May Day morning, a group of us went out on the hills around Goldroad and picked armloads of wild flowers for the step banisters and to mark the path of our entry from the school house onto the playground where the May Pole was standing.

The moment we had worked so hard for had finally arrived! We stand with our first long dress in place and red, white and blue bunting tied across our chest. Our hair is freshly washed and curled. And the May Pole's pastel streamers flutter quietly and softly in the breeze. The beautiful wildflowers are strewn on the banisters and along our path. The music of the *Minuet* is heard and the door of the school opens.

A Well-Rounded Life

Out walk the queen and her attendants. She is declared Queen of May and leads the dancers along the path to the May Pole. Every dancer assumes her position and the Minuet is danced. Then a cord is struck on the piano and the braiding of the May Pole begins.

What a choice experience! Did we miss anything by living in Goldroad? No—but, oh, how much we gained!

Chapter 10

Other Friends

Arthur exaggerated his pain by screaming and falling to the ground, and then rolling around in the dirt on his back.

Helen Kristich had an older brother, Nicky, who rode the school bus each day to Kingman to attend high school. Others in camp who attended Kingman High and also rode the bus were Shirley Peeples, Helen Brough, Margie Duriez, Agnes Phelps and Elsie Redding. N.R. Dunton had the contract to provide the school bus to carry the high school students from Goldroad and Oatman into Kingman.

For a while, a few of us in grade school were allowed to ride the bus to the daytime football games in Kingman. But Arthur Motz told some of the parents about their daughters and sons smoking on the bus, and we were no longer allowed to go. Shirley Peeples was especially angry with him. Those of us who had been going on the bus were also very upset with Arthur for tattling and causing us to lose this opportunity to have fun.

On occasion we could coax Nicky to play softball with us. During one of those games I was playing first base. He hit a short grounder into my area, and I grabbed it and ran toward first. I arrived a few seconds before he did. But he was running so fast, he was unable to stop. He ran over me and knocked me a few feet into the air. That stopped the game. Although I did not cry, it did hurt. But I would have been too embarrassed to cry. And I did not play softball the remainder of the day.

Helen and Nicky had an aunt and uncle and cousins who lived in camp. They were the George Phillips family. Georgina was Vella's age; Arlene was my age, and there was a younger daughter as well. Very infrequently Arlene and I played together. Although we were the same age and should have been best friends, this never happened. Mostly because Georgina was always hovering protectively over Arlene inflicting swift punishment with a slap to the playmate if things did not go as Georgina felt they should for her sister. Friendships cannot flourish under those circumstances. And for some reason unknown to me, I never felt comfortable in their home, although her mother was always nice to me. George was very gregarious, but his wife was very quiet—almost meek.

Other Friends

The Phillips Girls with Joan Bird: left to right: Phillips girl, Joan Bird, Arlene Phillips, Georgina Phillips

Their home was spotlessly clean and attractively decorated. Below the rock wall of their house a huge mustard plant grew on the hillside. It towered many feet over my head. In many non-company houses such as the Onetto houses, water from the kitchen sink and bathtubs was allowed to empty outside. The mustard seed that had grown into the huge plant below their house had probably come in water from their kitchen. It had found good soil and plenty of water to keep it wet.

Nicky Kristich and Elsie Redding decided they would attend the Senior Prom together. They did not date and were just friends. But each wanted to go to the Prom and had no one else to go with. For the dance, Elsie's parents ordered from the catalog a long, light blue-green taffeta, formal gown with matching slippers and a short, white wrap.

Other Friends

When the clothes arrived, Elsie was very excited and happy. Clothes that beautiful and expensive were a rarity. And sometimes in the evenings after she arrived home from school, she would put on the clothes and wear them around the house and outside with her mother to talk to their neighbors. They would admire and comment on her beautiful clothes.

But a very sad thing happened a few days before Prom night. The Reddings received word of the death of a close relative who lived out of state. The family made plans to go to the funeral, and Elsie had to miss her Prom. I felt so badly for her, because I knew how excited she had been and how eagerly she had waited for this special night. It was good that she had worn and enjoyed the clothes as much as she had prior to the dance.

To get your *Goldroad legs* took a while. The steep mountains with the layer of loose, sharp rock made walking very difficult. But when you ran everywhere you went like I did, it was next to impossible. Sometime before I got my *Goldroad legs*, as I was running down the hill below the school grounds, I fell and my knee hit a sharp rock and I received a gash in my knee. I was glad my parents never considered taking me to a doctor to have it stitched, because I preferred having the scar. The kids in Goldroad felt about scars like soldiers felt about medals they received in battles. As we got each one, we showed them to our friends.

Margie Duriez carried me home one evening to the Onetto house with a cut in the arch of my foot. A group, including Johnny and William, was playing a game that required we run around the hospital. Margie was living there at the time. Because it was night and the lighting was poor, and I was running, it was impossible to see the broken piece of glass on the ground until my bare foot came down hard on it—and another battle scar was added to my body. Although Margie was in high school, she enjoyed having us around.

While they lived in the hospital, Margie's two older brothers, George and Philip, played basketball in one of the large unused rooms. George was a Senior and student body president of Kingman High in 1939 where he also played football. In 1940 Philip was senior class president.

Being a curious child, the medical equipment stored in a couple of the hospital rooms was of great interest to me and made it exciting for me to visit Margie. And my ability to walk on my toes intrigued her. I was always willing to perform for her whenever she asked me. Now that I look back, perhaps the reason I was so welcomed into the Duriez home might have been due to the friendship between Daddy and Mr. Duriez.

On a shopping visit to the Central Commercial, Billy accidentally knocked over a large can of popcorn, and it spilled.

Other Friends

Mother felt obligated to buy it, although she normally did not spend our grocery money on pre-popped corn.

Uncle Son and Henny were living with us at the time of the accident. And he was pleased Billy had spilled the popcorn, because he could eat the popcorn remaining in the can. The round metal can the popcorn was packaged in was about twelve inches high and six to eight inches in diameter. Vella and I saw a use for the empty can—we brewed our desert tea in it. Many evenings William and Johnny, Vella, Billy and I, and sometimes other kids, would build a fire, fill our can with water, and stuff it full of desert tea gathered from one of the nearby bushes. When it had brewed a while, we poured it into our tiny toy china cups and stood around the fire talking and drinking. We did this evening after evening. When we had finished for the evening, we did not bother to dump the can. But the next evening, we just added a little more water and desert tea.

During one of our tea parties, Arthur Motz' back was burned with hot tea. His father was manager of the Central Commercial, but this had nothing to do with our dislike for him. His brother Marvin, who was Johnny's and my age, was Johnny's best friend. But Arthur, who was William and Vella's age, was not liked by anyone.

At the desert tea-get-together when his back was burned, Arthur had done something that angered William. He probably showed too much attention to Vella. Then William showed his disapproval by throwing his toy cup of hot tea on Arthur's bare back. Arthur over-exaggerated his pain by screaming and falling to the ground, and then rolling around in the dirt on his back. And because we were only a short distance from the Sayer house, Mr. and Mrs. Sayer heard Arthur's yells and saw him rolling around in the dirt. They came off their front porch and called Johnny and William home. This made Arthur even more unpopular with us.

Once in a while we could coax him into playing a game of hide-n-seek with us, but he always had to be *it*. When his counting started, and he always had to count to at least a hundred, we would scatter over the side of the school playground en masse running as fast as we could go down the road to the mill. This was behind the hill and out of Arthur's sight. He was fooled a couple of times with this game, but he refused to be fooled a third time. Kids are so cruel!

The kids in camp understood that William and Vella were boyfriend and girlfriend—Johnny and I were boyfriend and girlfriend—Marvin and Marie were boyfriend and girlfriend. These relationships were strictly in name only and carried no rights or privileges. However, Helen Kristich still had a secret crush on William, and Arthur Motz still liked Vella.

Other Friends

One activity we engaged in as often as we tried playing softball together, and with the same results, was organizing clubs. Hours were spent by Joan and me setting up a club. Of course, we always put ourselves as the president and vice-president and assign the other less important offices to the other kids—without consulting them. Dues were always a part of the plan—two or three cents per week. A weekly meeting schedule was also set up. But usually the pre-assigned officer refused to be a part of the club unless she could be president or vice-president. That was totally unacceptable to Joan and me. Why have a club if you cannot run it. Right?

There was one exception to our record of failed club organizing. William and Johnny Sayer, Joan Bird, Marvin, Alma Dean Doolin, Vella, Billy and I decided to form a club, but we needed a clubhouse—a *real* club house—not the old refrigerator box we had used in the past. The decision was made to sell sandwiches and Kool-Aid to earn the money for a tent we had seen in the Sears catalog. It was bright yellow and made in the shape of an Indian teepee.

What were we going to make the sandwiches from and where were we going to get the Kool-Aid to sell? Mother was approached and she agreed to allow us to charge lunch meat, bread and Kool-Aid on our family account at the Central Commercial.

The site chosen for the stand was the flat area by our garage at the bottom of our hill, and was on the curve across from the Central Commercial. We figured we could sell to the few cars on Route 66, and the men walking to and from the store, gas station, and mine.

At 11:30 A.M. when the siren on the silver water tank sounded, we were prepared to do business. We expected people to flock to our stand. But we were disappointed when even those cars we yelled at did not stop.

Only one mine surface worker, probably taking pity on us, came over and ordered a sandwich and glass of Kool-Aid.

Then someone in our group suggested we go to the women in the homes and ask them for orders. On approaching them, the first thing we did was explain the reason for our enterprise. But the only woman willing to support our effort was Mrs. Rindlisbach. At first, she ordered one sandwich for that day. But then she placed an order for a sandwich and glass of Kool-Aid for each day of the week. And we faithfully made and delivered her order each day. Looking back, I feel certain she did not eat what we delivered—how clean are the hands of kids and the makeshift stand we used as a counter. But, she made us feel like she took seriously our efforts at the food supply business.

Other Friends

As we counted our money each day—the tent cost about two dollars—we decided our goal had been reached when we had the two dollars in our hands. We never considered Mother had provided the supplies for our sales-in our eyes we had *earned* the money for our tent. The tent was ordered. Each day we would go to the post office to see if it had arrived. How excited we were when it finally did come! And a get-together was planned for that evening. The tent was set up in our backyard.

We talked Vella into making her famous stew with the equally famous *secret* herb Mrs. Onetto had earlier given a cutting of to Mother. Of course, desert tea brewed in our popcorn can was part of our celebration.

The metal stakes used for holding the tent down soon bent when they were driven into the rocks on our hill. But we placed large rocks on the corners until substitute stakes could be found.

Everyone agreed the tent should be kept at our house because we had more of a share in it than anyone—and Mother had never been reimbursed for the food supplies we had charged on our family account at the Central Commercial. Looking back I realize Mother knew at the time she was providing the way for us to buy the tent and to have an experience as well and did not expect repayment.

When we would get together to have stew and desert tea, the tent was set up not only at our house but also on vacant landings on the hills where houses had stood in previous openings. I do not remember our ever going inside the little bright yellow tent at any of these stew-and-tea-get togethers. But it was always set up and admired because it stood as a symbol of our club. Joan and I used it many times as a playhouse, so it received plenty of use that way.

Chapter 11

Traveling Salesmen

The women eagerly bought from him because he charged a lot less than the Central Commercial for his produce.

On a regular schedule, a large, covered truck would pull off Route 66, come into our area of camp, honk its horn, and the women and children would come running. The driver sold fruit and vegetables from California. Mother usually bought a large box of oranges and a few vegetables. At the Onetto house, the oranges were stored in a box in the bathroom behind a curtain where our clothes were hung. The women eagerly bought from him, because he charged a lot less than the Central Commercial for his produce.

A variety of other salesmen stopped in Goldroad on their way to someplace else. A photographer made a Saturday appointment to take pictures of Vella, Billy and me. A Saturday appointment was necessary because our hair was always washed and curled on that day. But Mother was upset when the photographer appeared at our house earlier in the day than scheduled. Because our hair was long and thick and was rolled wet on rags, it took nearly all day for it to dry. When he appeared early, Mother had to remove the rags while the ringlets were still damp. As a result, our curls appeared very small and tight in our picture.

When Billy was a little older, a photographer came through the camp with a Shetland pony taking pictures of the younger children. Of course, Billy and most of the other little children had their pictures taken on the pony with all of the props—cowboy hat, red handkerchief and chaps. All of the older children were in school and missed the fun and pictures.

A man selling used sewing machines found our house, and Mother bought a *White* machine from him. When Mrs. Peeples heard about the sewing machine, she brought a couple of her old dresses down to the house and asked Mother to re-style them for her daughter Shirley who was in high school. Mrs. Peeples paid for this work by giving Mother two old dresses to make over for Vella and me. Mother was too shy the first time to refuse to do it, so she agreed. But this was a lot of work for Mother with very little in return. After re-styling the two dresses for Mrs. Peeples, Mother refused to fix anymore.

Traveling Salesmen

This sewing machine was used to make all of Vella's and my clothes during our growing-up years. And I took the machine when I got married and used it to make clothes for my three daughters.

Billy on pony with his long hair tucked up under hat.
This appears to be the same pony that Otis Willoughby
and his brother Richard had their picture taken on.

Chapter 12

Mother's Illness

This was a very unsettled time in our lives.

Not far into the summer of 1938, my mother spent a sleepless night with severe chest pains. They continued on into the next day causing extreme worry and concern to my father. On his trips to the mill, he would stop by the house to check on her. I remember the word *pleurisy* being mentioned. When the pain did not subside but got worse, Daddy loaded Mother and the three of us kids into the car and went to Auntie and Uncle Joe's house in Kingman.

Dr. Paup had pulled off a miracle a short time previous to this on my uncle when he had appendicitis, so Mother was taken to him. He took x-rays and found a spot on Mother's lung the size of a quarter—a spot that size meant almost certain death from tuberculosis.

Tuberculosis was a feared disease because there was no known cure for it. Bed rest and a hot, dry climate were the best the doctors could do. This was before the time of the miracle drugs sulpha and penicillin. At that time, TB sanitariums dotted the state of Arizona. Whisperings of having to put Mother in the Prescott sanitarium were overheard by Vella and me and caused us silent worry.

This was a very unsettled time in our lives. Auntie cared for Mother in Kingman. For a short time, Vella and I were taken on a day-to-day basis to Aunt Ruby's home also in Kingman. But we eventually ended up in Goldroad with Daddy. And Billy who was not yet four stayed in Kingman with Aunt Ruby and Uncle Tom—Daddy's brother and wife.

My sister was nine and I was seven—Daddy had to work from 7:30 A.M. until 4:00 P.M. with half an hour for lunch. One morning Vella sent me to the Central Commercial to buy something for our lunch. She did not tell me what to buy, so I arrived home with a box of assorted filled cookies. And she was upset with my choice of food. But I have since thought that my choice was a very normal one for a child of seven.

Neighbors tried to help. Mrs. Peeples brought two lemon meringue pies over—a pot of beans would have been much better for a family in our situation, with no mother in the home to cook a decent meal. However, I know that Daddy appreciated the pies—lemon meringue was his favorite pie.

Mother's Illness

But the ants got into them before we had finished eating them. At that time, we had no refrigerator or way to keep them from spoiling.

Daddy paid Mrs. Kirby to wash and curl our long hair, but she did not use rags as Mother did, so the ringlets did not stay in very well.

The old saying, *When the cat's away, the mice do play* applied to one thing I liked to do. I loved to jump on beds, and I got in plenty of jumping time. The most fun was jumping from the high metal headboard down on the mattress. Trampolines were designed and made for children like me. What a thrill I felt each time I bounced high into the air. But my ecstasy was short-lived, because Mrs. Onetto must have seen or heard me and came over to the house and stopped my bed jumping.

One of our favorite activities was to gather the tall, dry grass that grew around camp. We would take a small amount of the dry grass, roll it up in newspaper, light it, and smoke it. Vella and I became quite bold with Mother out of the house when we brought a small amount of the grass into the kitchen with the idea of smoking it later.

But time slipped away from us and before we knew it, Daddy was home for his lunch. The dry grass was lying on the drainboard. Daddy did not even notice it, but I felt so guilty and believed he surely must have known why it was there. I doubt that our parents would have objected to our smoking the dry grass, other than a concern over our burning the house down. But we felt we were doing something wrong and always sneaked around the backside of the hill to do it. Mrs. Onetto and Frank must have wondered what we were doing as they looked out from their back porch to the area where we hid.

With Mother away, Vella and I did try to carry on at our house doing what we remembered she had done. One day we were singing and sweeping the floor. I do not remember the song, but it must have been something sad, because we both started to cry. We realized that there was a possibility Mother might not return home to us and we were lonesome.

One afternoon near the end of the summer, Mama Bessie, accompanied by our young aunt, Dorothy, appeared at our home in Goldroad. Unknown to us, she had come to take Vella and me to her home in Solomonsville where she lived with our grandfather and Dorothy. We were to live with them and attend school until Mother either got well or died. Unaware of her arrival, on his way home from work Daddy had stopped at the Central Commercial to buy meat for our dinner. As he was walking up to the front of our house, Mama Bessie was pulling away with us in her car. She hesitated just long enough to exchange a few words with Daddy and then drove on out of camp with us. We went to Auntie's where Mother was staying.

Mother's Illness

I do not know if Daddy was aware Mama Bessie would be in Goldroad to pick us up. Or if he was even aware of her plans to take us home with her to Solomonsville the next day. But from the look I saw on his face as we pulled away from our house, I felt her being there was a surprise to him, and he did not know her plans.

He was completely at the mercy of the situation because he was doing all he could do to take care of his children, his wife, and his job. Even at seven years of age, I could see the pain and vulnerability on my father's face as he saw his children being taken from him. I felt sorry for him at that time because I knew how much he loved us, how hard he was trying to take care of us, and how hard he worked at his full-time job every day. All of these efforts were meshed together and made more difficult by the fear and uncertainty of Mother's fight for life. Children many times are not informed about matters such as these, even when they are very much affected by them. Needless to say, this was a very difficult time for my parents, and was also a very difficult time for Vella, Billy and me.

Early the next morning when Mama Bessie left with Vella and me, Billy was still asleep. The evening before he had begged to go with us, but of course, that was impossible. I felt sad leaving him asleep—it seemed like a betrayal knowing he wanted to go.

Because Billy had been temporarily staying with Uncle Tom and Aunt Ruby, at this time they took him on a semi-permanent basis. Their daughter LaRue was younger than I was, and they wanted a son. Because there was not much hope at this time Mother would recover, although this was not expressed by anyone, Uncle Tom and Aunt Ruby might have had Billy in mind to fill this spot. Of course, Vella, Billy and I were not aware of these adult concerns, or of the very real possibility of Mother's death.

Daddy continued to work hard everyday at Goldroad, and then each evening make the long, twenty-five mile trip to Kingman to see Mother. On one of his visits after we left, he found Mother crying. Dr. Paup had told her it would be very unwise for Daddy to sleep with her because of the very contagious aspect and the high mortality rate of her disease.

She was very young, only twenty-seven, and very frightened by what was happening to her and to her family. To see her children go off in all directions to be cared for by others and knowing she had a disease with no known cure, she felt a need to be held and loved and comforted by her husband. With a full knowledge of the dangers and consequences involved, Daddy chose to ignore the warning of the doctor. He slept with her that night and held her in his arms, loved her and comforted her. And he continued to do this throughout her illness.

Mother's Illness

Even though Mother did not like Dr. Paup, she respected his medical knowledge and followed his instructions. The instructions were simple and the only treatment known for TB at the time—six months of complete bed rest and inhaling the vapor from a brown medicine put into boiling water. A paper funnel was used to direct the vapor to her nose and mouth.

Her dislike for Dr. Paup came from a comment he had made to her on her first visit to him. He had said, "All you've been doing in Goldroad is having one baby after another!" This comment angered Mother, and she resented his inaccurate observation of the facts. None of us had been born in Goldroad. If his conclusions had been correct about the number of children Mother had, Mrs. Sayer, Mrs. Phillips, and Mrs. Kirby would also have had tuberculosis. Their children matched the ages of our family.

The resentment Mother felt toward Dr. Paup for what he had said did not diminish the gratitude we all felt toward him at the end of six months when his treatment had healed the spot on her lung and she was free of tuberculosis.

When Mother was well enough to be brought back to our home in Goldroad in late September or early October 1938, Vella and I were still in southern Arizona with our grandparents, and Billy was with Uncle Tom and Aunt Ruby. Mrs. Henline, the mother of Cloyd Henline, agreed to take care of Mother when Daddy brought her home. But she refused to take care of Billy, an active four-year-old boy.

After work Daddy would go to Kingman to visit Billy. One evening not long after Mother was back in our home in Goldroad, on one of his visits Billy got Daddy alone and said, "Daddy, don't you want me anymore?" Daddy did not say a word but immediately had Aunt Ruby pack his clothes. He took Billy home that night to Goldroad. When Mrs. Henline came the next morning to take care of Mother, she found Billy there. She was upset at first but relented. She probably felt sorry for Mother and Daddy's situation—they needed their son and he needed them.

But it was love at first sight on her part. And in the mornings when she combed his shoulder-length curly, blonde hair, she would put a bobby pin in the front of his hair to keep it from falling in his eyes as he played. He hated the bobby pin because he knew that only girls wore bobby pins. But he never said anything or made a fuss when she put it in but waited until he was out of her sight and then took it out. Later, when he would come back into the house after playing, she could never figure out how the bobby pin slipped out of his hair. And of course, he never told her. And if he had not worn blue stripped overalls and acted so much like a boy, from a distance you would have mistaken him for a little girl.

Mother's Illness

Vella and I were looking forward to coming home at Christmas. Mother would be allowed to get out of bed for the first time in six months. However, Dr. Paup had a stringent rule about an afternoon rest and a daily jigger of red wine to build up her blood. When school in Solomonsville was finally out for the Christmas vacation, we happily prepared for the trip home to Goldroad to see Mother and Daddy, Billy, and Auntie and Uncle Joe. We had not seen them for six months!

Mama Bessie and Papa Guy and Dorothy brought us home. They had purchased dolls for us, but, upon arriving, we were told Frank Onetto had wanted to provide the dolls for our Christmas. They had been ordered from one of the catalogs and looked like Deanna Durbin, a very popular young movie star. Probably because I was a year older, I did not feel the excitement I had felt the previous year when we had been sent to the Onetto's to wait for Santa.

This was my year to realize there really was no Santa Claus. Realizing this took a great deal of the magic and excitement out of Christmas and all my future Christmases. On Christmas Eve as we were walking from our house to wait for Santa Claus, I realized Santa would not really be the one leaving our gifts. Suddenly, logic took over, and I could understand the impossibility of the situation of Santa Claus.

Mother had ordered a green, upholstered, platform rocker from the catalog for Daddy's Christmas present. Billy found out about it, and, whenever he could not get his way with Mother, he would threaten to tell Daddy about the rocker hidden in the playroom. After Christmas he was hard-pressed to find a way to blackmail Mother.

I loved being home and being a family again. And our family slipped back into its normal routine almost as if we had never been gone, and our family had never been apart. All of us were happy to be together again.

But Mother's illness had been very hard on everyone—including Vel, Billy and me. Although Mama Bessie and Papa Guy provided a good home for Vel and me, we were put into a new school situation as well as a new home situation. And Vel grieved quietly. But I accepted my new surroundings and each new experience with optimism and did the best I knew how in each of them. But inside I was feeling very insecure.

All of the children in my class were friendly and accepting of me except Janice Kempton. Whatever her reason, over a period of time she tried to make my life miserable. When I was seated in a small chair in my reading circle, Janice would unbutton the back of my dress, and I was totally unaware she had done this until time for me to leave the reading circle. And then someone would mention it.

Mother's Illness

This dress had many buttons down the back. It had been given to Mother by Mrs. Peeples for her work altering dresses for her daughter Shirley. And Mother had altered this dress for me because I liked it so well. I was not embarrassed when I discovered my dress had been unbuttoned, just hurt and puzzled why anyone would do this to me when I had done nothing to them but try to be their friend. Later she did invite me to her home to play a few times. And we rode her bike that had no tires. All families were struggling.

But far more traumatic than what Janice Kempton did to me, was the fear of hypodermic needles I developed at the Solomonsville School that remained with me for the rest of my life. Because I did not have a written record with me of my vaccination history from Goldroad, and the school refused to listen to me or believe I had received them, and all the other children in my Solomonsville class had been vaccinated the previous year, I was taken alone from my class without any prior notice or warning into the nurse's office and vaccinated. It was more than fear that caused my cries when I was held and the needle stuck into my arm. It was a feeling of total helplessness and lack of control over my own body, which was caused by knowing my mother was not there to defend me if I needed her. Because when my first grade class had been vaccinated the previous year in Goldroad, I had not been afraid or cried. To me it was just another new and interesting experience.

Although Walt and Effie Elgin had no children, they were aware of how much the healing of his wife and the return of his children meant to Daddy. They showed this understanding when they invited him to their home for dessert one evening shortly after our return to Goldroad and asked that Vella and I come as well.

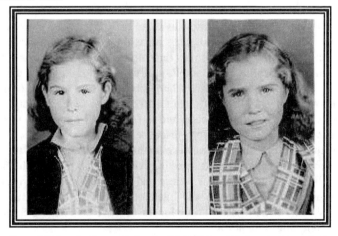

Norma Jean Richards-Second Grade Vella Mae Richards-Fourth Grade
108.

Mother's Illness

Sometime after the Christmas holidays, Uncle Son and Henny and their young daughter Bobby Kay came to stay with us. They had been living at the Katherine Mine about twenty miles northwest of Goldroad not far from the Colorado River. Daddy had secured employment for Uncle Son with USSR&MCo in the Crusher under Mr. Brough—a very hard taskmaster. They lived with us until they were financially able to move into an Onetto house below the school. While they lived with us their bed was on the eastside of the screened porch. Our family slept on the southside. But before they could move into their own house, friends came to stay with them at our house. We were all together in our little Onetto house. They did not stay long, but they were nice people, and their visit did not seem to create any problems in our home.

In the evening after work, my parents and the Johnsons next door would use our jump rope with us. There was not a lot to do for entertainment, especially when you did not have much money. Some evenings Daddy and Mother would walk around camp talking to friends who were outside their houses. My parents liked the Johnsons, and we missed them when they moved back to Joplin.

But Daddy and Gaylord Cudney had become friends, and he was married to Babe Barnes from Oatman. She had a small son Tommy by a previous marriage who was about Billy's age. She and Tommy visited often, and our families became very close friends. Every month Mother took Vella and Billy and me on her grocery-buying trip to Needles. Some of our Needles' trips were made with them. Our only purchases at the Central Commercial were for incidentals. Daddy had earlier chased Mr. Motz, the manager, around the store because he believed our monthly bill had been charged incorrectly, and Mr. Motz refused to listen.

But the mountains were really our playgrounds. And during the school year our hikes in the mountains were limited to weekends. On weekdays after school we played around camp. Most of our weekends were spent hiking over or around one of the mountains. Not long after our return from Solomonsville a group of us, including Vella and Billy, took a hike over and then around behind Saddleback Mountain. We did not gauge our time very well and found we were farther from camp than we had thought and were running out of daylight. We knew the rule that we were always to be home by 4:00 P.M. when Daddy got off work and before the sun got low. This time we were running behind the deadline and were concerned about Mother's reaction when we arrived home. As we came up the slope to our front yard, Mother and Daddy were waiting there for us. Mother was not completely well and was still required to spend time lying down.

Mother's Illness

But she was worried, and this worry changed to anger when she saw we were safe and had not fallen down an abandoned mine shaft or some other terrible fate. When we got close enough, she grabbed each one and gave us a good spanking and sent us to bed without any supper.

Later after her anger had subsided, she relented about the no dinner and bed. Billy and I were happy to get up and eat. But Vella was nine and offended by such discipline and remained supperless in bed. Mother explained the next day what had happened. When Daddy arrived home at 4:00 and we were not there, she became very worried and sent him to Saddleback Mountain to find us. We were not there. We had decided to go over the mountain and use the tailings pond trail on the west side of the mountain. Daddy had scuffed his nice dress shoes on the hike up over the mountain looking for us. His shoes had nothing to do with the punishment we received—but it had everything to do with our parents' concern for us.

Vella Mae—Summer of 1938　　　　*Norma Jean—Summer of 1938*

Not long after these pictures were taken of Vella and me, Mother was diagnosed with tuberculosis and we were taken by Mama Bessie to her home in Solomonsville AZ. The dresses we are wearing were made by Mother— white material with small, light blue polka dots and matching tied silk ribbons.

Chapter 13

Sunday School Comes To Our Camp

In our Sunday School, we were given pictures of Jesus to color, and we had stories from the Bible ...

A non-denominational Sunday School was organized by Mrs. Sayer and a few other women to fill the absence of a Protestant church in camp. The only church building in Goldroad was the Catholic Church in Mexican town. Our Sunday School met each Sunday morning in the school. Their intent was to provide at least minimal Christian teaching for the children of the camp. In our Sunday School, we were given pictures of Jesus to color, and we had stories from the Bible, but what I enjoyed the most were the songs we sang—*In the Garden*, *Onward Christian Soldiers* and *The Old Rugged Cross* were my favorites. I loved those songs, and the words still remain with me.

Each Sunday Mother gave us ten cents to take as a donation. I decided one Sunday if I gave the dime and asked for five cents in change, I could take the five cents and go to Fortner's grocery store in Mexican town and buy candy. Fortner's was chosen because the Central Commercial was closed on Sundays. Mother did not say much when she saw the candy and I explained what I had done. But I got the message and never did it again.

The Sunday School continued for a short time, and one Easter program was held with real Easter lilies. I do not know why it was disbanded but lack of attendance by the children was probably the reason.

On the last Sunday it was held, Mother and Daddy were away, and we were staying with Uncle Son and Henny. There were no plans for us to attend Sunday School that morning. Henny had fed us but had not cleaned us up for the day. We had gone outside and were walking along the road below the school where we met Mrs. Sayer. She insisted we come to Sunday School with her, although we told her we had not been dressed to attend that day. But she continued to insist, and we went with her. And we found they were not holding the regular Sunday School but were giving the unused Sunday School supplies to the children in camp.

Sunday School Comes To Our Camp

A short time later when we arrived back at Henny's house and proudly showed her the pictures we had received in Sunday School, she was very embarrassed by our appearance and that we had been seen in Sunday School so unkept. Because Mother did not allow Vella and me to comb our own hair, it had not been combed that morning before we left the house to play. Billy still had part of his breakfast egg on his mouth and was wearing a girl's old, beige, bear fur coat two or three sizes too large for him. It was held together in the front with a large safety pin, and he looked like a little teddy bear when he wore it. This was a coat he loved to wear, because he normally had a difficult time staying warm, but this coat did the job.

Usually he had to nag Mother for awhile before she allowed him to wear it outside to play. When she did relent and let him, he could not venture very far from home in it—and this Sunday, he had gone to Sunday School wearing it!

Chapter 14

Beginning To See The Light At The End Of The Tunnel

Mother ordered a tank-type vacuum cleaner from the catalog to clean the new upholstered furniture.

At Lee's Lumber Co. in Oatman, Mother and Daddy purchased a rust colored living room couch and matching upholstered chair. The couch made into a bed and was the forerunner of the present day futon. Unlike other sleeper couches where the bed pulls out of the bottom of the couch, the back of our couch snapped loose and lay flat making one large bed.

Lee's Lumber Co. is the white building on the right as you round the curve entering Oatman from Goldroad.

Lee's Lumber Co. loaded the couch and chair onto their large, flatbed truck normally used to deliver lumber and supplies. They were tied securely in place with ropes. And with my parents' permission, I was allowed to ride to Goldroad on the back of the truck with our furniture. There was never a thought about liability insurance—what's that?

113.

Beginning To See The Light At The End Of The Tunnel

Lee's Lumber Co. knew that if anything happened to me on my ride to Goldroad, my parents had given their permission for me to ride on their truck. And my parents assumed full responsibility for me and my safety—an idea completely foreign to our society today.

That day I learned one important lesson on the short ride to our home—the danger of walking around on the bed of a truck while it is moving. When I got up to move from the couch to the chair, I was startled and frightened by my inability to control my legs as they took me towards the back end of the truck bed. When I got up from the couch, my mind had one destination—the chair. But my legs were taking me toward another—the edge of the back of the truck bed. Had I not consciously stopped myself, I would have walked off the back of the moving truck. This lack of control I felt over my body during the experience frightened me so badly I stayed seated for the remainder of the trip.

Mother had ordered a tank-type vacuum cleaner from the catalog to clean the new upholstered furniture. After it arrived, Babe Cudney came to visit and was anxious to try out the new vacuum with its various attachments. But in her exuberance she cracked the attachment designed to clean the deep crevices around the cushions. But this was no problem. With black electrical tape wound around the crack, it served its purpose for many years.

Soon after we bought our couch and chair at Lee's Lumber Co., Henny and Uncle Son also bought a green couch and a table radio fronted with blue mirrors there. And I secretly wished we had a radio like theirs.

But by this time, they had moved from the Onetto house below the school to the Onetto house on the road to the Mexican swimming pool. This house had a bathroom with an inside toilet, but water from the kitchen sink did not go into the septic tank. It drained outside and down the hill. And cooking was still done on a wood cook stove.

One summer the kitchen water carried a tomato seed and deposited it in the ground down the hill where it drained. A large tomato plant grew and flourished providing tomatoes for their family—much like the mustard tree grown by the Phillips' kitchen water.

Chapter 15

Gold Road Or Goldroad?

The cockroaches were so numerous they hung in large clumps from the ceilings of the drifts.

An ingenious and low profile method was found to haul the gold concentrate out of Goldroad to the railroad in Kingman for shipment to the USSR&MCo smelter in Midvale, Utah. Milk cans were filled with the gold concentrate and hauled in the back of a company pickup into Kingman.

Route 66 east of the mountains on the flat land between Goldroad and Kingman was crossed by many washes that ran deep and swift when heavy rains fell. After one bad rainstorm, the pickup carrying the milk cans filled with gold was caught in one of these water-filled dips. Two or three of the milk cans were washed out of the bed of the pickup and lost. Needless to say, the company put forth an all out effort to find these cans, and eventually all of them were retrieved with the gold intact.

In previous operations of the Gold Road mine, burros had been used to pull the heavy ore cars. When the mine reopened in 1936, the corrals that had been used underground to hold the burros were still in place. But burros were not used in the 1936 operation—electric motors replaced them. But the legacy left by the use of the burro underground was a mine filled with large, brown, cockroaches that had fed on their manure.

The cockroaches were so numerous they hung in large clumps from the ceilings of the drifts. Daddy contrived a device to electrocute them. A long rod was connected to a miner's lamp battery, and as he walked down the drift and stuck the rod into a clump of cockroaches, the clump would immediately fall to the ground with a loud thudding sound. This was more of a game than an earnest effort on his part to rid the mine of the cockroaches—this would have been impossible. And the miners used metal lunch boxes to keep their food safe from these armies of cockroaches. Because of the cockroaches in the mine, the houses had a similar problem with them—except they did not hang in clumps.

Although many miners were jokingly teased about using their lunch boxes for *high grading*, a few were actually guilty of doing it. The term meant to secretly put a few of the small high-grade ore rock from the site where they were working into their lunch box.

Gold Road Or Goldroad ?

And then at the end of their shift leave the mine with the stolen ore unnoticed and undetected.

My father and other supervisors were aware this activity was taking place. And they also knew the rocks were later hammered into a finer form at the miner's home and then sold to a prominent well-known man who lived in Oatman. This man had many mine diggings around Oatman that had no gold in them, but whose rocks, when mined and put into trucks, were wet down and *salted* with the *high-graded* ore from the Gold Road Mine. Then, when the *salted* rock was hauled to less-than-scrupulous processors, though they were aware the property listed on the form presented to them was not a producing gold property, they closed their eyes to what was happening, and processed the *salted* rock.

One Mexican boy was heard to say he could play no longer because he had to get home to hammer out the gold before his father arrived home from work, or he would be in trouble.

The mine was called *Gold Road Mine*--the town was called *Goldroad, Arizona.* The Post Office rubber stamp read *Goldroad.*

First post office in Goldroad looked like a large bird house sitting in front of the unfinished crusher in background
(Courtesy of Mohave County Historical Society)

116.

Gold Road Or Goldroad?

When we first moved to Goldroad and before the Central Commercial was built, our outgoing and incoming mail was placed in a small, roofed box built on stilts on the south side of Highway 66 almost directly north of the mine shaft. A large rock was placed on the mail to keep it from blowing away. After the store was completed, the Post Office was located in the right corner in the back of the store. Later, a separate room was built on the north side of the store. Both buildings faced east and had outside entrances.

Gold Road years of operation were: 1904 through 1918
1922 through 1924
1936 through 1942

(Gold Road or Goldroad and Operation Dates Courtesy of Cloyd Henline)

When Goldroad reopened in 1936, the men who went into the older areas of the mine expressed respect and admiration for the high quality of timbering they found that had been done by the *Brits* (English) in previous openings. It reflected the pride they had in their trade.

Daddy said he earned *good money* when he worked for the power company climbing poles and stringing power lines before he took the job in Goldroad--$1 an hour for a ten-hour day. The following wages paid in Goldroad at that time verify his statement:

Mine
Muckers -- $4.50 per day
Miner/Driller -- $5.00 per day
Hoistman -- $5.50 per day
Powderman -- $5.00 per day

Mill
Crusher Operator --$5.50 per day
Ball Mill Operator -- $5.50 per day
Mill Helper --$4.50 per day

(Wage Information Courtesy of Morris Bird—Timekeeper 1937-1942)

117.

Gold Road Or Goldroad?

Two extremely qualified and dedicated Mexican men—Candelario B. Mendez, a small man, and Matias Calderon, a very large man—were general foremen in the mine under Guy Gardner. These two men were respected by their Mexican peers, and their influence on them and their families was manifest in the peaceful, stable climate of the Mexican community. Each man had his own following in the Mexican community and wielded great influence over them.

Carmen Mendez, the youngest daughter of Candelario, played with me on a number of occasions when we first arrived in Goldroad and were living in the Onetto house. When we were older, we sang an Easter hymn together in Mexican for the Sunrise program held on the school grounds. I remember when Candelario died a few years later. His death was a great shock to his wife, but the greater shock came when her older son died a few months later. At the graveside after his casket had been lowered into the grave, she picked up a handful of dirt, held her fist high, looked upward and cursed God for taking both her husband and her son.

The Fortner Store in Mexican town fascinated me. The Central Commercial Store was larger, but to me Fortner's merchandise was much more interesting. The first time we ventured into Mexican town to visit the store, we were met with barking dogs and rock-throwing kids. However, we were too stubborn and proud to retreat and finally made it to our destination—the store.

Our next trip sometime later was a different story. No one threw rocks and not even the dogs were allowed to bark and chase us. Daddy was very much liked by the Mexican miners, and I have always felt somehow they learned of the rocking incident and told their children to leave us alone.

A few Anglo families bought the bulk of their groceries at Fortner's. Henny and Uncle Son did, but they used the dirt road off Route 66 that passed by the Catholic Church. When we went to Fortner's, we did not go in a car but walked west over the embankment at the curve of Route 66 as it passed under the conveyer belt.

One night our family and some friends went to a home in Mexican town for dinner. Daddy had made prior arrangements with the husband for his wife to prepare enchiladas for us. And Daddy paid them the same as he would have paid a restaurant. On occasion Mother paid the woman to make tortillas for our supper. And they always arrived warm from the stove wrapped in a clean, white dishtowel. We had lived among Mexicans for a number of years before Mother learned to prepare Mexican food for our family.

Gold Road Or Goldroad?

And it did not happen until we were living in Vanadium, New Mexico, at the USSR&MCo mine. Even then, she used canned chili and tortillas. Not until many years later did she learn from her mother, who had learned from Mexican women, how to blend red chili pods to make enchilada gravy.

One night the entire camp was awakened by the siren that was normally used only to signal the 11:30 A.M. lunchtime. Daddy was the first of our family to leap out of bed. But it did not take any of us long to realize what the problem was—the change room at the mine was on fire. From our vantage point on the hill, we could see the flames coming from the building. Daddy was dressed and at the site in a minute. His responsibility was to disconnect all electrical wires from any burning building—which he did in this case.

Not much could be done to save the building—Goldroad had no fire department. But efforts to keep it from spreading to the lamp room and mine office were successful. And our family had front row seats on the front porch of our house directly across the canyon from the change room.

Controlling the fire was going well. But suddenly a loud noise startled everyone. The large hot water tank in the change room had exploded. It shot straight into the air and landed in the bed of Dunton's dump truck that was sitting at his garage close to the burning building. Had it landed somewhere other than there, much damage, possibly killing or injuring someone, could have been done.

Mother allowed us to stay up as long as we wanted to watch what was happening. When the change room was just a pile of smoldering embers, and light was beginning to appear around the mountain behind our house, we gave it up and went to bed.

Every mine has a change room. It is a building usually close to the shaft. When miners arrive for work at the beginning of their shift, they change from their street clothes into their dirt and sweat-soaked mine clothes, which includes rubber boots. These work clothes are lowered by a rope from the ceiling where they had been pulled at the end of the previous shift. The street clothes are then attached to the rope and pulled to the ceiling. The miner is now ready to be lowered by skip into the mine for his shift. Because of the smelly, wet condition of the work clothes, if a miner is negligent in pulling them to the ceiling before leaving the change room, he may return for his next shift to find the legs of his pants have been cut off. And he must work his shift in these shortened pants, because there is no way to replace them before the shift begins. Miners do this to teach the careless miner a lesson. His thoughtless behavior makes it necessary for others to walk through the foul-smelling clothes left hanging at face level.

119.

Gold Road Or Goldroad?

When a miner finishes his shift, he showers, retrieves his street clothes, attaches his mine clothes to the rope, pulls them to the ceiling and leaves. When he arrives for his next shift, he has dry work clothes. They dry out between shifts when properly pulled to the warm ceiling area. Change room fires are not that uncommon. The change room at the Bullfrog Mine in Vanadium also burned.

A new bigger and better change room was built in Goldroad to replace the one burned that night. The fire and new change room gave everyone in camp a lot to talk about for quite a while.

Dunton's trucks not only hauled ore from Line Road to the mine, but they also picked up the camp garbage. The families burned their garbage in large metal barrels. One careless driver failed to realize a barrel he had dumped into the truck contained smoldering garbage. The movement of the truck must have fanned a small spark, and before he realized what was happening, he had a truckload of burning garbage behind him.

Realizing his problem, he made a beeline to the Dunton garage where a fire hose was used to douse the flames. My, we did have a lot of excitement in our little camp!

The garbage dump was below Flora and Frank Onetto's house on the curve of the road leading to the mill. But soon after the reopening, it was relocated outside of camp. Because bottles and tin cans made up most of the garbage that remained after burning, the dump had no odor and did not attract animals.

Carmen Garcia was the man responsible for building many of the beautiful rock walls for the yards of the new company houses and offices in the 1936 re-opening of Goldroad. They were at the Morris Bird house, the warehouse-office building and the assay office area. A few of the houses built in the re-opening were not built on rock walls made by Carmen Garcia, but were built on sites remaining from previous openings. But the walls built by Carmen Garcia were far superior to those walls. The beauty of his workmanship is still available to those who travel through Goldroad. These remaining rock walls are located along the south side of Route 66 in the assay office area.

Carmen Garcia was from Mexico and could not speak English. After our transfer from Goldroad in 1942 to the New Mexico site, he built the rock walls for all of the houses. No rock was hauled in for his use on these walls. He blasted the rocks he needed from the area around the house where he was building the wall. And this was done with us living in the house. Our yard had three levels of rock wall in the front and one in the back.

Gold Road Or Goldroad?

All steps were made of rock as well. He worked alone and many of the rocks were very large. These larger rocks were placed at the bottom and they became progressively smaller toward the top. The Walt Elgin house next to ours had a wall at least eight feet high on one side.

Looking west toward mine. Assay office and rock walls are at the left of dark car. Change room is directly ahead with white-framed window in end. Dunton's garage and trucks are to the right of the change room. Steps in left corner led to homes on the hill. (Courtesy of Mohave County Historical Society)

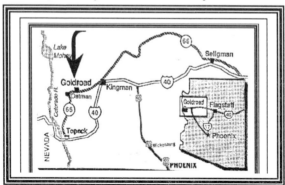

Map Showing Historic Route 66 As It Winds From Seligman To   Kingman and On Through Goldroad and Oatman To Topock

Gold Road Or Goldroad?

Goldroad Mill in 1937-1942
(Courtesy of Mohave County Historical Society)

Chapter 16

Historic Route 66

Westward from Kingman, Arizona

Early in the history of our country, we became a people on the move. The adventurousness of the early American people and the seemingly unlimited resources to the west, reached out to this nation on the move. Although there were no established trails, the westward expansion followed used by the Native Americans, early groups of trappers, and the westward migrations of wagon trains.

The gold rush of 1849 caused thousands of people to search out these trails in their journey to the gold fields of California.

One such trail that would become Route 66 across Arizona was the Beale Wagon Road. A Lieutenant Fitzgerald Ned Beale was commissioned by Congress in 1857 to survey and build a wagon road from Fort Defiance, New Mexico that roughly followed the Whipple trail across Arizona through Kingman to Fort Mohave on the Colorado River and into California.

Beale's survey report was approved and by August 1857, Beale and his survey crew exceeding 100 men and 22 camels as pack animals in a unique desert surveying experiment, left Fort Defiance and by late fall of that year reached the Colorado River. The Beale survey trail would become known as the Beale Wagon Road across Arizona and about 70 years later would be followed by Route 66. This unique desert surveying experiment used camels instead of horses or mules because camels were very well suited for these desert conditions and capable of carrying heavier loads than horses or mules and also they were able to travel for days without water. The Syrian camel driver Hadji Ali (Hi Jolly) worked for Beale and later lived in western Arizona. His grave can still be seen in Quartzsite marked by a stone pyramid with a camel on top.

Perhaps this unique desert experiment of camels and their drivers explains why a giant fig tree was growing in the area of the hot springs on the east side of the Black Mountains north of Route 66. At one time there was a resort there with a large swimming pool where people would bathe in the healing mineral waters of the hot springs.

Historic Route 66

The following pictures courtesy of Curtis Bonelli.

Fig Tree at Fig Tree Springs Claimed to be the World's Largest FigTree by Ripley's Believe It or Not

Remains of Resort and Swimming Pool Today

Historic Route 66

I remember visiting these springs on a number of occasions. One time was when our family met Auntie and Uncle Joe for a family picnic. At that time, all that remained at the site was the empty swimming pool and giant fig tree. For entertainment, while the adults ate and talked, Vel, Billy, and I climbed on the tree and played inside its branches.   The diameter of the limbs was the size of a man's thigh, and could be seen for miles from Route 66. At this time, the fig tree was reported to have been the largest fig tree in the world.

On the another occasion, mother gathered some of the figs to take home to make fig jam. Daddy loved fig jam. The figs from the giant fig tree were dark figs, which are required to make jam—light figs cannot be made into jam. When a friend of Mother's and her five children stayed with us for a month while her husband was searching for housing in Needles for the family, the family ate most of the fig jam. Daddy was not happy! He did not like the family to begin with, and especially did not appreciate having to house and feed six extra people. And, eating his favorite jam only added injury to the insult!

The Giant Fig Tree At Fig Tree Springs
(Courtesy of Mohave County Historical Society)

Returning home to Goldroad from our picnic, other points of interest we would pass were: Cool Springs Camp, Fish Bowl Springs, Ed's Camp, and up the hill to Sitgreaves Pass. On this high elevation perched a service station called the Osman Shell.

Historic Route 66

Cool Springs Camp

Ed's Camp

The Osman Shell Station at Sitgreaves Pass
(Courtesy of Mohave County Historical Society)
126.

Historic Route 66

The Great Depression was still creating jobless families, and thousands of people were being driven off their farms in the mid-west, especially Oklahoma, by what was called the Dust Bowl. The Dust Bowl was the result of prolonged drought and high winds. This weather condition left the farmer with unproductive land and no way to provide for his family.

Route 66 was the main artery which funneled these poor homeless people from their destitute home state situation to California—a place they hoped and believed would provide the way for them to make a living for themselves and their families. These were good honest people who had always provided for themselves, but who now were caught up in a terrifying situation over which they had no control. The word *Okie* was used to identify these people and is still in use today to convey poverty.

We watched as these displaced people passed through on their way to a better life, they hoped, in California. Regretfully, I must admit we did not look upon them and their situation with the sympathy and understanding that should have been given. Perhaps, the lack of concern was due to the hard times most had experienced or were still experiencing themselves. Most of the people had enough of their own problems to handle and had no time or money to help others in such large numbers. And I do not know of any help that was asked for by these people from anyone in our camp. But Mother always fed any hoboes who came to our door asking for a meal—that was the way she was raised. Our house on the hill must have been marked for them to find us. Because the last hobo she fed complained about the pancakes and eggs she served him on a pie tin rather than a plate. She ran him off, and we were never bothered again by any hoboes.

Their old trucks and cars were loaded with all their possessions, and they passed almost daily through the camp. The treacherous curves and steep inclines of the highway were a particular hazard because of the age and condition of their vehicles. N.R. Dunton, the owner of the Standard Station and garage, took advantage of this situation and stationed a truck on the east side of the mountain range and, for a fee, pulled many of them up and over the high mountains into Goldroad. The brakes went out on an old, unassisted, heavily loaded truck on its descent down the mountain and around the many S curves into Goldroad. The shaft and mine offices were up an incline on the corner of one of these S curves. The highway turned but the road up to the mine and offices went straight. By the time the truck reached this S curve, it was going too fast to turn the corner, so the driver did the only thing he could do—he went straight on up the mine road. The road had enough of an incline to bring the truck to a stop before it hit the head frame or hoist house—acting as a modern day runaway truck ramp.

The men working in the mine area were startled to see the truck rolling by with the frightened, pale-faced driver and his family inside. Without brakes to hold the truck on the incline, it rolled back to the relatively level area where the highway made the turn. The weak-kneed driver crawled out of the truck as soon as it had slowed sufficiently for him to safely exit. And he and his family were grateful their lives had been spared. All of the workers in the area who had seen the old truck go by gathered around and discussed what had happened, and the tragic way it could have ended.

The Dunton garage was located on this *S* curve. Bill Russell was the manager for Dunton and Roger Williamson was his mechanic. Other Okies stopped at the service station to get water for their steaming trucks and cars and any free or low-cost repairs they could get that would enable their worn-out vehicles to take them on their way to California.

When our family saw the movie *The Grapes of Wrath* at the Oatman theater, we were not surprised at what we saw, because we had been watching it pass through Goldroad on an almost daily basis for years.

The Tom Redding family whose house set below the rock wall of the schoolyard was a displaced family from the Dust Bowl of Kansas. Rosie was a little older than I was, and her sister Elsie was in high school. Rosie and I played together periodically during the years we lived in Goldroad.

One evening we were together outside her house before the sun had completely set, and she began to cry. She told me when they lived in Kansas there had been times when she had not had enough to eat. There were two other related Redding families in Goldroad—one was *Sundown* Fitzpatrick who worked at the mill. And although they were farmers, they were very happy to have jobs with a mining company.

Sundown wore bib overalls—a carry-over no doubt from his farming days. He had two young sons and built his house down the road from Uncle Son and Henny's house. I was in their house a few times with Rosie and was impressed with the ingenuity of the toilet he had installed on the back screened porch. The lack of privacy was one unique feature of the toilet—the other was the faucet placed on the wall over and above the toilet bowl that was used to flush it. I had to admit the set-up was better than an outhouse.

Goldroad had a small restaurant when we arrived in 1937. It was located in the same area as the Standard Station and the garage. Business must not have been good, because it closed a short time later. We bought candy bars there before the Central Commercial was built.

Much excitement was stirred when it was whispered around camp Helen Brough had eloped with her boyfriend Barney Roberts.

He lived in Oatman and attended high school with her. William and Johnny and I were not too surprised when the elopement happened. Obviously, Barney was not welcome at the Brough residence, because he enlisted the help of William and Johnny to contact Helen with notes. He worked each evening after school cleaning the Goldroad School. Johnny and William had carried notes from Barney at the school to Helen at her home a number of times before their elopement.

For a few days after they eloped their parents did not know where they had gone. Then the rumor circulated around camp that Mr. Brough had gone after them in his car and had caught up with them in Flagstaff.

The Paris Brough House With The Silver Water Tank In The Background
(Courtesy of Mohave County Historical Society)

When I heard this rumor, my first thought was how terrible it would be to be caught by Mr. Brough in a situation such as this—a fate worse than death.

Both Mr. and Mrs. Brough had a reputation in camp for being sharp with people and very strict with their children. I just knew Mr. Brough would return to Goldroad with Helen in tow and the marriage would be annulled and Barney would not be seen again in the area. Contrary to my expectations, Mr. Brough returned to Goldroad alone, and the marriage remained intact. Barney and Helen moved to Silver City when our group left Goldroad in 1942. They had two daughters after their move.

My own experience with Mrs. Brough occurred when Bobby Brough and I were six years old and I gave him a haircut. Mrs. Brough indicated her displeasure over what I had done when I returned to play the following day. She did not yell or scream at me or tell me not to return. But in a sarcastic way said that she really liked the haircut I had given Bobby. And for just an instant I thought she meant what she said, but then I realized she was being sarcastic—something I had not experienced from an adult before. I left without saying a word and never returned again to play with Bobby.

My Very Best Friend Of All
Norma Jean Richards, Joan Bird, Vella Mae Richards

130.

Chapter 17

My Very Best Friend Of All

His first job with the company paid him more money than he had ever earned in his life.

After Marie Kirby left Goldroad, I tried to fill the gap left in my life by playing with the few Anglo girls in camp. But no one filled the spot of best friend until Joan (pronounced JoAnn) Bird moved to Goldroad with her father, Lamar, and her mother, Fern, from Mapleton, Utah. They arrived in the early part of 1939. When Alma Dean Doolin introduced me to the new girl in camp, we immediately became best friends and were never apart.

Joan's uncle and aunt were Morris and Margaret Bird, and the company had built them a second company house up on the hill not far from the house we were to move into very shortly. Morris had secured a job for Lamar, and also later a job for his other brother Floyd. While Joan's father was building their two-room house just up the hill from the Doolins', her family lived in a tent-house behind Morris' house. When their house was completed, they painted it white with red trim like the home they had left behind in Mapleton. But the home in Utah was stucco, and the home in Goldroad was wood.

Like everyone in Goldroad, they were grateful for the opportunity to work. They arrived in Goldroad driving a Model T sedan. They had come from Mapleton by way of Las Vegas, Nevada, and across Boulder Dam. When they stopped at the dam to take the tour, they, and others who were in the tour, were advised not to go on to Kingman that night because the roads were flooded from heavy rains.

The highway between the dam and Kingman had many dangerous dips that filled with swiftly moving water when heavy rains fell in the area.

Joan's family, as well as others in the group, did not have the money to spend the night in a motel in Boulder City, and it was decided by this group to go on to Kingman. Their entire group made it safely through that night. And they were grateful because the swift water running over the highway that they had gone through had created a very dangerous situation for them.

Joan's family had left a very difficult economic situation in Utah. In his first job with the company, Lamar pushed a surface ore car at the mine. The ore car was filled with waste and he pushed it on tracks to a place where he emptied it over the side of the dump.

My Very Best Friend Of All

Many times Joan and I waved to her father as he worked. After a time, he was transferred to a better job on the conveyor belt. His first job with the company paid him more money than he had ever earned in his life.

In the evenings while we were still living in the Onetto house, I could hear Joan, Alma Dean Doolin, and others playing hide-n-seek under the street light in front of the Doolin's house up the hill from us. Hearing their excited voices made me even more anxious to move to our house on the hill so I could join in the fun.

Mother and Fern Bird were not too pleased about Joan and I playing with Alma Dean. In fact, Mother had told us not to go to her house. When we continued going, she threatened to send Vella and me to a boarding school for girls if we did not stay away from her house. When I found literature on the table Mother had received from one of the schools, the threat worked for a while. But it was very difficult to stay away. So many different and interesting things were always happening at the Doolin house.

They had older, married children who would occasionally come back home. One of the married daughters lived down the hill from them with her husband and child. This married daughter and the sister who was close to her age took several vacations together. That would not have been an unusual happening except these two girls hitchhiked wherever they went. During the married girl's absence, her husband and mother took care of her child. After a time, she and her sister would arrive back home, and she would pick up her life with her husband and child again as though she had never been away. Through Alma Dean's stories about this sister, Joan and I heard more about sex than we should have at our age.

Alma Dean had an older brother, Dutch, who lived at home. He should have been in high school but had dropped out. On Halloween night on our way to our own Halloween party at the school, Joan and I stopped by Alma Dean's house to check out her costume. We did not recognize Dutch when he walked into the room. And it was not until we heard his voice that we would believe it was Dutch. He was dressed as an old prospector. The costume had been made by several members of his family for him to wear to a community-sponsored Halloween party in Kingman. A prize was to be given for the best costume, and they were hoping he would win it.

His mustache and beard were made by untwisting sisal rope. The untwisted rope looked so natural and real it was difficult to tell it was fake. And his light hair coloring made the beard appear even more natural, because it blended perfectly. With an old beat-up hat on his head, grubby clothes, old worn out boots, a gold pan and a prospector's pick, he looked exactly like an old prospector.

My Very Best Friend Of All

The day after the Halloween party, Joan and I checked back with Alma Dean on her brother's success at the party. We were pleased to learn he had indeed won the prize for best costume—an electric toaster.

After Dutch won the toaster, Joan and I noticed several new household items appearing at different times in their home. When asked about them, Alma Dean told us Dutch had won another contest with his costume. This seemed a little strange to us since Halloween was over, and he was still winning contests. But we accepted her explanation without question. However, not long after all of these new items began appearing in the Doolin house, we learned Dutch had been arrested for breaking into homes in Kingman and stealing items from them. He was sent away to jail, and I do not remember his ever returning to Goldroad.

The Halloween party Joan and I attended that night was held at the school and was for both adults and children. Joan and I were dressed alike in southern belle costumes with ruffled leggings coming from underneath our skirt. The adults also wore costumes. Daddy went as Don Juan; Mother went as a witch; Bill Hicks went as a scarecrow with straw sticking out around his hands and neck; Maureen Hicks, the wife of Otis Hicks, went as a black cat. She was so small and trim, I later wore her cat costume when I was in the eighth grade. Everyone, children and adults, had a good time together that night.

Mr. Doolin was a carpenter with the company. And he built the house his family lived in. When he enlarged the house, he used discarded wooden powder boxes from the mine. They were heavy boxes made with dovetailed corners and a figure of Hercules pressed into each side. When the boxes were flattened to nail into place on the side of the house, they were left dovetailed together. Although he painted the wood, the pressed figure of Hercules could still be seen.

Furniture—bedroom sets, large chairs and tables for the living room—was built in the open work shed located in his front yard. It was filled with expensive electric woodworking equipment. Because no one in the family knew how to upholster, bed blankets with an Indian pattern were thrown over the chairs. He was very artistic and talented in working with wood.

To hold the matches for a game his family played, he made a very elaborate and decorative holder. On a board approximately 16" x 16", he bored holes to hold the individual matchsticks. On the remaining board space, he built a detailed replica of the Gold Road headframe. Small shovels and picks were made by finely grinding gray stone to represent the metal parts of these tools.

My Very Best Friend Of All

Many times when Joan and I went to Alma Dean's house, her father had moved inside walls creating new rooms. One room had been painted white decorated with gold paint designs that had been blown by mouth through a paper funnel.

Mother was very particular in our home. And I was always amazed at the large globs of dried fingernail polish on the nice bedroom dressers Mr. Doolin had made for his family's use. The Doolins smoked. But rather than putting their burned match in an ashtray after lighting a cigarette, it was thrown carelessly on the floor.

Alma Dean had two younger brothers, four and under, living at home. Mrs. Doolin did a lot of laundry. To accommodate the volume of wash, Mr. Doolin built heavy metal clothesline poles. These poles were approximately six feet across. The other women in camp had the smaller, regular size *T*-pole clothesline poles.

The size and strength of the Doolin poles made them perfect for us to use in our play. Two kids could get on each end. We would spend hours spinning forward and backward on these poles. Marie Kirby's pipe under her porch could not compare to them. And if we fell, which we never did, soft dirt was under us not a large boulder.

One day a significant experience happened as we were walking from the Henline Apartments past the main Office building. We saw a dog under the edge of the back of the building. Upon closer examination, we discovered she was a mother dog with several small nursing puppies. She obviously was a stray and belonged to no one and was in need of nourishment. She wanted to be friendly but was more concerned with protecting her pups than receiving the food she needed. After much coaxing, she ventured out a few inches. Only when she was convinced we would not harm her or her puppies, she allowed us to pet her and the puppies.

We immediately felt concern and compassion for them. And we also felt a responsibility to provide nourishment for her so she could feed her puppies. The problem was how we would be able to do this. Even though all the men in camp had jobs and were providing for their families, there was not an excess of money. Being children of the Great Depression, we also realized our parents would not be willing to provide food on a permanent basis for an extra animal.

Our solution to the problem was to work to earn money to buy food for the mother dog. Our plan was to approach our own mothers first and then the other women in camp and offer to work at odd jobs for pay. A name was selected for our group—*The Handy Helpers.*

My Very Best Friend Of All

Not many women had the extra nickel or dime to pay *The Handy Helpers* for odd jobs. Or it could have been they did not want to be bothered with us. As it usually happened on these projects with our friends where money was involved, Mother was the only one who gave us any help.

We did a small job for her, and with the money she gave us bought a can of evaporated milk at the Central Commercial. A container was found and the milk was poured and diluted with the proper amount of water. But in our desire to provide more for the dog with what little we had, we decided to add more water. This extra water diluted the milk to a point where it was too weak to be of value to the dog. She refused to drink it.

We were discouraged. And we knew our prospects of providing for her were not good because of the response we had received on our first soliciting attempt. But children are optimistic beings, and we left the mother dog that day feeling that somehow everything would work out—a phrase Mother had taught us that hinged on our willingness to do our best to find a solution to the problem.

No dog approached us the next day when we returned to the spot where we had left her and the puppies the day before. We searched under the building hoping against hope she had perhaps moved her family of puppies farther under the building. After much searching, we finally had to accept the fact she wasn't there!

We never knew what happened to her and the puppies. I have always felt a meddling parent under the guise of taking care of a bad situation had the mother and puppies killed. That would never have been my parents' solution to the problem. We were allowed to solve our own problems in matters such as this. And I believe because my parents did this, I am probably the only *Handy Helper* who remembers this mother dog and her puppies and have been able to relate her situation to similar situations in human lives.

When I see or hear of mothers left with children to raise alone, whose husbands have fathered and left, as happened in the case of the mother dog, I am reminded of the determination I saw in the eyes of the mother dog the day we found her. It was a determination to protect her puppies with her life, if necessary. And there was always the choice available to her to leave her puppies helpless to die from hunger while she fended for herself. But she chose to remain with them even if it meant sacrificing her own life to do it.

There are so many single mothers now who are struggling to provide the necessities for their children to survive—love, food, housing, clothing, Christmas—and they are doing it alone. Even those few fathers who provide the minimum of money for physical survival of their children are not willing to sacrifice their time and concern for the happiness of their children.

My Very Best Friend Of All

These fathers have abandoned them and have gone on with their own lives convincing themselves that they have a right to happiness even at the expense of the children they have fathered.

I learned a great lesson of life in my brief encounter with the valiant mother dog who had been willing to sacrifice her own life to save her puppies. She certainly filled *the measure of her creation*. And as I read about and observe first hand human mothers willing to do the same, I honor and have deep respect for their determination to fill the measure of their creation.

One day I thought my eyes were deceiving me when I saw a black jackrabbit. But it did not look quite like a jackrabbit—no long ears and the wrong color. As I studied the strange animal, I realized it had to be a cat! A black cat with no tail using its hind legs like a rabbit when it ran. Someone must have cut off its tail, but why did it run like a rabbit?

At our dinner table that evening when I mentioned what I had seen, Daddy told me it was a special breed of cat called *Manx*. I also learned this strange looking cat belonged to Shirley Peeples. He was rarely seen and spent most of his daylight hours inside their house. He was very unfriendly when I tried getting close enough to pet him. He always quickly ran away. Most cats in camp welcomed a good petting—not him.

This cat fathered the kittens found under the Henline woodpile that were adopted and tamed by Morris and Margaret Bird. He also fathered my Gray Kitten. Although she looked nothing like him and had a sweet, friendly disposition like her mother, I knew he was her father—in the same litter were two or three Manx kittens. But they were not black like their father; they were an orange tiger stripe.

The Gray Kitten came out from under our porch on her own without any coaxing and wanted to be loved and fed. But the Manx kittens hissed, scratched and bit Joan and me when we tried to hold and pet them. We even tried wearing an old pair of Mother's gloves to protect our hands, but they bit and scratched through them. And after several attempts, we gave up and left them alone.

When not in school, Joan and I filled our days with many activities other than swinging on Alma Dean's clothesline poles, playing paper dolls and games, or organizing clubs. To add adventure to our lives, William and Johnny shared the location of a fun place to play just west of the mill. It was an old tailings pond left from a previous opening. And what made it different from the other old tailings ponds in camp was that it was sand. And we spent many hours jumping off the top of the tailings into the sand on the side of the hill. But our game came to an end when the company decided to re-mill these tailings.

My Very Best Friend Of All

One day when we came back to our place of play, a huge ore bucket was rigged on a heavy cable to scoop the sandy tailings and haul them to a bin at the mill. Once the operation was begun, it was not long until there was no more sandy area to play in.

Another activity William and Johnny shared with us was the opportunity to experience in a small way the fun Tom Sawyer and Huckleberry Finn had on a raft. A large tailings pond had been deliberately built in the canyon by the mill to dam the water that ran down the wash when it rained. A lot of water was required to run the mill and the water caught behind this tailings pond helped to supplement the normal supply.

But we found a more important use for the small pond—we nervously pushed our wooden pallet a few feet from the shore, alongside an old partially submerged car body, and felt we were actually afloat. The pond was probably not more than 5 feet in its deepest parts. But after an afternoon of play, a mill worker, probably at Mr. Brough's request, came over and asked us to leave.

When this large tailings pond was no longer used and had completely dried and hardened, we played many baseball games on it—one of the few flat places in camp—not caring that adults had warned us about the danger of cyanide in its tailings.

But we were in the mill area often where we always hefted and tried throwing the heavy metal balls used to crush the ore in the very large ball mills. And we dug through the remaining bits and pieces of the balls after they had done their job in the ball mills and were dumped by wheelbarrow into piles on the ground. Many were the right size for throwing. And they threw a large plume of water up into the air when tossed into the mill pond.

Much cyanide was used in the milling process. The unusual metal barrels used to transport the cyanide were used everywhere in camp, but especially at the mill. I do not know the composition of the metal, but it had the appearance of aluminum. And I am sure it was not. All the years we lived in Goldroad, two of these barrels were part of the Oatman sign on Route 66 near the junction of the dirt Silver Creek Road. And they remained there as part of the sign until a few years ago. What happened to them and the sign, I do not know.

Mother, and most of the other women in camp, used cyanide barrels for packing dishes and many other household items when we left Goldroad in 1942. Mother wrapped her canning jars in newspaper and placed them in cyanide cans hoping they would arrive unbroken at their destination in New Mexico.

My Very Best Friend Of All

Although Joan's parents were grateful for the job he had in Goldroad, they always had a desire to return to their home in Mapleton. Fern would joke and say if she had a refrigerator and a new car, she would be happy in Goldroad. She got the refrigerator. And in March or April they went to the Old Trails Garage in Kingman and bought a black 1941 Chevrolet sedan. And although Joan and I preferred the pale green Oldsmobile on display, her parents felt they could not afford the higher-priced Oldsmobile.

With a new car they planned a trip to Mapleton. A few weeks before Easter when Lamar got off work at 4:00 P.M., they loaded Joan and me in the back seat and we left for Utah. We drove through the night and arrived in Mapleton early the next morning.

Joan's Grandma Bird was visited. But we stayed with Fern's relatives the few days we were there. And Joan and I visited her old school for half a day before leaving for California to visit other relatives. The class was asked to draw a picture about Easter. A prize would be given for the best picture. Then the winning picture would be posted for all the class to see.

I busily started my drawing, and when it was finished, I noticed the other children in the class, without exception, had drawn pictures using Jesus as the main theme. My picture was a chicken with Easter eggs. I had never associated Jesus with Easter. I was not embarrassed, but was impressed with their knowledge and their understanding of the true meaning of Easter. When the children in the class learned we would not be returning in the afternoon, many of them wanted my picture to keep and copy for their entry in the contest.

California was a very exciting place for two little girls from Goldroad. Everything was different, especially the number of people and stores. At one of these large department stores Fern bought the red, white and blue cheese cloth used as ties for our May Pole dance.

But one of the saddest things that could have happened to me happened— in late summer, my best friend moved back to Mapleton. We had been together everyday for over two years, and her leaving left a big hole in my life that could not be filled by anyone else. But little did we realize at the time, everyone except a few caretakers would be leaving Goldroad in little over a year, and our lives would never be the same again. In a few months, one of the largest wars in history would begin. No one would escape untouched. Everyone's life would be changed by it. And the entire world would be in turmoil.

Chapter 18

The LDS Church Comes To Goldroad

No, you can't join the Mormon Church, but you can go.

After the ladies in camp gave up on the Sunday School they had been holding, there was no church to attend, except the Catholic Church in Mexican town.

Some of those in camp who were Catholic, such as Ella Watkins, attended this church. Although Mrs. Plummer had been raised Catholic, she did not attend. As far as I know, no one in camp knew she was Catholic. But she felt Miss Watkins needed a companion on her weekly visits to church, so she sent Madeline with her. And maybe that was her way for Madeline to receive training in the church without divulging her own membership.

Rosie Redding and I attended the Catholic Church one time. And we had made plans to attend the following week together. But when I walked to her house the following Sunday so we could go together, she told me her family was going on a picnic to the Colorado River that day and she could not go to church with me. I was disappointed she had changed our plans to attend church. But I accepted it and went on home. A short time later Rosie came to my house and asked if I wanted to go with them. I accepted, and Rosie and I never attended the Catholic Church again. My parents did not care if I went to the Catholic Church, but if they had, they would have told me directly that I could not go. But the surprise picnic to the river provided by the Reddings might have been their way of ending Rosie's desire to attend the Catholic Church.

Morris and Margaret Bird were members of the Church of Jesus Christ of Latter-day Saints, commonly known as the Mormon Church. Joan and her father and mother were also members of this church. The closest Church of Jesus Christ of Latter-day Saints met in the Odd Fellows Hall in Kingman twenty-five miles away. Because the Goldroad men worked on Sunday, they could not meet with the Kingman Branch. This branch was presided over by Conway LeBaron.

A few inactive church members lived in Goldroad. They were Bert Rindlisbach (his wife, daughter, son-in-law and grandson were active); Guy Gardner and his wife; Don and Yvonne Johnson and their two young

The LDS Church Comes To Goldroad

daughters; Rube Farnsworth, an assayer for the company, whose nephew Philo Farnsworth, developed the first television.

In 1939, with Morris Bird as presiding Elder, the Goldroad Dependant Branch was organized and met each Sunday evening in the school. When Joan told me they would be starting the meetings, we ran down the hill to our house to ask Mother if I could join. She was standing in the kitchen, and I said, "Mother, can I join the Mormon Church?" She said, "No, you can't join the Mormon Church, but you can go." I was satisfied.

Young missionaries between the ages of 19 and 21 were sent into camp. Elder Stoddard of Logan, Utah, with his missionary companion, was the first.

Young missionary, Lamar Bird, Joan Bird, Orson Wright, Dale Wright

A full Church program was offered—Sunday School, Sacrament Meeting, Primary-Mutual, and Relief Society.

The LDS Church Comes To Goldroad

Sunday School and Sacrament Meeting were held Sunday evening in back-to-back sessions. Mutual-Primary was for children primary age through high school and was held on a week night. Relief Society was for women and was held on a week day, either in Goldroad or with the Kingman group. Mary Anderson and Mrs. George Phillips, and several other women who were not members of the Church, attended Relief Society.

Goldroad Relief Society in front of Mary Anderson's house with Joan Bird's house on hill behind: Left front row-Mrs. George Phillips, white purse; Fern Bird, dark purse; Mary Anderson, checked dress; Mrs Guy Gardner, white dress. Left back row-Jane Wright, second face; Naomi Bird, third full face

I was the only member of my family who participated in the Church. Our family went to the movies in Oatman every Sunday night, and this created a problem for me. I wanted to be a part of both activities. A few times Joan and I convinced her parents to allow her to miss part of the meeting and attend the movies with us. But one night they refused to allow her to do this, and I left the meeting alone and went with my family to the theater. Many years later I learned Joan's parents had not been the ones opposed to her leaving the meeting early to go with us to the theater on Sunday evening.

The LDS Church Comes To Goldroad

It had been the disapproval expressed by Morris and Margaret Bird to her parents that had caused them to refuse to allow her to go.

George Phillips and his family attended Sunday School and Sacrament Meeting quite frequently. One of the tenets of the Church is abstaining from tobacco. Before one of the meetings started, George Phillips sat and smoked a cigarette. Although my parents were not Latter-day Saints, when I returned home after the meeting and told them what Mr. Phillips had done, they were surprised and disapproved of his actions. However, he must not have meant any disrespect or had any thought of offending when he smoked the cigarette, because he told Morris Bird that he was interested in the Church but would get too much pressure from his family if he joined. He was Catholic, and his sister was married to Pete Kristich, who also was Catholic.

Morris and Margaret Bird, Terry and Jimmy Bird on back steps of their home on the hill.

Morris and Lamar's brother Floyd also lived in Goldroad. His wife's name was Naomi and they had four children. Their oldest son, Duane, was Joan's and my age. He had a beautiful voice and was asked to sing with Elder Stoddard at the all-day Conference we attended in Kingman. We had nothing to eat all day. Restaurants were too expensive for us to use, and I was very hungry when we arrived home later that afternoon.

The LDS Church Comes To Goldroad

When Joan's family arrived in Goldroad, her father smoked. In order for him and his family to go to the Temple and be sealed, he had to stop smoking. Lamar determined he would do this, and he did. He substituted gum for a cigarette. Some time later their family went to the Arizona Temple in Mesa where they were sealed together as a family. Joan was eight years old, and was baptized in the Temple while they were there. This was one trip I was not a part of, and I felt left out.

Many activities were held in conjunction with the Primary-Mutual evening program. One of the fun activities held was a party at Morris Bird's home. Games were played and good food was served. Several skating parties were held in Kingman. After their daughter joined the Church, the Deming family hosted an evening picnic at their dairy.

The first convert to the Church in Goldroad was Homer Howard. A large group from the Church went to the Colorado River where he was to be baptized. Before the baptism, Joan and I had climbed to the top of a small mesa near the river. Unaware of what was happening, we came running down the hill about the time the baptismal prayer was being said. I felt badly about disturbing the proceedings, but we had no way of knowing it was taking place at that time.

A local woman politician attended this first baptism. She was a Catholic. When the baptism was over and everyone was socializing, the Elders were joking around and started to chase her. She fell and broke her leg and had to wear it in a cast all through her political campaign. When she was asked about her cast, her reply was, "I got it while being chased by two Mormon missionaries," and then she would laugh.

When the time came for Elder Stoddard to return to his home in Logan for his mission release, he asked the Deming girl he had baptized to marry him. After his release, he returned to Goldroad, and they were married.

He was given a job with the company working for my father as an electrician helper. He built their house on the side of the hill on the road to the mill. And before the walls were up, they moved in and had to get up and dress before the sun came up. The men at work called him *The Preacher.*

Eventually all of the Deming family joined the Church—father, mother, adult children living at home, and Howie, who was my age. They lived in two houses across the road and up the hill from Uncle Son and Henny.   They sold milk from the dairy they ran located at the base of the mountains east of Goldroad. The little pickup used for hauling the milk had a wooden cover over the back with lettering that read, *Deming Dairy--You Can't Beat Our Milk, but You Can Whip Our Cream.*

The LDS Church Comes To Goldroad

Our family did not drink milk, so we never bought milk from them. Mother preferred and used canned milk for cooking.

Chapter 19

The House On The Hill Was Very Special To Me

There truly was not a happier child on the face of the earth during those times I sat alone with my kitten and surveyed my world.

Shortly after the death of Daddy's brother, Norman, in February of 1940, we made our move to the house on the hill with the fifty-seven steps up to it. A road wound around the hill and came to the back of the house. But when I wanted to get down to a friend's house in a hurry, or to the Central Commercial, I always took the steps. I could run up and down them almost as fast as I could run up and down the mountains. I think Joan and I were the only people who used those steps.

The house on the hill was very special to me, and I loved being there. Many special experiences happened to me and to my family during the time we lived in that home. To the world they would not be exciting because they were everyday, quietly lived, bonding and welding experiences special only to our family because of their ordinariness.

All that we had experienced in the years prior to our move to the house on the hill, the unsettled years spent trying to find a stable job to provide for our family; Mother's tuberculosis attack and the six or seven months Vella and I spent with our grandparents in southern Arizona; the time Billy spent with Uncle Tom and Aunt Ruby in Kingman; Mother's stay with Auntie and Uncle Joe in Kingman, were all smoothed out and made right by the life we were able to live in   *the house on the hill.*

One very ordinary thing I liked to do in summer was get up in the morning and go out on our front porch and sit on the table that was as high as the railing on the porch. And there I would love my gray kitten with the gold eyes, and watch everything going on in the entire camp (except those houses on the hill behind us).

What feelings of wellbeing and contentment I felt—I was totally and completely happy and satisfied—life could not have been better. There truly was not a happier child on the face of the earth during those times I sat alone with my kitten and surveyed my world.

The House On The Hill Was Very Special To Me

There are few times in our lives that we can look back on and remember as total and complete happy situations. But those times on the porch were added to the other simple experiences I carry in my mind from our few years in Goldroad. The following experiences provided by my mother and father make all of the other meaningful experiences I had in Goldroad possible:

Running into our home anytime of the day and finding my mother there cleaning, maintaining and beautifying our home—cooking good meals—washing and curling our long hair each Saturday no matter what else happened—keeping our clothes washed and ironed—taking us with her to Needles each month for our monthly grocery and clothes shopping—making and bottling root beer for our family—insisting on proper behavior in our home as well as out—supporting us in everything that was important to us—devoting her full time and energies to our family by putting us first above anyone or anything else no matter what the world's expectation might have been of her.

Seeing my father get up every morning to go to his job—knowing he would be home at 11:30 when the siren sounded for his noon meal—knowing he would be home soon after 4:00 P.M. when the whistle blew and our family would sit down together for our supper—knowing he was respected and liked by the men he worked with—knowing he expected a certain level of behavior from us, but also knowing he would go-to-bat against anyone or anything if the need arose—knowing he would always be there as a father for us and a husband to our mother no matter what the difficulties—knowing he *was* what he projected to the world, an honest man with integrity and compassion for the underdog.

One spring before our school was out for the summer, Mother decided she would make root beer for our family. She had a few beer bottles she had saved from the one beer Daddy drank each evening during the summer months when he came home from work. Mother, who normally was against all drinking, agreed with the one-beer-a-night rule because of the Goldroad heat—Daddy had become quite thin, and she felt the beer might put some weight on him. She planned to make a large batch of the root beer and needed more beer bottles than what she had.

In order to get more bottles without having to buy them, Mother sent us to different families in camp to ask them for their used beer bottles. Some bottles were more interesting than others. Daddy's *Apache* bottles were very ordinary compared to the bottles Joe and Ethel Peeples gave us. They drank the more expensive *Pabst Blue Ribbon* beer.

146.

The House On The Hill Was Very Special To Me

The blue ribbons on these bottles were real blue ribbons tied around the neck of the bottle and held in place with a gold sticker—very pretty. I begged Mother to leave the blue ribbons on the bottles because I thought they looked so pretty. She refused, maybe because in the sterilization process the ribbons and gold seal would have been destroyed anyway.

Our family enjoyed the root beer she bottled. Not only at home, but also on our trips to Kingman and Needles. We drank it wherever we happened to be. No thought ever came to our mind it might look a little strange for a mother and her children to be drinking what appeared to be beer. This thought never came to Mother, either. *She* knew we were not drinking beer and that was all that concerned her—what the world thought never bothered her because she knew she was not doing anything wrong.

This was the principle we were raised with. We were taught we could go anywhere as long as we behaved ourselves—the place did not determine our actions, *we* determined our actions and controlled them—and she expected this from us throughout our lives—even as teenagers.

The root beer in beer bottles was one of many teaching experiences enforcing this principle of behavior. I do not want to imply I always made the right choices when placed in less-than-desirable situations—I did not. But I always had it as a standard of expectation to live up to and eventually was able to do it.

New furniture was in order when we moved to the house on the hill. Our new couch and chair and Daddy's platform rocker were brought with us to our new home. But new bedroom sets were purchased for all members of the family. Vel and I received a pretty rose-trimmed-in-black set for our birthday (ordered from the Sears catalog). Billy's set was made of knotty pine and was purchased from the Central Commercial in Kingman—a close-out item. Mother and Daddy's set was ordered from the catalog and was walnut veneer. Although Mother and Daddy had a bedroom, they always slept on the canvas-covered back porch on the brass bed brought from the Onetto house.

The bedspread on our bed was a blue sheer fabric that required a white sheet as a lining to keep the blanket underneath from showing through. Two blue glass lamps sat on our dresser. Mother and Daddy's bedspread was the same as ours except the color. It was dusty rose. And their lamps were cut glass.

Mother made curtains from monks cloth, a heavy, light-beige material, for the many windows across the east and south side of the house. If we had opened these windows in the summer at night, or even during the day, our house would have been a little cooler.

147.

The House On The Hill Was Very Special To Me

The House on the Hill with its 57 steps and landings leading up to it; our garage at the bottom of the steps where we sold sandwiches; bottom center building with dirt-covered roof is the powder room used in previous openings; left side is Henline house with garage. This picture was taken before the Sayer and Peeples houses were built. Route 66 can be seen in the bottom left corner as it turns to go under the conveyor belt on its way to Oatman.

But Mother was adamant the windows which swung up to open and had to be held open with a hook hanging from the ceiling would *not* ever be opened—this would make curtains an impossibility and Mother was determined to have curtains at our windows. And the windows *never* were opened no matter how hot the summer got.

One of the most exciting purchases made by our family was the Philco radio-automatic record player. About six records could be stacked on the player, and they would be played automatically one by one. *Amapola* was one of our favorite records. Johnny and William Sayer were taught to dance by Vel and me on our front porch to the music played over and over again on this record player. Our family friends—Gayle and Babe Cudney and Bill and Rosie Hicks—also enjoyed the music played on it.

The House On The Hill Was Very Special To Me

Before leaving for their Saturday night dance in Kingman, they would gather at our house and listen to the records.

Daddy bought Mother a desk for our living room. And then Vel and I bought a gold-colored pendulum clock for her birthday to sit on it. Mother still has the clock at her home in Bayard, New Mexico.

Not long after we moved into the house on the hill, a living room was added to the north end of the house and connected with the kitchen. Vel and I moved our bedroom into what had been the living room. A green carpet was purchased for the living room, and Bill Hicks manually scrapped and varnished the outer boards not covered by the carpet.

Mother kept the floors throughout the house heavily waxed and polished. And if you did not remember to slow down when you came to a corner your feet would slide out from under you. White Priscilla curtains were on the living room windows. And a small fuel oil stove provided heat for the entire house. Our house was never uncomfortably cold, but later at our new home at the USSR&MCo mine in New Mexico, the small heater was inadequate and would not heat the bedrooms in winter.

Over Daddy's objections, Mother purchased an electric oven. Because the company paid for all electricity, he was concerned it would make our electric consumption too high. But at least one other supervisor's wife used an electric *stove*, and because of this, Mother felt she could very well have her electric *oven*. But she did purchase a butane stove to do the bulk of her cooking. Periodically the butane truck from Kingman made its rounds to fill the tanks in Oatman and Goldoad, and points in between.

I remember when Daddy laid the new kitchen linoleum Mother had ordered from the catalog. It was dark blue with a black foot-wide border around its circumference that had to be cut and laid separately. All jobs such as this were done after work, because the men worked seven days a week. The floor had a professional look when Daddy finished.

Memories of our evening meals are especially happy ones. Daddy sat at the head of the table opposite the kitchen window; Mother sat on his left in the first chair, Billy in the second; Vel was on Daddy's right and I sat across from him with my back to the window. The golden hue created by the lowering sun coming through the shaded window filled the room each afternoon at 4:00 during our supper. This was the time our family touched base with each other on the happenings of our day. Daddy always shared work experiences or any happenings in camp offered by the men at Dunton's service station as he walked from his work at the mine area to the mill. This is where he learned about Vel's lunchtime fight with Rosie Hernandez at the Central Commercial.

149.

The House On The Hill Was Very Special To Me

Our family also ate dinner together at 11:30 A.M. Daddy came home from work and the children came home from school. And this was nice. But the evening meal was more relaxed because there were no time constraints. My belief is that by doing just this one simple thing together as a family each evening, a lot of the troubles the children of this country are experiencing could be eliminated. Great and important results come from very simple acts such as this. The simplicity of this one act is lost on most people seeking solutions to problems with young people, because they are looking for the more complex, the more difficult and the more costly solutions to the problems.

Our house was one of the few connected to the local telephone system. No calls could be made out of Goldroad—just to company offices, and a few supervisors' homes, such as the Duriez home. These phones were not to be used for idle chatter by anyone, but were to be used only for the business of running the mine and mill, or an infrequent short personal call. Our telephone hung on the wall in the hall between the kitchen and my bedroom. It was an antiquated wood phone with two outside bells and a black speaker on the front. A crank turned on the right side of the phone dialed the desired party. The black receiver was attached to the phone by a black cord and looked like an inverted Coke glass. It hung on a hook on the left side. Such was our Goldroad telephone. Mother did not like the incessant bell ringing and the interruptions it caused in our home. So—she stuffed paper towels inside the bells changing their sharp ring to a low, almost inaudible muffled tinkle. Margie Duriez attempted calling me at our house one day. Daddy had told us our ring was four and a half. But when Margie's call came, we did not answer it. Mainly because the sound was so muffled by paper towels it was difficult to hear. But also we were not listening, because we assumed all calls were between the mine and mill offices. When I saw Margie a few days later, she asked why I had not answered our phone. I told her we never answered the phone when it rang because Mother considered it a nuisance.

Before Daddy took his shower after work, the manual gas heater was lighted. When enough shower water was warm, the heater was turned off. Water for washing dishes and other needs was heated in a teakettle on the kitchen stove.

Kenneth Guy Massey, the son of Uncle Son and Henny, was born while we lived on the hill. He was the only baby I had ever had in my life, and he was special to our family. Before his birth, Mother embroidered a very pretty white dress for him. All babies, boys or girls, wore dresses and bonnets with satin ribbons. Before his arrival, Mother held a baby shower for Henny at our house.

150.

The House On The Hill Was Very Special To Me

We had made plans to go to Solomonsville in southeastern Arizona to spend a month with Papa Guy and Mama Bessie.

But we kept delaying our trip hoping the baby would be born before we had to leave. Finally, Mother decided we had to go even though the baby had not yet arrived. And we were up bright and early on the day of our departure to take advantage of the cooler morning air for our drive over the hottest part of the desert before the temperature got too high.

When we arrived in Solomonsville later that afternoon, we learned Henny had delivered the baby that morning at home with the company doctor in attendance. After the delays we had made in our trip, we were very disappointed at missing his birth by just a few hours. All of us had eagerly anticipated his arrival with much excitement. And now it would be a month before we could see him. This made us very anxious to get home. All of us loved and enjoyed him, but Vel especially spent many hours with him at his home as well as many afternoons at our house.

Dunton's garage had a Coke machine just inside the garage on the right side of the large doors. When Kenny Guy was older and could drink and eat regular food, we would take him to the garage, put a nickel in the machine and get a Coke for him. We also gave him a Hershey's chocolate bar with the Coke—he loved both. Later, he was not doing well and the doctor diagnosed anemia. During the time we gave him the Coke and chocolate, we did not realize the amount of caffeine we were putting into his small body. We also were not aware Coke and chocolate were harmful. When we stopped giving him these things, his problem went away.

About this time Uncle Son decided to try his hand at making *home brew* in a wash tub. I do not know how successful he was, but I believe he only made one batch.

When the siren signaled dinnertime at 11:30 A.M. for the workers, Daddy would be home a few minutes later, and our family would be seated ready to eat. This is when our young cousin Bobby Kay would come flying through the door huffing and puffing saying, "I didn't think I was going to make it!" She was only about four years old, and had to climb the hill to get to our house.

Bobby Kay also made many trips to Kingman with us. She loved to sing. But like most children her age could not sing on key. When she started singing, Billy would say, "Mama, make Bobby stop singing!" Of course Mother did not make her stop, and an argument between Bobby Kay and Billy usually lasted the twenty-five miles from Goldroad to Kingman. Mother contended with a lot on these trips to Kingman, because I always got carsick.

The House On The Hill Was Very Special To Me

And I finally learned that if I would lie down this would not happen. But when I stretched out on the back seat it left no place for Billy, Vel and Bobby to sit. Their outcry was, "Mama, Norma Jean is lying down. She's taking all the room, and we don't have any place to sit!" When Mother had enough of all our complaining, all she had to say was *dammit!* No more complaining was heard, and we quietly handled the problems ourselves.

When Mother ordered the electric heater to warm our bath water at the Onetto house, Daddy ordered an electric hairbrush. As a young man he had beautiful, thick, wavy hair. But as he grew older, it started thinning on top. The hair loss concerned Daddy, and the electric hairbrush was supposed to stop the balding process. Each evening after his shower, he would sit on the couch in the living room patiently combing his hair with the brush for the recommended amount of time. The brush was connected by an electric cord to a small, brown cylinder-shaped control unit that sat on the floor. The amount of electricity sent to the metal bristles in the hairbrush was regulated by the dial on top of the unit. Although he faithfully used the hairbrush, his hair continued to thin. And later the unit was discarded.

Many unusual situations kept our lives interesting. One afternoon several Mexican boys came by the Sayer house where we were playing. They had three baby chipmunks. Their dog had killed the mother. And I wanted those chipmunks! I talked until they gave them to me. Joan and I took them to my house and made a place in the big, refrigerator box we had moved from the Onetto house to the house on the hill.

By this time, the box had seen much use and one end had come loose from the bottom at the corner leaving a space large enough for my cat to grab one of the chipmunks, even though we were sitting in the box with them. After the cat succeeded in getting two of them in this way, we decided the only safe place for the remaining chipmunk was in our house.

Being an immaculate housekeeper, Mother would not allow my cat in the house, but she allowed the chipmunk to live with us. When I asked if it could come inside, I was totally shocked when she said he could. But the most surprising part was that she seemed to enjoy him and would tell us the cute things he had done during the day while we were at school.

Now, Daddy was a different story. He loved any baby—whether it was a human or an animal. Each morning as he prepared for work, he would get the baby chipmunk from its little box, put him inside his shirt above his belt, and carry him around and talk to him. A few years earlier, he had done the same thing with the little green chick I had received for Easter.

152.

The House On The Hill Was Very Special To Me

Because he was a baby when brought into the house, a small box lined with a cloth and covered with another was his home at night. But it was not long before he was in and out of the box at will and running freely throughout the house. What do you feed a baby chipmunk? Nuts, of course! Mother was not too thrilled to share her expensive pecans and walnuts with him. Soon pinon nuts were purchased at Fortner's Store. Pinon nuts were very inexpensive at this time, and were gathered in the fall by Indians in the Hualapai Mountains.

A small bowl of pinons was kept under the utility cart in the kitchen for him. We started noticing that the nut bowl was always empty. And we wondered how such a small chipmunk could eat so many nuts. So we decided to watch him. He would fill his mouth with nuts and disappear for a short time, and would reappear again and do the same thing. We did not find the answer to the mystery until later when Mother cleaned the house, and found pinons in the creases of the couch, under dressers and in other strange places. He was storing nuts for the winter! Parts of dress patterns had also been disappearing and were found made into little nests.

When he would get too aggravating and mischievous, Mother would put him in the bathroom and close the door. Normally, she made certain the hall throw rug was away from the bathroom door. But one time when he was into things and was put in the bathroom, she failed to check the edge of the rug before leaving. Later, when she went back to let him out, she noticed the edge of the rug had been left under the door. When she opened the door and checked the rug, the edge had been chewed. This was another surprise to me, Mother did not take destruction of any part of our home lightly—but she did not ban the chipmunk from the house, nor did she seem upset with him. Mother excused what he had done by saying he chewed the rug in retaliation for being put in a place where there was nothing exciting for him to do.

The chipmunk never had a name. He was just *The Chipmunk* like my two cats were just the *Mother Cat* and the *Gray Kitten*. House life must have agreed with him, because he grew larger and stronger. He also liked our family and would let us hold him. However, one day when Joan picked him up, he bit her. Because she was so shocked by this unexpected change in his behavior, she dropped him. He fell on his head and was knocked unconscious. Quickly we ran to get a cold, wet, wash cloth to put on his little head. Shortly, he revived and was his old self again, but we realized he was too large to be allowed to run wild through our house.

Because Mac and Sue McConnell had two chipmunks in cages with running wheels, Daddy approached them about taking our chipmunk, so he would have the company of others like himself.

The House On The Hill Was Very Special To Me

They agreed and *The Chipmunk* went to live with the McConnells down the hill from us. We visited him in his new home, but the tie had been broken, and soon his memory faded from our minds and probably ours from his.

Each Saturday night, many of the couples in camp went as a group to the White Palace in Kingman where they danced. Mother did not drink and neither did her friends, but the men in the group would have a beer or two. But the drive back over the steep, winding highway home discouraged excessive drinking. A few of the couples who were a part of this group were Babe and Gaylord Cudney; June and Cloyd Henline; Rosie and Bill Hicks; Maureen and Otis Hicks, and Mother and Daddy.

Rosie and Bill Hicks

All of the men had to work the next day but felt being tired was worth the night out, except Cloyd. He grumbled a little over the late hour. On these nights when my parents were gone, Joan spent the night with me. Vella, Billy, Joan and I would play around the house until we got tired, and then we would go to bed.

The House On The Hill Was Very Special To Me

On one of these sleepovers, we were frightened by a noise at one of the bedroom windows. When we gathered enough courage to peek out, we saw Duane Bird standing there. Joan had told him she would be spending the night at my house, and he had sneaked out of his house and had come by to see us. When Mother arrived home and we were still up and not asleep, she let us know she was not pleased.

Although Goldroad was a desert town, the number of natural springs in the area was surprising. Every spring, water would seep from under many of the huge boulders on the mountains and moss would grow on their sides. Many of the springs ran only at that time of year, but others ran year around. Three of the year-round springs I was aware of were Fish Springs on Route 66 on the eastside of Sitgreaves Pass. It is still running. Another was in the same area in the high, white cliffs directly across the canyon from Fish Springs. I have not been back to that area but assume it is still flowing. And the third, Onetto Springs on Route 66 on the westside of Sitgreaves Pass whose opening is full of water and still marked by the tall cottonwood tree as it was when we lived in Goldroad.

The Onetto Spring

On one of our family trips to the white cliffs, we found a spot where a house had obviously stood in previous years. Watercress grew in the clear, cool spring that ran close by. The covered well had a hand pump on it; several fruit trees still grew; and a rock fish pond still held beautiful, three-tailed gold fish. We took several of the gold fish with us and they thrived in a large fishbowl on a shelf on our kitchen utility table. Fish Springs on the side of the mountain also held goldfish in its rock pond.

155.

The House On The Hill Was Very Special To Me

In the area near the white cliffs, cedar trees grew. Lamar Bird cut one of these trees for their Christmas. We had never thought of doing this, but it made a beautiful Christmas tree.

Closer to home in one of the canyons where we played was a beautiful spring flowing down between two solid walls of rock. We spent many hours playing there. But one day when we arrived, we found the spring had been dynamited. The water still ran, but the beauty of it had been marred. The loose rocks in the streambed ruined the fun we had enjoyed walking in the water between the solid rock walls. We never knew who destroyed our play area.

One custom the Mexicans had that I vowed to copy when I was old enough to get married was that of decorating the cars of the bridal party with beautiful crepe paper flowers and streamers and driving through Goldroad and over to Oatman—with horns blaring. The bride was beautiful in white, her attendants looked lovely in their brightly-colored, long, silk dresses and hats, and the men were handsome in their dark suits. I had assumed this was a custom everyone followed and was very disappointed later in New Mexico to learn that not everyone did it.

Although we spent much of our time in the mountains, there was only one time we met Mexican children. And it was on the same afternoon when we arrived home late and were met and spanked by Mother and sent to bed without supper. Our chanced meeting was at the old Goldroad cemetery. After talking briefly with them, they confided that we should never come to the graveyard after dark, because at that time a headless horseman rode through the cemetery. No worry there. We were not allowed that far from home at night.

A month before our 1940 Christmas, Mother and Babe Cudney decided to make a Christmas-present-buying-trip to California. Babe had relatives there and they were invited to stay with them. Our parents believed we were old enough to stay with Daddy while Mother was gone. During this time Mother was to be away, Daddy continued working each day, but he was always home for lunch at 11:30 A.M. and a little after 4:00 P.M. in the evening. We knew he was only as far away as the mine or the mill, and anyone in camp would have been willing to help us in an emergency. Babe and Mother were to be gone three days—just long enough for them to do their shopping. This Christmas of 1940 was a very special Christmas to me. The next Christmas would be marred by the fresh trauma of the December 7 Japanese attack on Pearl Harbor and would be clouded by the looming specter and insecurity of all that World War II was to bring. Our age of innocence would then be lost forever.

The House On The Hill Was Very Special To Me

But for this Christmas of 1940, all of the special people and feelings in my life were still intact. Mama Bessie, Papa Guy and Dorothy were coming from Solomonsville and Auntie and Uncle Joe from Kingman. Henny, Uncle Son, Bobby Kay and Kenny Guy lived down the hill from us. These were the people who provided the security bubble for my life.

Christmas Day 1940-On the front porch of the house on the hill—Left to Right: Henny, Daddy, Billy Massey, Mother, Vel, Papa Guy, Auntie, Uncle Joe's head, Dorothy ,MamaBessie, NormaJean

When the presents were opened on Christmas Eve, Vel and I received beautiful red fur robes, and red fur hoods to keep our ears warm on the few cold blustery days when we were running around the hills of Goldroad. Also, a pair of white cowboy boots with gold leather scrolls up the sides of the boot top were a part of our Christmas. Mother had done well on her shopping trip to California. Especially the red fur robes. We wore them into our teen years.

Our house was full of people. Vel, Billy and I were spending the night with Henny and Uncle Son because Auntie and Uncle Joe and Papa Guy and Mama Bessie were using our bedrooms.

The House On The Hill Was Very Special To Me

As I stepped out of our back door in my beautiful red fur robe and my white cowboy boots, the most exciting thing that can happen on a Christmas Eve, especially in a desert town, happened—SNOW! It covered our car and lay lightly on the large rocks and coal box in our backyard. Feelings of complete peace and wellbeing filled my heart. And many times I have drawn deeply on those feelings when a need for them has arisen in my life. Also, every time I hear the song *Silent Night* the feelings and the picture of what I saw that night, along with my father's image, come into my mind and I am comforted. It has been said, and it is true, we need the happy memories of our summers to give comfort in our winters of despair. Goldroad, the golden years, has been the source of that comfort to me.

The Cyclopic Mill stood across the wash from Uncle Joe and Auntie's new ranch headquarters. The building in the lower right corner is the change room where Uncle Joe and his cowboys tore out part of the wall to get the honey stored there by the honey bees who got their water from the sink drainage from the ranch house .

Chapter 20

Summers At The Cyclopic Ranch

Uncle Joe had been willing to run his horse to death that day to find me.

The Cyclopic—what an interesting place to explore! Our first look at Uncle Joe and Auntie's new ranch headquarters was very exciting. A mill site with four houses, a mess hall, change room, mill, and four or five tent houses. The mining company had left everything in place: stove, dishes, utensils, and refrigerator in the mess hall; the bedroom sets and other miscellaneous furniture in the houses; all machinery and equipment in the mill. And a pumping station a few miles over the hills pumped water to fill the large water tank on the hill for the domestic water supply at the ranch headquarters.

White *Boulder City* houses were scattered all over Mojave County, and four or five of them stood on the ranch a few miles from the mill site. Families lived in two of them one summer before being sold by Uncle Joe. During my first summer at the Cyclopic an officer of the mining company came to the ranch. He asked if we knew of a corporate seal that had been carelessly left when they moved. Uncle Joe and Auntie knew nothing about it. But I knew it was in one of the houses and quickly took him to it. Earlier I had found and played with it. Needless to say, he was very relieved to have it in his possession again.

For three summers, beginning in 1940, I was with Auntie and Uncle Joe at the Cyclopic Ranch. At the end of May when school was out, they would be in Goldroad to take me to the ranch where I would spend the summer.

Summers At The Cyclopic Ranch

Uncle Joe and Auntie June 1940-The back of the house on the hill on the day they came from the Cyclopic Ranch to take me with them for the summer

Summers At The Cyclopic Ranch

Billy and Norma Jean June 1940-The back of the house on the hill on the day Uncle Joe and Auntie came from the Cyclopic Ranch to take us with them for the summer. The electric cord behind us went from the house to the washing machine in the wash shed. Mother's hollyhocks can be seen in the background. A part of Vel can be seen on the left.

The ranch headquarters was located in a canyon on a wash at the end of a dirt road in the White Hills west of Kingman.   A turn north from Highway 93 on the Dolan Springs road approximately 25 miles west of Kingman wandered 35 or 40 *cowpuncher* miles to the ranch—it was not just over the hill from Goldroad. Because of the ninety-mile distance from home, I saw my family at the ranch only on my birthday in July and on short visits

Summers At The Cyclopic Ranch

in Kingman when Mother knew we would be in town for the day. But I was content and happy on the ranch with Auntie and Uncle Joe and looked forward to each summer there.

Daddy on Badger with Milton & Ruth McCall. Ranch House is in background.

Uncle Joe's partner in the Cyclopic Ranch was Mr. Peterson. He was an Anglo married to a Mexican. His wife and children lived on their ranch in Mexico. Mr. Peterson traveled between Arizona and Mexico. On one of our trips from the Cyclopic to Kingman, we arrived in town earlier than planned and met Mr. Peterson at the house where he and Mrs. Peterson were staying for a few days. Normally, we would have met him for breakfast at the Beale Hotel. But we were introduced to Mrs. Peterson and visited for a short time with her and their three or four small children. She was a very pretty, Spanish-looking lady. And Uncle Joe made plans with Mr. Peterson to meet later in the day to take care of their business. I never liked Mr. Peterson. He was different from Uncle Joe's other cowboy friends who were open and friendly.

Located west of the Beale Hotel on the main street (Route 66) were two other cafes frequented by Uncle Joe and his friends, and sometimes me—the Gaddis and Lockwood cafes.

Most of the steers on the Cyclopic were black Mexican steers, but the bulls and cows were white-faced Herefords. The Cyclopic was unique in its use of Mexican steers. Other ranchers in the area ran only white-faced Herefords. The Mexican steers were shipped directly out of Mexico to the Cyclopic. And the brand used on all Cyclopic cattle was cross drag—a Christian cross with a drag down the right side of the left hind leg. Probably the brand used on the Peterson ranch in Mexico.

Summers At The Cyclopic Ranch

Many different jobs kept the ranch running. And providing water for the ranch headquarters was one of them. When the marker on the ranch water tank indicated the water level was low, Uncle Joe, Billy, and I would jump into the pickup and head several miles over the hills to the pump station—another fascinating place. The large pump was in a tin building and had a large and small water tank attached. Two one-room buildings with a couple of old cots and dozens of old magazines strewn around inside—and a three-hole outhouse—completed the pump station.

The pump required lubrication before use. And Billy and I were always excited about filling the large lubrication cups with heavy grease—it was the consistency of butter—and filling the container on top of the pump with oil. After this was done, Uncle Joe started the pump. When he was satisfied it was running properly, he would head for the pumpman house, lay on a cot and read the magazines, or take a nap.

When Billy was with us, we found other interesting things to do while Uncle Joe slept or read. Early in the summer we found a nest with several eggs that had been built in a very unusual spot. The nest was located under the eaves of the pump house on a small ledge above the small water tank. This tank must have been the cooling tank for the pump, because the water pumped from the well for use at the ranch went into the large tank.

After we discovered the nest, each time we went to pump water, Billy and I hurriedly ran to check on the progress of the eggs. When the eggs finally hatched, there were four baby birds in the nest. And each time we went to the pump station and checked on their progress, they were safe from any predators and seemed to thrive in their unusual location. But as they feathered out and became more active, we became aware of the problem they would encounter when the time came for them to learn to fly—they would have to fly out of their nest over the water tank. The stronger birds that made it beyond the water on their first attempt would be all right. But if any had a problem learning to fly, they would certainly fall to their death in the water below and drown.

On our next trip to the pump station, Billy and I were extremely anxious to learn the fate of the baby birds. As soon as the pickup stopped, we hopped out and ran quickly to check on them—the nest was empty.

Our hope was all of the little birds had made it out of the nest and over the water tank. But as we looked more closely, we found two small bodies in the bottom of the water tank—two had made it, two had not. We felt sad for the unsuccessful baby birds and wondered why the mother bird had not been wiser in her selection of a site for her nest. Maybe she would know better next Spring—we hoped so.

Summers At The Cyclopic Ranch

The outhouse was an entertaining place to visit—almost as good as TV. It seems those who had previously used it had quite a sense of humor and a bend toward the poetic—and time to sit and think. The inside walls were covered with verse, surprisingly, none of it pornographic. Billy and I spent much time reading and enjoying all that had been written. The only rhyme I remember is cute but not something I want to be remembered for, therefore, I will not quote it here.

When the large water tank was full, which was an indication the tank at the ranch house was full also, we hopped in the pickup and headed off for other interesting and challenging experiences. One thing we did while in the area of the pump house was check on the many smaller gasoline pumps on other wells. And Uncle Joe stopped at each one checking if they were operational.

Of course Billy and I were always excited about the prospect of filling the grease cups and oil container on each of these pumps before Uncle Joe made his attempt at starting them. And he started all of them except one. He had a pump repairman from Kingman come out, but he failed also.

Later in the summer, we stopped at this pump on one of our frequent trips through the area—Uncle Joe refused to give up on this pump. He had plans to sell all of these smaller pumps and knew a non-working pump could not be sold for as much money as a working one. And he gave the wheel a few half-hearted turns, although he had no hopes of starting it himself after the pump repairman had failed—and nothing happened.

So he gave up, mumbled something and wandered off a short distance to take care of another problem. This gave Billy a chance to play with the pump. And after a short time, we were all startled by the noise of the pump as it coughed and sputtered and then took off running! We could not believe our eyes...and ears! How excited the three of us were—Billy, because he had done something not even a pump man could do, Uncle Joe and I because we were proud of him. When the pumps were later sold, *Billy's* pump was among them.

Water was vital to the cattle. Water lines had been laid from the source of water many miles over the ranch, and they emptied into watering troughs for the cattle. In the heat of the summer one important job Uncle Joe, Billy and I did was check on these troughs to make certain the water lines had not become air-locked and were still delivering water. And most of the checking was done in a pickup.

No roads led to the watering troughs, and the *Jeep* used so effectively in the war had not yet been developed. But Uncle Joe did not need a *Jeep* to get where he wanted to go. He had a pickup.

Summers At The Cyclopic Ranch

From the road, he would pinpoint the location of the trough. And off the road we would go, out through the brush, cactus and Joshua trees, over small hills and gullies making our own *road* as we went. This was great fun, and Billy and I loved it when Uncle Joe would decide to do his off-road driving! Looking back, I realize the three of us were all the same age in our summer-time adventures—Uncle Joe was 57, Billy was 7 and I was 10.

Drinking water for our use was not carried in the pickup on our trips away from the ranch house. Our thirst was quenched in the same way the cattle satisfied theirs—from the trough. The troughs always had green algae growing on the sides and bottom and water bugs walking on the surface of the water or swimming on the bottom, depending on the type of water bug.

We never gave a thought about whether this water was a threat to our health. From birth, we had always drunk from creeks, springs or watering troughs when the need arose. When we were on horseback, our horse drank at one end of the trough, and we drank at the other. However, we never drank from a trough recently muddied and polluted by a herd of cattle.

Unlocking air from the water lines was not an easy task. It was a hot, frustrating job, and Uncle Joe spent hours our first summer on the ranch doing it. But by the next summer, vents on the water lines had been installed at designated intervals eliminating the air-lock problem.

The water flow to the trough was controlled in the same way the water flow is controlled in a toilet tank—by a float. To save money on material costs, Uncle Joe wired empty square metal cans with screw-on lids as floats to shut off the flow of the water when the troughs were full.

And he always had something interesting for us to do. If there were no real jobs to be done, he would create one to get us out of the ranch house area. One rainy afternoon Billy, Uncle Joe and I hopped in the pickup to check on a problem several miles from the ranch house. After the problem had been taken care of, Uncle Joe decided to kill a jackrabbit or two for our dogs. One was spotted, and we took off in hot pursuit over the brush and cactus dodging Joshua trees as we went—Uncle Joe driving with one hand and his gun pointed out the window with the other. He was an excellent marksman with any type of gun, and after a short chase, the rabbit was bagged and thrown into the back of the pickup. Another jackrabbit was spotted and we took off after it. But before we knew what was happening, our pickup made a full circle—we were now headed in the opposite direction of the way we had been going. What fun! Billy and I assumed Uncle Joe had done it purposely, and we were impressed, but when the pickup came to a sudden stop, and we looked over at him, we realized he was as surprised by the sudden change in directions as we were.

165.

Summers At The Cyclopic Ranch

Obviously, the pickup had hit slick mud throwing the truck into an uncontrolled spin. After assessing the situation, Uncle Joe decided we had experienced enough fun for one day and headed back to the ranch house.

When the rabbit was thrown to the dogs, they would have no part of it. And eventually Uncle Joe had to throw the carcass in the back of the pickup and dump it out of the ranch house area.

Late one afternoon Uncle Joe and I drove down the road a few miles from the ranch house to corrals where he had penned a steer he planned to butcher for our use. When we arrived, he roped the steer and pulled him tightly against the side of the corral. He hit the steer in the forehead with the blunt end of an ax. The steer did not go down the first time, and Uncle Joe had to hit him again. This time he went down. Uncle Joe quickly cut his throat and blood flowed into the loose corral dirt and disappeared. I felt sorry for the steer and determined I would never be around when another steer was killed.

Each morning and evening the cowboys and other hands were served steak, milk-gravy and biscuits. Jerky was taken on their all day horseback rides over the ranch to check the cattle. They had no ATVs or four-wheel drive vehicles to use. In summer the heat was intense, and the winter brought numbing cold. Unlike the cowboys I tried to imitate, I disliked steak and ate biscuits and gravy instead. However, I did love jerky and would grab a handful whenever the opportunity presented itself.

Most of the meat from the steer was cut off as steaks and used for the cowboys' breakfast and supper. A smaller amount was cut into strips and hung for jerky.

Beef was all right, but being a true Southerner, Auntie loved chicken fixed anyway it could be cooked—fried, boiled, roasted, or chicken-and-dumplings. Her favorite part was the back with the tail left attached. She was not beyond killing a prime laying hen for supper. Since a young child, my job in the chicken-killing operation had been to hold the chickens until Uncle Joe was ready to chop off their heads with the ax—Auntie had a different way, but with the same result, she always wrung their necks.

The last time I did my job in the chicken-killing operation was at the Cyclopic when I was ten. Two hens had been chosen. I had one hen under each arm holding them until Uncle Joe had the ax and the wood stump ready for the first kill. He took one hen from me and walked over to the stump to do the job. The eyes of the hen under my arm were almost level with mine. When I looked into her eyes, I could feel she knew what was in store for her. But she accepted her fate and did not struggle or make any effort to escape from me. But I determined that day as I had done earlier with the steer, I would *never* again hold another chicken and participate in the killing process.

Summers At The Cyclopic Ranch

The steps to prepare the chicken after it was killed were very interesting to me, and I looked forward to watching as it was done. First, Auntie poured boiling water from the teakettle over the chicken. This loosened the feathers and they were easily plucked from the chicken. After the plucking, a piece of rolled paper, usually newspaper, was set on fire over the kitchen sink to singe the fuzz remaining on the chicken.

Cutting into a chicken with Auntie, especially if it were a hen, was an exciting adventure—it was like being led on a treasure hunt as she explored and commented on each organ of the chicken. The egg bag was always carefully examined to see how many undeveloped eggs remained in it. She counted them and was pleased when the count was high. The craw with its sand and gravel inside was examined to discover what the chicken had been eating that day. The gizzard was also cut open and examined carefully, and I was allowed to peel off its lining. Peeling the feet after they were scalded with boiling water was another activity I enjoyed.

After the chicken had been carefully scrapped and all pinfeathers removed, Auntie turned her attention to preparing delicious soup from the undeveloped eggs, gizzard, heart, neck and feet.

Many birds flocked to the Cyclopic to eat the hay and grain left on the ground by the horses when they finished their daily feed rations. This area was in front of the former mess hall where the hay and grain were stored. On occasion, Uncle Joe used his shotgun to kill the dove eating there. He always skinned, gutted and dug the shotgun pellets out of the birds, and Auntie then fried them for our dinner. Several times I helped him with the cleaning chores but decided I wanted to clean dove all by myself.

He agreed and shot into the flock. But after the birds had been shot and I picked them up, several were not dead, just wounded. I asked Uncle Joe what I should do with them. He told me to just pull off their heads. Without questioning, I did this. How shocked I was at the terrible sensation I had in my hands as I felt the head pull away from the neck! I had never killed any living thing except bugs before, just watched. I felt so badly about killing the injured dove, I never asked Uncle Joe to kill anymore for me to clean. This must have been my summer to realize what killing a living thing really was about. Since birth, I had grown up watching and being a part of the killing process. When our family had chicken for dinner, it was always one of our own killed by us. No store-bought chickens in our family, they were too expensive. Killing animals for food was a part of life—like breathing.

Perhaps one of the reasons I loved Uncle Joe so much was because he always took time to do the things that were important to me even though they might not be important to him.

Summers At The Cyclopic Ranch

How I felt was more important to him than what anyone thought no matter what position they held in his life. He loved me unconditionally. It might be thought by some this would create a spoiled child—it did not. I always knew when I was wrong and never took advantage of a situation when I was. His support of me made me better.

One experience at the ranch supports this. Chick and Edith McKnight had been friends of Uncle Joe and Auntie since their arrival in the Kingman area in 1936. On several occasions I had been with them when they visited Chick and Edith, and I liked them. When Uncle Joe acquired the Cyclopic Ranch, he hired Chick and they lived in the smaller house across the wash from Auntie and Uncle Joe.

Late one morning Auntie approached me visibly upset. Chick had taken her aside and told her I had commanded him to saddle my horse. He had not liked the way I had asked and was offended by it. Auntie believed him and felt I had done something wrong. When she told me what Chick had said, my feelings were hurt and I was embarrassed. I had not intended my request for him to saddle my horse to sound disrespectful—I felt I had merely made a request. Uncle Joe always saddled my horse, but he had left the ranch headquarters earlier in the morning and was not available at the time to do it for me.

On Uncle Joe's return to the ranch, Chick must have approached him, because when Uncle Joe came into the house, neither Auntie nor I said anything to him about what had happened. I am sure he perceived and could tell by the look on my face that I was disturbed. When he started talking to me, he did not mention the horse-saddling situation directly, but asked me if there was something wrong, had someone hurt my feelings. Close to tears, I bowed my head and lied and said they had not. He asked me again, and I shook my head. His next words were: "If someone has hurt your feelings, I'll put him on his horse and run him off down the creek!" In other words, the person would be fired. With those words, he turned and left the house. Uncle Joe meant what he said, and by the edge of anger in his voice, *I* knew he meant it. He was not making an idle threat just to comfort a hurt child.

Nothing more was said between Uncle Joe and me about the matter, but I know now he must have confronted Chick after leaving me at the house or sometime later in the day, because Chick and Edith soon left the Cyclopic.

When I asked Uncle Joe why they had left, he did not elaborate but said something about Chick misbranding some of Cyclopic's cattle. Chick and Edith had no children of their own, and Edith seemed to enjoy the time I spent at their house at the Cyclopic. On several of my visits we had baked biscuits together.

168.

Summers At The Cyclopic Ranch

I was sorry they were no longer there, but never thought at the time that the problem between Chick and me had been the cause of their leaving. Uncle Joe was not blindly defending a spoiled, disrespectful child when he defended me against the charges Chick made. Uncle Joe and I had been together since I was a toddler sharing hours and days of doing many different things. He knew I had always been obedient and never disrespectful to adults, and if my request for Chick to saddle my horse had come across as such, it had not been intended in that manner.

One spring Auntie ordered a hundred baby chicks, and raised them to pullet size. At this age, they were turned loose to wander around the area to feed off the spilled grain from the horses' feed bags and hay. These pullets grew rapidly and as they grew, they became wild and would not allow anyone to approach them. This was in sharp contrast to the hens living in the chicken house. They allowed us to walk up and touch them.

When Auntie needed a chicken for dinner, Uncle Joe would get his .22 rifle, take a bead on the head of the chicken, squeeze the trigger and kill it— no easy task as these pullets were far away and not a stationary target.

On the ranch each cowboy had his own string of horses for use on his daily rides over the ranch. Contrary to what cowboys do in Western movies, a horse cannot be ridden all day two days in a row in the summer heat over a period of time and live. A cowboy on Uncle Joe's ranch rode a horse from his string once every four or five days.

Several horses on the ranch would allow a child to ride them. Horses are like people. They like certain people, and certain people they do not like. Some horses do not like women. And there are horses that do not like men. There are horses that will buck when a child is put on their back. And there are horses that do not care who gets on them. But it is important to know how a horse feels about people before climbing on its back. But sometimes the only way to find out how it feels is to put the person on the horse. Uncle Joe did not want to experiment with me. And there were three horses he knew liked children: Wagon, a huge gentle bay horse, Tex, a sorrel, and Skipper, a pacing palomino.

Wagon was my horse the first summer I spent on the ranch. One morning while he and the other horses were eating their hay, he accidentally stepped on the side of my foot while I was petting him. Uncle Joe had warned me before not to stand by Wagon while he was eating with the other horses, because they nip each other on the rear to get to that horse's hay. This is what happened to Wagon, another horse nipped him, and he moved. And my foot happened to be in the way. Luckily, he did not step directly on my foot.

Summers At The Cyclopic Ranch

But his hoof slipped off the side taking a small amount of skin and slightly bruising my foot.

Kingman was quite a distance from the Cyclopic. But Auntie insisted I be taken to see Dr. Paup to make certain nothing was broken in my foot. He x-rayed it and found no broken bones. But he insisted on my receiving a tetanus shot. The other treatment given was a heating pad applied to the area for a period of time to reduce the swelling. The injured foot did not slow me down much, and I was my old self in a day or two.

Tex was a very pretty horse, and I rode him occasionally as a change from Wagon. He never misbehaved while I was riding him alone. But horses were scarce one day, and it was necessary for Billy to ride behind me on Tex. He behaved perfectly on the ride until we were on our way back and were a short distance from the ranch. To show his displeasure at being ridden double, he bucked ever so slightly. Not enough to try to throw Billy off, but just enough to let us know he was unhappy with our riding arrangement.

The next summer when I arrived at the ranch Uncle Joe had a pacing palomino named Skipper in the corral. He was to be my new horse, replacing Wagon and Tex. Skipper was shipped from Mexico with a load of cattle. And when he arrived, his beautiful blonde mane and tail were so badly chewed by the cattle, to make him presentable, Uncle Joe trimmed his mane down close to his neck and pulled his tail very short. He was a very pretty horse and good with children. But his pacing gait made an all day ride very tiring.

At the same time Skipper was shipped from Mexico to Kingman, Pal, a beautiful, picture-perfect palomino was also shipped, but not in the cattle car. And he had a problem with two-legged riders, because he had been broken and trained by a Mexican man with only one leg. As a result of this training, Pal kept his head slightly turned to the right watching the rider's leg. And then when he caught the cowboy off-guard, he would pitch violently, usually throwing him.

Chapo, Uncle Joe's horse, was a powerful bay with a large scar on his left hindquarter. This scar had been caused by the attack of a wild animal when he was a colt. Chapo could walk all day in the summer heat, carrying Uncle Joe, at a pace faster than my horse could trot—he was a tremendous cow horse. And although I admired Chapo and wanted to ride him, I knew he was not a horse a child should be riding.

There was a smaller version of Chapo on the ranch. His name was Little Britches, a small but powerfully built bay. My goal for the summer was to be allowed to ride this horse. As mentioned before, Uncle Joe allowed me to ride only the horses he knew were gentle and would not hurt me. And he was not certain about Little Britches.

170.

Summers At The Cyclopic Ranch

Most good cow ponies behaved with the cowboys, but did not like children riding them. But with much coaxing I finally succeeded in convincing Uncle Joe that I could handle Little Britches on the cattle drive we were to have with the other ranchers in the area. Uncle Joe, Billy and I were to round up cattle in the corner area on our northeastern boundary and drive them to the adjoining Jim Smith Ranch headquarters at Gold Basin—a very old abandoned gold mining site with two or three vacant houses. We were to meet other cowboys with their gathered cattle. Everything was going well. We had our cattle headed up the east fence toward the north corner. Uncle Joe felt comfortable in leaving Billy and me to herd the cattle up the fence the mile or so to the northeast corner where he would meet us. The problem began when a white-faced Hereford cow with a calf decided to break away from the herd and head west. A few of the Hereford cows with calves were quite wild, and this particular cow was a very spooky one. I left Billy moving the herd along the fence and went after the cow and calf to bring them back. But being wild and determined, she refused to be brought back, although I spent time chasing and trying to head her back toward the herd. But I soon realized success was impossible. And I headed back toward the fence to a spot where I felt Billy and the herd should be.

The Cyclopic Ranch was in a Joshua forest. This made it impossible for me to see very far. When I arrived at the fence, Billy and the herd were not there. I assumed he was ahead of me, so I rode to the designated meeting place, the northeast corner—no one was there. Because the Joshua trees obstructed any long-distance viewing, I remembered a small hill located a mile or so west of the fence beyond the graded dirt Pearce Ferry Highway. I felt I had a better chance of seeing Billy and the herd from the hill than I did on flat land looking through a forest of trees—even if they were Joshua trees.

By this time I was frightened and a little unsure about how this situation was going to turn out. But I headed Little Britches in the direction of the hill making my own path through the trees. When I reached the bottom of the hill, I dismounted and left Little Britches tied there. I knew it was easier for me to climb the rock-strewn surface than for the horse to go around each boulder. I had not gone very far up the side of the hill, when I saw Uncle Joe on his horse running full speed toward me. Again, contrary to what is seen in Western movies, cowboys do not run their horses for miles and miles everywhere they go, especially in the summer heat. Horses are run only short distances to do a particular job with the cattle. But contrary to this rule, Uncle Joe had run his horse a good distance in the full-heat of the summer sun in his panic to find me.

Summers At The Cyclopic Ranch

When Billy arrived with the herd at the meeting place and I was not with him, Uncle Joe was alarmed. Billy told him how I had gone after the cow and calf, and Uncle Joe immediately assumed Little Britches had thrown me in my efforts to do this. He was able to track me for a distance although my trail at times went in circles. Later, he said my trail wound around through the Joshua trees like a drunk Mexican. This erratic trail had intensified his fears and conjured up visions in his mind of a rider less horse wandering aimlessly and me alone somewhere seriously injured.

These thoughts only made him more convinced he had to find me quickly. And this determination ultimately brought him to a point where he could see me on the side of the hill. When he saw me standing there alive and uninjured, a tremendous flood of relief surged through him. And he jumped off his horse and rushed up to me grabbing and hugging and kissing me. What a sight we must have been! An old cowboy with an exhausted, sweat-lathered horse standing in the middle of nowhere hugging and kissing a young girl with a dusty, tear-stained face wearing an old battered sweat-stained cowboy hat several sizes too large for her head! Uncle Joe had been willing to run his horse to death that day to find me.

After discussing what had happened and what brought me to the side of the hill, we got on our horses and rode over to meet the others who were gathered at the northeast corner with the cattle. Uncle Joe told me how pleased he was with the way I had handled the situation by staying with my horse and going to higher ground where I could see out over the countryside, and where I could be seen by him.

We completed the job we had set out to do. And Little Britches proved himself that day. None of the experience had been his fault. He had been obedient to every command I had given him.

In patching together why I had not found anyone at the meeting place, we decided I had somehow arrived before they had. On our ride back to the ranch house that afternoon, Uncle Joe suggested we say nothing to Auntie about what had happened. She might not allow Billy and me to ride again. We knew how concerned and worried Auntie always was about our safety, and agreed with Uncle Joe's suggestion. Before the summer was over, though, she was told about the incident and understood that riding Little Britches that day had not put me in any danger.

As mentioned before, the headquarters for the Jim Smith ranches was at the old abandoned Gold Basin mill site. Holding pens for shipping cattle had been built there. One of the smaller houses was occupied at this time by the Tyree family.

Summers At The Cyclopic Ranch

I played with their daughter while Uncle Joe and the cowboys loaded the previously gathered cattle into large cattle trucks. Eroded tailings were evidence of past milling activities. And the old cemetery with broken-down wooden fences held together with square nails also was proof that people had lived there long ago and had stayed long enough for many of them to die at the site. The Tyree girl and I explored the larger vacant house and discovered a large brown leather brief case with the name *Jim Smith* stamped on it in gold letters. Bedrolls were spread among the rubble on the floor. He and several of the cowboys were sleeping there during the round-up.

Mr. Tyree—Cowboy on the Cyclopic. Tack Room in Background

Uncle Joe had known Jim Smith in the Safford Valley and later in Phoenix. And when he was a candidate for the Democratic nomination for Governor of Arizona he asked for Uncle Joe's support.

At the Cyclopic, three cows provided milk for the ranch—a red white-face, who gave little milk of average richness; a petite, pretty but very unfriendly Jersey who gave rich milk in small quantities; and a large, friendly Holstein who gave quarts of what would be sold today as 2% milk. And my goal was to learn as quickly as possible to milk these cows.

Summers At The Cyclopic Ranch

Milking looks simple, but it is not. Just squeezing the tits will not bring the milk out. Learning to squeeze and pull at the same time is the key. Before long, I was helping milk the three cows every morning and night. After I finished milking a cow, Uncle Joe would come behind me and completely empty the cow's bag. This was a necessary procedure if she did not have a calf to suck it dry. It kept the cow producing milk.

If a cow had a calf, it was kept in a small pen next to the milking corral. Both corrals were joined to the side of the mess hall where the hay and grain were kept. The milk cows were given a portion of cottonseed cake each day. They loved it, and so did Billy and I. We spent a lot of our time in and around the cow pens and mess hall, and used the cottonseed cake as a snack. And we were never concerned about germs or how clean it was. To us, if it looked clean, it must be clean!

The ranch had a mother cat whose job was to keep the mice out of the feed in the mess hall. One day Billy and I were playing there and noticed her chasing a mouse. The mouse got lucky and outran the cat and got behind the refrigerator that had been left behind by the mining company.

The cat could not get the mouse where it was hiding. So we decided to give the cat some help by moving the refrigerator away from the wall. After we did this, the cat grabbed the mouse and ate it. That experience was not too bad to watch, because we had been taught that a cat was supposed to catch mice and eat them. But we were not ready for what we found under the edge of the refrigerator protected from the cat—several small, pink, hairless mice who did not yet have their eyes open! Guilt and regret flooded over us as the full significance of what we had done hit.

At that moment, if we had been given the chance to turn the clock back five minutes, we would have grabbed it. But we realized that was impossible and we must face the problem we had created—several small, helpless, motherless mice needing care.

The first need of any living thing is a home, a place to be sheltered. Billy and I created a nest of soft hay and leaves in a large, empty, discarded coffee can. We placed the baby mice in the nest and covered the can with a small square rag to protect and keep them warm. We knew the cat would eat them if she found them.

Our next responsibility was to find food for the baby mice. The most logical food was milk from the cows. Without alerting Auntie to what we were doing, we quietly slipped into the kitchen, took a small amount of milk from the huge containers cooling in the large refrigerator and ran to our baby mice in the mess hall.

174.

Summers At The Cyclopic Ranch

Having no other way to feed them the milk, we dipped our finger in it and put the drop of milk on the mouth of the baby mouse. I do not know how much got inside the mouse, but we tried.

We told no one about the baby mice or what had happened to the mother. We determined we would raise them ourselves. When we left for the afternoon, we put their covered coffee-can nursery on some bales of hay in the corner of the mess hall. The next morning we anxiously ran to the mess hall to check on our mice. Upon entering the mess hall, we were encouraged by the fact the can was where we had left it and appeared not to have been disturbed. But, when we took the cloth cover off the can, we were surprised and mystified by the absence of our baby mice. We emptied the hay and leaves from the can unwilling to believe they were not there. Our first suspect was the cat, but we immediately eliminated her as the guilty party. If she had eaten them, the can would have been knocked over and the contents would have been in disarray. No, the only way the mice could have been removed from the can was by a person.

Billy and I were upset by the loss of our baby mice. But neither the person who destroyed the mice nor Billy and I ever said anything about the baby mice in the coffee can or what happened to them.

Much of our time was spent in and around the mess hall when we were not off someplace with Uncle Joe. The calf pen not only held the milk cows' calves, but also held any dogie calf brought in from the range. We felt very fortunate to have a number of the dogies to play with, and we each chose one to be our special pet. And each was named. Mine was Minnie and Billy's was Mable. The only bull in the pen belonged to the red milk cow, and we named him Mickey. But he was true to normal boy behavior and did not like to be hugged and played with, so we left him alone.

One afternoon when we were playing in the pen with the calves a light summer shower hit. Hurriedly we retrieved several empty burlap grain bags from the mess hall and threw them over the backs of the calves to protect them from the rain. But the storm was over by the time we got them covered. Our hearts had been in the right place, though.

Cats and kittens as well as a puppy made the mess hall their home. The puppy slept under the building where several boards were missing. The first tick I ever saw was on the chest of the puppy. When I noticed it, I thought it was an exposed blood vessel, and was afraid to touch it. But the more I studied it, the more certain I was that it could not be a blood vessel—the puppy was not injured in anyway and was playful and happy. He just had this grayish-purple oblong thing sticking out of his chest.

Summers At The Cyclopic Ranch

Finally, I got up the nerve to give it a pull. But in my surprise at having it pull loose, I dropped it in the dirt. Curious, I knew I wanted to find and identify whatever it was. And after a few minutes of searching, I found it.

I examined it carefully. It was a bug of some sort with barely identifiable legs on its fat, bloated body. I did what most kids do when they find an unfamiliar bug—I smashed it with a small stick against a rock. To my surprise, the spot where the smashed bug lay was bloody. When I later described the bug to Uncle Joe, he said it must have been a tick.

This encounter with the tick was not to be my last one. Billy began complaining to Uncle Joe about a noise in his ear. So what does a cowboy do to solve the problem? What every good cowboy does with a medical problem. He pours coal oil (kerosene) into Billy's ear. The noise stopped. Problem solved? No! Because the next time we were in Kingman Uncle Joe—probably at Auntie's insistence, she was a worrier—took Billy to see Dr. Paup. He saw nothing unusual in Billy's ear. He must have been blind that day. Because after the summer was over and we returned to Goldroad, Billy complained to Mother that he could feel something rolling around in his ear.

Mother took him out on the back step of our house, laid his head on her lap, saw something in his ear, and took him to the Goldroad company doctor just down the hill from our house. The doctor filled Billy's ear with water and guess what came floating out—the skeleton of a dead tick! Uncle Joe really did solve Billy's problem. Well...maybe half of his problem—the tick was killed before it could cause pain or injury to Billy's ear. After much discussion, we decided it had probably crawled inside Billy's ear while he had his head against his calf Mable's side while he was loving her.

One little dogie in the pen had obvious lice and fleas, but we were wise enough not to hug or pet her. She was not with us for long. Sadly, one morning we found her dead with her head caught in the water bucket. Too weak to free herself and no one there to help, she had drowned.

Toward the end of the summer not long before time for Billy and me to return to Goldroad for the opening of school, Uncle Joe sold all of the calves, including Mickey the bull calf. Billy and I were aware of the plan to take the calves and felt we had accepted it until Minnie and Mable were loaded into the trailer. About that time, Auntie came out of the house and over to the corral where we were standing. And when she made a comment to us about the loaded calves, we both broke down in tears.

When Uncle Joe saw what was happening with Billy and me, he hurriedly came to where we were standing and asked what was wrong. We both sobbed out how sad we were at losing Mable and Minnie. He turned on his heel and said, "Well, we'll just unload the calves!"

176.

Summers At The Cyclopic Ranch

Again, as he had been with the Chick McKnight incident, Uncle Joe was serious about unloading the calves. Billy and I both shook our heads, because we knew he had committed to sell them and probably needed the money.

It would not have been right for us to ask him to unload the calves just so we could play with them—and we did not.

When Billy and I were not playing at the mess hall or the dogie pen, we were usually in the small building between the house and the large corral. This was the building where the saddles, bridles, horse blankets, oats, feed bags for the horses, burro grease, shoeing equipment and other sundry items used in the care of the horses were kept.

The saddles were hung from the exposed rafters by ropes strung through the opening behind the saddle horn. Hours were spent swinging back and forth on these made-to-order indoor swings. We sang as we were swinging, or we pretended to be cowboys chasing cattle. While we played, we ate the oats kept in a gunnysack on the floor. They were so good! When we tired of the swinging saddle game, we busied ourselves rubbing burro grease into the leather of a bridle harness and reins, or a saddle. The burro grease was homemade from burro fat and was used by ranchers as a leather preservative. I kept my own small saddle well greased. A few years earlier Uncle Joe had paid $25 for it so I could ride with him in the Kingman Dig n' Dogie Days parade. It wound through town and ended a few miles away at the fairgrounds east of town.

Huge bowls topped with heavy cream were kept in the commercial size gas-powered refrigerator in one end of the kitchen. When there was no more space, the milk was poured into large pans for the chickens to eat. This abundance of milk created an unlimited supply of cream. And Auntie allowed me to make butter for our meals in a small glass churn.

Although I never drank milk, and disliked having it even touch my skin, I enjoyed whipped cream. Frequently, I skimmed the inch-thick cream off the huge bowls of milk and made whipped cream with the eggbeater. With a little sugar and vanilla added, it tasted good on crackers.

The refrigerator, stove and hot water heater ran on butane gas. All houses and other structures at the Cyclopic were wired for electricity. But for reasons unknown to me, there was no electricity coming through the lines. Many hot summer days were spent wishing we had electricity to run a small fan to cool the house. And electric lights to replace the inadequate light generated by the Coleman lantern hung from the ceiling in the living room would have been great. A large wood-burning stove sat in one end of the living room and provided heat in the winter.

Summers At The Cyclopic Ranch

The bathroom had a shower, toilet and washbasin. Frequent trips were made to Kingman although the ranch was about sixty miles away. After Mother complained about the horsey odor she smelled on Billy and me on one of our meetings with her in Kingman,   Auntie made certain on subsequent trips we took a shower before we left the ranch.

On one of these trips to town, we were a few miles from the ranch when we realized there was a possibility the gas water heater had not been turned off before we left. We had all showered. The heater was not automatic and would have exploded had it been left on until our return to the ranch later in the day. So, we turned around and went back to make certain the heater was not on—and luckily it was not.

My first summer at the Cyclopic, on one of our trips to Kingman, Uncle Joe bought a tan cotton shirt just like his for me at the Central Commercial. He also bought me a straw cowboy hat, spurs with yellow rhinestones on the leather strap and small metal hearts on each side of the spur—and a pocketknife. The pocketknife was a smaller version of his. Both knives were faced with white stone. Later that day when we arrived back at the ranch, he made a case for both our knives from a piece of buckskin stored in the tack room. The sides and bottom of these cases were bound together with strips of buckskin. The knives fit snugly inside. And a strip of buckskin was left long on one side so it could be tied through the loop on Uncle Joe's Levis, or the buttonhole on my shirt. By pulling on this strip of buckskin, our knife could easily be retrieved from our pocket.

Most of our trips to Kingman were made by just Uncle Joe and me—and Billy if he was there. Auntie probably enjoyed the time alone at the ranch. When she did not go, our first stop was to buy comic books. And then Uncle Joe would drop us with our comic books at the Beale Hotel lobby. We would sit and read while he went about his business. This business was done over a cup of coffee at one of the restaurants or in the Sump—a below ground bar west of the Beale Hotel. On occasion, Uncle Joe would play a few hands of cards at the Sump. But he never drank anything but black coffee. If I had an extra nickel, I would put it in the slot machine in the hotel lobby. Minors were not supposed to play the slots unless accompanied by an adult. When I finally noticed and read the sign prohibiting *minors* from playing alone, I thought it strange only *miners* were not allowed to play. When I finally mentioned this discrimination to Uncle Joe, he explained what a *minor* was, and it had nothing to do with a person's vocation.

Summers At The Cyclopic Ranch

When Auntie went with us, we had a different routine. Uncle Joe would park the truck where we could do grocery shopping at the Central Commercial. And when we had finished there, we would go back to the truck and watch people—one of Auntie's favorite pass times. But before we would settle down to watching people, Auntie would buy several different kinds of candies at a nearby candy shop. Each kind was put in a separate bag. Her favorite candies were candy corn, jelly beans (or rabbit tracks, as she called them), cockleburs, and chocolate drops. Until Uncle Joe returned, we entertained ourselves by the hour eating candy and watching people go by.

For many years Auntie had carried a small chamois square in her purse that held the diamond from her engagement ring and several gold jewelry items. In the summer of 1942, on one of our trips to Kingman, she took the little chamois out of her purse, opened it and took out the diamond expressing how very much she wanted to have the stone mounted. I do not know how many years she had carried the unmounted diamond in her purse. The original mounting had worn out. But on this day, she was torn and having a difficult time. One part of her knew they could not afford to have it done. But the other part had waited so long and wanted it so badly. Perhaps, she had come to town that day with the resolve to do it irrespective of their financial situation. Money *was* the problem, but she decided there could be no harm in asking the jeweler in the small shop close by what a new mounting would be. Asking would not cost anything. She was told $30 would remount the diamond.

I watched as she struggled between her strong desire to have the diamond mounted and whether that much money should be spent at this time on a seemingly frivolous item—a cowboy's monthly wage was $30. But, in the end, her heart won out, and she told the jeweler to mount the diamond.

When Uncle Joe returned to the car a few hours later, Auntie put her hand with the newly mounted diamond ring up so he could see it. She did not ask him directly to understand how important it was to her to have this stone mounted again. And she did not ask him not to be angry about it. But she did convey these two messages through her body movements and the tone of her voice. And because he knew her well, he *did* understand how she felt, and because of his love for her, he was neither angry nor upset—he said nothing.

Five years later Uncle Joe would be dead. And some time after his death, this was the ring Auntie pointed to on her finger in our kitchen at the USSR&MCo Mine in Vanadium, New Mexico, and said, "When I die, I want this ring to go to your mother, then, I want it to go to you. It isn't a large diamond, but it is a good one. It came from the Peacock Co."

Summers At The Cyclopic Ranch

A few years ago my mother wanted the diamond remounted and Vel took the ring to Blackwell's Jewelers in Silver City, New Mexico, to have it done. The gold had worn through on the back of the ring. When Vel returned to get the remounted diamond, she was told by Blackwell's the ring had accidentally been given to an unidentified woman customer at the time she got her own rings. Supposedly when they contacted the woman about the ring, she denied receiving it with her jewelry. Blackwell's replaced it with a diamond of comparable size, but it is very doubtful it is of the same quality. But more important than that, it was not the ring Uncle Joe had given Auntie in 1911 for their engagement.

Obviously, the electric washing machine Auntie had at their rent houses in Kingman could not be used at the Cyclopic. And Auntie washed all of the clothes on a scrub board. Taking responsibility for my own clothes, I washed them by hand in the kitchen sink and hung them outside the kitchen door on the wires strung between two Joshua trees. Because I was young, I would forget them and they would hang in the hot sun all day. When I returned home at the end of the summer, the pretty turquoise dotted Swiss dress Mother had made for me earlier in the spring was several shades lighter when hung in the closet next to Vel's dress.

Auntie never seemed to be concerned about what I did in the kitchen. The sugar and salt were kept in identical unmarked large wide-mouth jars. One day I was making a milk drink and added two cups of what I thought was sugar into the mixture. But when I tasted it, I realized I had used the salt instead. Reluctant to tell Auntie I had made a mistake and had ruined the drink, I tried to fix it by putting in large amounts of sugar.

But she soon realized by watching my activity that there was a problem and asked me about it. I told her what had happened. I was surprised she was not upset and just told me to pour out the milk and start over. I learned two things that day—sugar will not reverse the flavor of salt, but more important than that, I learned sometimes it is just better to realize some mistakes cannot be fixed and move on and start over. But the difficult part is being wise enough to recognize when a problem just needs more work on our part to correct it.

The words to most of the popular songs of that era are familiar to me, and I can still sing most of them all the way through. Radios were not effective in cars and most did not even have one. Radio stations at that time were used primarily for news and programs, not music. And songs could not be learned from that source. So it was the hours spent riding over endless miles of rarely traveled dirt back roads with Uncle Joe singing that taught me the songs.

Summers At The Cyclopic Ranch

It was on one of those trips when he revealed to Billy and me the dream that he had had as a younger man to go to Hollywood and be a part of the westerns being produced there. If he had pursued this dream, I believe he would have been successful. He had a good singing voice and genuine friendly personality. And his riding and roping skills would have been a definite plus. Throughout their marriage Auntie had followed him anywhere he wanted to go and in everything he had wanted to do. But there were two things Auntie stood firm on. One was that he always wore pajamas to bed, and the other was she refused to allow him to go to Hollywood to be in the movies. Auntie had told me about the pajama rule. But it was not until the summer of 1942 when Billy, Uncle Joe and I were riding along one of those endless dirt roads with him singing that he told us about the dream he had years earlier to be a singing cowboy star. When asked why he had not gone to Hollywood, he told us simply that Auntie had refused to go.

Can you imagine this motherless, uneducated cowboy who ran away from a Catholic convent when he was ten and was raised by Texas cowboys, pulling on a pair of pajamas each night to please his wife? But that is what he did. My dad never wore a pair of pajamas until his first visit to a hospital when he was in his seventies. And he was raised in a home with indoor plumbing, two cars in the garage and was sent from his home in Bowie, Arizona, to Tempe Normal School to complete high school.

In the three summers I spent on the Cyclopic, I never trained myself to recognize the sound the wind made as it came through the Joshua trees on the small hill behind the ranch house. I *always* turned around expecting to see water rushing down the hill. But it was always the wind.

One summer Billy decided to pound a long piece of steel he had found into the ground in the wash in front of the ranch house. Somehow this set his imagination going and he began digging his own mineshaft. And he spent many hours scooping the damp sand and gravel out of the hole next to the piece of metal. He planned to dig it deep enough to tie a rope around the metal bar and pull himself out of the hole. But before this dream could be realized and the hole was only about three feet deep, a sudden cloud burst brought deep water rushing down the wash and over the hole. When the storm had passed and the water subsided, Billy checked his hole. It was no longer there. The water had deposited sand and gravel into the hole completely filling it. This discouraged Billy and he did not have the heart to start digging again. But Uncle Joe used the wash's power to his advantage. He had deliberately built the large corral across it. And the swift water periodically swept the piles of manure down the wash and out of the ranch house area.

181.

Summers At The Cyclopic Ranch

Honey bees came to collect water where the sink and shower water drained in front of the house. And before I realized the bees were on the ground, I was stung several times on the bottoms of my bare feet. I soon learned to watch where I placed my feet when I walked in that area.

This brought the bees to Uncle Joe's attention. And he decided the hive must be close by and spent much time following their flight path as they left the watering spot.

After many false leads, he finally located the hive in the wall of the old change room below the mill and across the wash from the ranch house. He decided to raid the hive. And with the help of a few ranch hands, he filled the room with smoke. Later, when the bees were dead or dazed, they went inside and tore the boards from the wall exposing the honeycombs. Much honey was retrieved. And it was very good and I enjoyed eating it. But my favorite part was chewing the honey-filled wax combs.

In the White Mountains where the Cyclopic was located, many closed mines dotted the hills. And a few, such as the Cyclopic, were left with buildings, houses and equipment intact. At the Cyclopic an old ungraded and unused road wound up the hill from the ranch house behind the mill and up over the top of the mountain. Located on this road a few miles from the Cyclopic was one of these closed mines. Uncle Joe, Billy and I visited this mine several times, both by horseback over the old road behind the mill, and the longer route by way of a maintained dirt road. A family lived at the site, but I do not know why they were there. It was not being used as a ranch headquarters like the Cyclopic. But perhaps, the company planned to reopen soon and had hired him as the watchman.

On one of our visits there, while Uncle Joe talked with the man, Billy and I busied ourselves in one of the vacant buildings picking up small *Wings* cigarette cards left behind by workers. They were pictures of airplanes and were packaged with the cigarettes. Daddy smoked *Wings* so the cards were not a novelty to Billy and me, but it gave us something to do while we waited for Uncle Joe.

The horseback ride over the mountain to the mine was very interesting. Many large pieces of equipment were strewn around the hills. One large abandoned wood-burning cook stove was in such good condition it appeared ready to cook a meal just by adding wood, a match and food.

Another interesting place Billy and I enjoyed was the Spear Ranch headquarters over the mountains a few miles southwest of the Cyclopic. It was not an old mine but had always been a ranch and had large corrals.

Summers At The Cyclopic Ranch

In one of these large corrals, Uncle Joe and other cowboys were working cattle. He was riding Badger, the special horse he had brought to the Kingman area when he and Auntie sold their ranch near Solomonsville. Badger was running fast when a short, sharp, loose wooden stake thrown up by his front hooves was impaled near his groin.

Uncle Joe immediately recognized Badger was badly hurt. And he reigned him in and hopped off. After assessing the injury, he hurriedly proceeded to remove the imbedded stake. A reasonably clean handkerchief from his jeans' pocket was saturated with ointment used by ranchers to treat injured horses and cattle. Then the saturated handkerchief was swabbed in and around the bleeding hole.

Billy and I were not with Uncle Joe when the accident occurred. But when he returned later in the afternoon to the Cyclopic, he told us about Badger's injury. Naturally, we were very upset and concerned. He had always been Uncle Joe's horse—we had never known a time when he had not been around.

Because of the seriousness of Badger's condition, Uncle Joe had not brought him home to the Cyclopic that evening. He had been put in one of the smaller corrals close to the ranch house. Understandably, we worried about him all that evening. And early the next morning we hopped in the pickup and drove to the ranch to check on him. Because Uncle Joe had told us Badger would recover if he survived the night, as we approached the ranch, and before the pickup stopped, we were anxiously searching the small corral to see if he were standing.

Our hearts dropped. We could not see him! But as our eyes frantically searched all of the corrals, we finally saw him standing in one of the back corrals. Uncle Joe did not say much. But, from the look on his face, we knew he was very relieved to see his loyal, longtime friend still alive and doing well. Badger remained at the Spear Ranch for a time until Uncle Joe was convinced his wound had healed sufficiently to be safely brought back to the Cyclopic. But until that time, we made daily trips to the Spear Ranch to dress the wound.

On one of our trips to the Spear Ranch, I saw the first owl I had ever seen up close. I thought my eyes were deceiving me when I noticed a bird sitting on the fence post with its head on backwards. Although I immediately recognized it as an owl, I had not known owls had the ability to turn their heads around backwards. When the owl allowed us to approach within a short distance of him and did not fly away, Uncle Joe knew the bird was either hurt or sick and cautioned us not to move any closer to it.

183.

Summers At The Cyclopic Ranch

The fact that it was out in the daytime in an unprotected area further convinced Uncle Joe it was not wise to bother the bird. And soon the owl flew a short distance away into the cover of some trees.

The wife of the cowboy who lived in the Spear Ranch house was an unusual woman for the times. I do not remember her husband, but she was a younger woman, probably in her late twenties or early thirties. And she dressed in men's clothing—cotton button shirts and blue jeans, and her hair was cut short and straight. But the house was neatly kept.

And every time we visited, green onions stuffed in a large glass jar were on the faded oil cloth-covered table. Spoons in a glass container were also on the table. They were conveniently available for the coffee drinkers who poured coffee from the pot left brewing on the stove all day. And the onions were eaten with the beans kept warm on the back of the stove.

The last time I saw the woman from Spear Ranch was on a street in downtown Kingman—she was wearing a dress, her hair was longer and she was very pregnant. For some reason she appeared embarrassed we had seen her, whether it was because she was in a dress or because she was pregnant— or both—I do not know. The dress and being pregnant were both inconsistent with the image I had of her from the Spear Ranch.

Uncle Joe drove an *International* pickup. At the ranch, he kept a fifty-gallon drum of gasoline and used a hand pump to fill the trucks—the International and a larger flat bed Chevrolet. When the drum was almost empty, Uncle Joe would load it into the back of the pickup and take it to the Mobil station in Kingman.

For a cowboy who loved ranching, Uncle Joe also liked city life, and we made a trip into Kingman about every two weeks. Many times as we were driving down a dirt road or highway, Uncle Joe would turn the steering wheel over to me while he rolled a cigarette. This was not as dangerous as it sounds, although I was only a ten-year-old girl. The highway between Kingman and Las Vegas was not heavily traveled. And we might meet one car from the time we left Kingman until we turned off onto the Pearce Ferry Road leading into the Cyclopic Ranch area. We pretty much had the highway to ourselves—a common thing on Arizona and New Mexico highways at that time.

Summers At The Cyclopic Ranch

On every trip we made to Kingman, the pickup would sputter and stall at least one time. Uncle Joe would pull over to the side of the highway, lift the hood, and put the small metal sieve from the gas pump to his lips and blow off the collected residue. That is all it took, just one puff, and he would hop back into the pickup and down the road we would go—until the next time it became clogged. Somehow dust and small leaves found their way into the drum of gas, and this was what was clogging the sieve.

Several herds of mustangs—wild horses—roamed Cyclopic Ranch land. These herds of wild horses were considered a nuisance by Uncle Joe and the other ranchers. They ate the grass needed for their cattle. And the ranchers would have rid their lands of these horses if the law had allowed them to do so. But at this time it was illegal to destroy or remove them. Later, after Uncle Joe left the Cyclopic, many truckloads of these horses were hauled out of the area.

One afternoon after an all-day ride over the ranch, Uncle Joe returned to the ranch house with a colt following him. As I watched them come down the wash toward the house, my mind was trying to come up with an explanation of how Uncle Joe could leave the ranch in the morning on a gelding and return at the end of the day with a colt.

He answered my question by explaining that he had jumped a herd of mustangs and had given them chase. The colt was young and could not keep up with its mother and was soon left behind. Uncle Joe could not abandon the colt. And there was no possibility that the mother would return for it. He roped and led it gently for a short distance. Then he removed the rope and the colt followed his horse on into the ranch.

The colt was a bay mare with black mane and tail. She was very wild and backed away from me when I tried to touch her. And I spent many hours trying to tame her, but she never responded to me or to anyone else. When she was older and Uncle Joe left the Cyclopic, many cowboys in the Kingman area tried to ride her but with no success. The name Uncle Joe suggested for her—Ginger—truly fit her. She had a lot of *ginger*.

Later in the summer, after another long, hard day riding the range, I again watched as Uncle Joe approached the ranch house with a colt following behind his horse. This time I knew where the colt had come from—a mustang herd

Although the colt was black with just a touch of white on her head, Uncle Joe said the mother had been white. When asked, he suggested several names for the colt. One was Doll Baby. I liked that name and gave it to my new mare colt.

185.

Summers At The Cyclopic Ranch

Ginger and Doll Baby with Vel at the Cyclopic

Vel with Doll Baby at the Cyclopic

Summers At The Cyclopic Ranch

Unlike Ginger, she immediately allowed me to approach her, although she was a little nervous. But it was not long before I was loving and petting her. And she was following me around the ranch house area like a little puppy. We spent many hours together. She lived up to her name—she really was a doll baby.

When the two colts were introduced to each other, Ginger was immediately drawn to Doll Baby and bonded with her. They became inseparable. One colt was never seen without the other, and Doll Baby was always the leader with Ginger following closely behind. When I played with Doll Baby, Ginger stood a short distance away but followed us wherever we went, but she never allowed me to touch her.

The Cyclopic mill site looked as if the workers had packed their belongings at the end of their shift and left—everything was left in place. And the large tanks at the mill were still full and ready for the processing of the milled gold ore—the solution in them contained cyanide and was deadly.

On one of the many trips Uncle Joe and I made up the hill to the mill, we noticed dead birds by the tanks, but thought nothing about it. But later when the cyanide water began to leak from the pipes at the bottom of the tanks, almost immediately a couple of yearlings found the water and drank it. They fell over dead in their tracks without even a kick—indicating the potency of the poison in the tanks. To keep other cattle from dying, Uncle Joe quickly fenced them off.

On our trips to the mill, we rummaged through the assay office and found hundreds of ground ore samples. One of the large engines in the mill exploded when it was started by the man who had come to buy it. The many holes in the tin building where the engine was housed made it difficult to understand how he had not been killed or badly injured by the blast. I was not at the ranch when it happened, but I learned later when I inquired about the many holes in the tin building.

The war had made equipment and supplies scarce. Uncle Joe took the copper wiring out of the mill and sold it to a business in Kingman. Everyone was collecting and selling scrap metal to help the war effort. Billy and I retrieved every piece of metal we could find and sold it at a small store on the highway in west Kingman. The store also sold candy. And Billy and I spent all of our scrap metal money on candy there.

The ranch dog was a black female shepherd named Fussy. Her home was under the far corner of the house. The house stood two or three feet off the ground and was used not only by Fussy as a home, but during the day the chickens were also protected from the hot sun and occasional rain.

Summers At The Cyclopic Ranch

Fussy was a working dog and did not want to be loved or petted by children. However, when she had a batch of puppies, I chose a little male who had the same markings on his forehead as Mickey Mouse—thus, he was named Mickey Mouse.

Mr. Peterson did not come to the Cyclopic often, and he never paid any particular attention to Mickey. But for some reason, he bonded with Mr. Peterson. And on one of his infrequent visits to the Cyclopic when Mickey was full-grown, he followed Mr. Peterson and Uncle Joe off one morning on their full day ride over the ranch. When they returned in late afternoon, no one noticed Mickey was not with them.

But after a day or two, I noticed Mickey Mouse was not anywhere in the ranch house area, and I began to question others about him. Uncle Joe told me Mickey Mouse had been with him and Mr. Peterson all day on their ride until they were about a mile from the ranch house. At that time he noticed Mickey left the road and lay down in the shade under a small bush. But Uncle Joe had not been concerned because he had assumed he would rest a while and come on into the ranch later. And he had not thought about the dog again until I told him he could not be found.

On our next trip away from the ranch house, we stopped at the bush where Uncle Joe had last seen Mickey Mouse—and there he lay—dead. He had obviously died from heat exhaustion and fatigue. Dogs will follow those they care about until they drop dead.

Coyotes were a part of our lives on the ranch. Our sleep was disturbed many nights by their mournful howling and the excited barking of our dogs as they responded to them. The coyotes would not come into the ranch house area because they feared the dogs. But they positioned themselves high on the mill-site hill just far enough away to be safe from Uncle Joe's gun and the dogs, but close enough to disturb our sleep.

Coyotes, like mustangs, were also disliked by the ranchers. But they were killed whenever the opportunity presented itself, because there was no law protecting them. When I questioned why one of his grown cows had only part of a tail, Uncle Joe said a coyote had grabbed the tail when the cow was a small calf. The tail had been bitten off in the coyote's attempt to drag the calf down to kill it. The attempt had probably been thwarted by the intervention of the calf's angry mother.

However, late one afternoon after a full-day's ride, Uncle Joe approached the ranch house with a coyote slung over his saddle in front of him. He had roped the coyote and brought him home for me to see.

188.

Summers At The Cyclopic Ranch

We kept him a few days but then gave him to a family living in one of the Boulder City houses a few miles down the road. They kept him on a chain attached to a clothesline. This allowed him to run up and down the length of the lines for exercise. An animal that I could not play with and love was of no interest to me. I knew the coyote would never be a pet.

Mojave County had an ordinance requiring Negroes traveling through to be out of the county before the sun went down. Not surprising then was the outcry of anger raised by the residents of the area when they learned the United States Government had plans to station Negro soldiers at the new air base outside of Kingman. They cited this county law regarding Negroes remaining overnight in the county. But their protests fell on deaf ears, and the Negroes were brought in anyway. At first local merchants refused to serve them. This created more problems and dissension. But at this point, the Government stepped in and required the local merchants give the same service to the black soldiers as they gave to the white soldiers.

What point do I have in bringing up this incident? Because when I read stories stating there were many Negro cowboys in the early West, I question, because of my own experiences and that of my family, the validity of such statements. Uncle Joe knew all of the ranchers in the Kingman area, and I visited many of them with him over the years we lived in Goldroad. And I never saw a Negro on any of the ranches.

Further, my Grandfather Richards owned two ranches in southeastern Arizona during and after the Wyatt Earp-Doc Holliday-Tombstone-OK Corral era, and my father never knew or heard of a Negro cowboy. Also, Grandfather Whelan was a rancher in the Aravaipa in 1865 and on the Sierra Bonita Ranch, and he never knew a Negro cowboy.

The only Negro I ever saw on a ranch was the black man who arrived late one afternoon at the Cyclopic. He was riding on a wagon pulled by two beautiful black mules. These mules looked so much like horses I studied them carefully before I was convinced they really were mules.

This man had been hired by Uncle Joe to drag a shallow ditch for a water line that was to be laid on the ranch. He had brought his own hay for his mules; he did not eat in the ranch house with the other cowboys; he did not sleep with the other cowboys. He camped over by the wash near the milking pens. He did his job, and when it was completed, he left.

Summers At The Cyclopic Ranch

These comments are not made as a judgment on the right or the wrong of the social structure or how it was handled. But they are made to set the record straight on the presence of Negro cowboys in Arizona—northwestern and southeastern Arizona, anyway. They might have been cooks, handymen, line-draggers, perhaps—but not cowboys. I dislike seeing history being rewritten in any area. But it is especially upsetting to me when the facts as I know them and have lived them are deliberately changed to project a false and untrue picture to the world—whatever the reason.

After my summer on the Cyclopic Ranch in 1942 was over, I returned home to Goldroad and entered the sixth grade. Soon Uncle Joe and Auntie also left the Cyclopic. But I did not know they had plans to leave the Cyclopic after we went home. They gave no reason to me or any of our family, at least that I heard. And no questions were asked by us.

But I suppose I was so excited and caught up with the big move we were about to make to New Mexico, that I did not even think about their plans. Nor did I stop to realize our move would end my summers on the ranch as well as being close enough to continue to see them frequently. But they moved to Kingman into their large house on the lot with the Boulder City house and the other smaller rental.

Chapter 21

War Clouds Gather

...that's when the whole world seemed to explode around them.

Hitler started his move across Europe. Country by country was being crushed under the onslaught of the German blitzkrieg. My father walked the floor the evening we heard the radio broadcast of France's surrender to the Nazis. England now virtually stood alone against the massive German war machine and was teetering on the brink of defeat. The newly developed German *buzz bombs* were literally raining terror upon the people living in London and the surrounding areas. My father was deeply concerned about the fate of his fathers' homeland.

At this time, the United States' entry into the war would have given the British the support they needed so badly, but, as a country, we were not ready to commit ourselves to an all out declaration of war against the Germans. However, the American people supported the British cause over the Germans, and our loyalties were with them.

In the summer of 1940, after graduation from high school, my mother's cousin, Billy Massey, came to Goldroad to stay with Uncle Son and Henny. His goal was to enlist in the Navy but he was not yet eighteen. And this made it necessary for him to secure written consent from his father—but his father refused to give it. Billy thought of every conceivable way to get his father's signature on a consent document, but failed. By Christmas of 1940, he had turned eighteen. He spent Christmas with our family on the hill, and, a short time after the holidays, Mother and Daddy paid his bus fare to San Diego where he joined the Navy. If they had not done this for him, he would have had to hitch hike.

Approximately one year later, on December 7, 1941, when the news was broadcast of the Japanese attack on Pearl Harbor, one of our first thoughts was concerning Billy Massey's whereabouts—if he had been in Pearl Harbor, was he dead or alive? Word did finally come that Billy's ship, the *USS Patterson*, a destroyer, was in the harbor at the time of the devastating Japanese aerial attack and was tied up alongside two sister ships and a destroyer tender.

The attack happened right after breakfast. Billy had planned to visit a cousin on a nearby PT boat because they were on a holiday routine—and that's when the whole world seemed to explode around them. Only one—third of the crew members was aboard the *USS Patterson*. The rest were on leave. Each sailor on the destroyer was doing more than a single job, but they got the destroyer under way and out of the harbor.

In describing the scene before him as his ship moved through the water he said, "There were big ships going down—I saw a battlewagon (battleship) heel—there were men in the water—the noise was awful—fire was everywhere." He looked across the water to Ford Island, a big U.S. seaplane base, and saw it go up in flames.

Nineteen ships were sunk or severely damaged. The enemy destroyed 80 Navy planes and 97 Army planes at Hickham and Wheeler fields on Oahu Island.

The Patterson's gunners blasted one enemy plane out of the air and shot down four others after the destroyer cleared the harbor. "We were fortunate. We were never hit, and no one was injured during those horrible hours," he later related.

They *were* fortunate. Navy and Marine Corps casualties amounted to 2,117 people killed, 960 missing and 876 wounded. Within the first hour, the Patterson was scouring the ocean for enemy submarines. Billy said, "We sank a two-man Japanese sub with depth charges." The enemy sub was later mounted in front of the base at Pearl Harbor.

Relating the destruction the crew viewed when they came back in to get fuel and supplies and pick up the rest of the crew, Billy said, "I knew the harbor would be in bad condition, but I was still shocked when I saw it again. Ships were shambles—some were sunk. Just a little bit of the battleship *Arizona* could be seen above the water. I was only a 19-year-old boy when the Japs bombed Pearl Harbor, but I grew to be a man in a couple of hours on that day."

He believed the lesson learned there should not be forgotten today—"Americans should be sure that our armed forces are strong. We'd better tighten up and start working together."

This terrorizing sneak attack on Pearl Harbor struck all Americans with horror and fear, and we in Goldroad were no exception. We were not far from the Pacific coast. And our logic led us to the natural conclusion that if the Japanese could launch an attack of that magnitude on Pearl Harbor from their homeland thousands of miles away in Japan, they could certainly bring it a few miles farther on to our American shores as well. Our family was gathered around the radio in the living room listening to President Franklin D. Roosevelt when he made the declaration of war against the Japanese Empire.

War Clouds Gather

The fear Americans felt was very real. Uncle Joe's Cyclopic Ranch was located in the White Mountains not many miles from Boulder Dam. The dam was high on the list for possible enemy sabotage. Measures by the government were taken to protect the dam. One of the obvious measures that affected us was the restriction on stopping our car within a heavily guarded area surrounding the dam. A heavy cable was strung a few hundred feet behind the dam from one side of the canyon to the other to prevent the possibility of enemy aircraft flying low enough to damage or destroy the dam. Cleverly camouflaged machine gun nests on high points overlooking the dam again made us very aware of our country's recognition of the seriousness of our vulnerability against a determined and powerful nation—Japan.

Even though our country was now at war, and all of us in Goldroad knew that by the end of 1942 the camp would be closing and some of us would be going to New Mexico with USSR&MCo, I again did as I had done the previous two summers. I spent the summer of 1942 at the Cyclopic with Auntie and Uncle Joe.

Several months into the summer, business matters came up and Uncle Joe asked his brother and sister-in-law, Fred and May Boscoe, to spend a few nights at the ranch while he and Auntie were away. Billy and I returned to Goldroad. Later, when all of us returned to the ranch, Fred told Uncle Joe he and May had spent a fear-filled, sleepless first night on the ranch. As mentioned before, the mill was on the side of the mountain in the canyon across the wash from the main house where Auntie and Uncle Joe lived, and it was in full view from the house.

As darkness deepened their first night on the ranch, and they were preparing for bed, Fred looked out of the front screened porch where he and May were to sleep. Something caught his eye in the mill on the hill. Enough light from the moon made the mill buildings quite visible to him. In one of the open windows of the mill he saw something white—and it moved as he watched. Becoming concerned and frightened, he alerted May to what he had seen. To insure their safety, they felt compelled to constantly watch the movement of the white object in the mill window all that night. They feared the moving white object could possibly be enemy agents using the high mill window to signal to others in the area, and they feared for their lives.

When daylight came and they were still unharmed, Fred determined he would confront whoever or whatever was in the mill. He saddled a horse and cautiously made his way up the hill to the spot where the white signal had moved all night. As he moved forward towards the building, he did not encounter any resistance. He then moved closer until he was at a point where he could identify through the open side of the building the cause of the movement in the window the previous night. A piece of white canvas that had been tacked or nailed above the window had fallen loose on one corner and was hanging over part of the open window. A slight breeze on the hill, but not felt at the ranch house below, had created the sporadic movement of the white canvas.

People living today will probably not understand how a situation such as this could have created such fear in two mature adults. How they could have been gripped with fear of this magnitude by the movement of a piece of fabric in the window of an abandoned mill. How illogical and foolish, they might say. My response is this—those who would make such a determination did not live through the surprise Japanese attack on Pearl Harbor as we had. We felt the Japanese were capable of doing anything, and in fact, they had done it at Pearl Harbor.

The only time I ever saw Uncle Joe speak in an angry tone to Auntie was over an incident relating to the war. After our return to the Cyclopic and Fred and May's experience, one evening before bedtime Billy, Auntie, Uncle Joe and I were talking about the war. Auntie made the statement, "I don't know why we have to be in this war!" Uncle Joe turned on her with anger and, pointing to me, said, "That's why we have to be in this war!!" He did not elaborate, but even I knew what he meant. I had seen the newsreels in the theaters showing the raping and killing done by the Japanese in China and other areas where they had entered and conquered. Not another word was spoken as we made preparations to go to the smaller house with the large screened porch where we all slept.

When we left, Auntie did not go with us. Nothing was said. Billy and I got into bed but Uncle Joe did not. Five or ten minutes passed and Auntie still did not come to the sleeping porch. Finally, Uncle Joe walked back to the main house. A short time later he and Auntie emerged from the house and came to bed. Nothing more was ever said about the incident. Before Auntie and Uncle Joe were married, they had made a promise to each other that they would never go to bed angry. Auntie had stayed at the main house and Uncle Joe did his part by returning to the house. They fulfilled the promise made to each other many years before.

Present generations find it difficult to understand how Americans could have been so fearful regarding our country's safety both from the military power of Japan as well as the danger existing from so many first-generation Japanese living along the coast in California. Hindsight is always 20/20 when the scenario has been played out to its conclusion and all of the pieces fall into place in the end and the complete picture can be seen.

War Clouds Gather

The difficulty of the problem is *not* having all of the answers and *not* knowing the outcome but still having to make decisions based on the information available at the time. This was what was done in the case of the relocation of some of the Japanese people in California who were considered to be a threat to the security of our country. The only hurt these people might have experienced from their relocation was the disturbance of their lives for a short period of time, and, perhaps, feelings hurt from not being trusted by their adopted country. They were humanely treated — adequately feed, housed and doctored.

Americans caught in the reverse situation in Japan or territories they conquered were treated with cruelty, harshness and death. Most of the Japanese relocated probably were loyal to the United States, but some probably were not. We were teetering on the edge of defeat after an unexpected devastating blow and felt all areas of our vulnerability had to be covered wherever possible. The saying, "War is Hell" is true, but sitting in a relocation camp while having every need met is not exactly *Hell* when compared to what our troops were experiencing in the Pacific.

The summer of 1942 in Goldroad, Vella and all of the other kids in camp gathered the old, worn-out rubber tires for the war effort. Uncle Son offered his horse trailer to haul them to Kingman for recycling.

Everyone was very much aware there was a war going on. And we were not sure at this point in time if we had the ability to win it. Japan was hop-scotching island by island across the Pacific Ocean toward Hawaii and our shores. We did not have the war machine or trained troops to stop them.

The Japanese had caught us unaware and totally unprepared with their fine-tuned, well-trained, well-equipped and experienced armed forces. They definitely had the upper hand, and we knew it. Our National Guard units were being trained with wooden rifles. All other equipment was World War I vintage, and the training received was minimal. At this time, we had no war machine and no factories in place to build one.

The United States was not the world power in 1942 that it became before this war was over.

Japan had been preparing for the attack on the United States for years and was completely mobilized. And had they known the extent of damage done at Pearl Harbor, they easily could have invaded our country, and we would not have been able to do anything to stop them.

The boys eighteen years and older in the National Guard in Grant County New Mexico who went off to summer camp for training in 1942 were called directly into the Army and were shipped off to the Pacific

War Clouds Gather

Theater with little or no training. Most of them were on Corregidor when it fell to the Japanese and were part of the Bataan Death March. Those who survived, and many did not, spent the war in Japanese prisoner of war camps under cruel and inhumane treatment.

One of my friends in New Mexico had two older brothers taken when their National Guard unit was called-up that summer of 1942—one survived the Bataan Death March and the other did not. Another Grant County boy, Joe Goforth survived Bataan and became an art teacher at Cobre High School after his return. But his life and health were forever ruined by his experiences on the Bataan Death March and in the prisoner of war camp— both inhumane experiences were totally unnecessary.

It is not my intention to sound bitter, because I am not. But I spent many days during the war years in movie theaters watching newsreels showing the atrocities inflicted by Japanese soldiers upon captured people. I realize a lot of propaganda was disseminated at that time, but a lot of what was shown actually happened and was corroborated later through records as well as visual observations made when the Americans went back into territories conquered by the Japanese.

And because of the lighted conveyor belt running from the mine area down over the hill to the mill, those in authority felt Goldroad could be mistakenly identified as the Boulder Dam (Hoover Dam) and could possibly be bombed. Blackout drills were held with all outside lights in camp turned off and blackout shades or curtains drawn over home windows.

Every month when we made our shopping trip to Needles we were visually reminded of our closeness to the coast by the Military Police with bayonets strapped to their thighs who stopped each car approaching the Topock bridge before allowing them to proceed across the Colorado River into California.

If the MP's presence did not convince us our country was at war, the machine gun positioned across the river in rocks with its gun barrel aimed at the bridge brought the reality home to us. Route 66 spanned our country from the west coast to Chicago and was vitally important to the war effort and had to be protected from possible enemy sabotage.

One morning as I looked down on the camp from my perch on our front porch, I saw two Marines in full-dress uniform standing in the shade of the conveyer belt as it crossed over Route 66. John and William Sayer and my brother Billy had also noticed the Marines and had engaged them in conversation. The Marines asked John and William for a drink of water. The Sayer home was a short distance from where the Marines were standing. They quickly ran home and brought two large jars filled with ice and water

War Clouds Gather

for them. The Marines barely had time to drink the cold water before a car stopped, offered them a ride and they were on their way. Servicemen were so highly regarded and appreciated, it was not necessary for them even to put their thumb out to hitch a ride.

John was so impressed with the two Marines after his meeting with them he wanted to be a Marine—that is, if the war lasted long enough.

Thousands of soldiers were shipped into Needles for desert training. After their training, they were sent to North Africa to fight against the great German General Rommel—dubbed by the Allies as the *Desert Fox*. A grudging tribute to his expertise and successes in the armored tank battles he waged in the sands of the vast Sahara Desert against the British General Montgomery—no slouch himself at desert fighting.

Later Hitler called General Rommel back to Germany, and he was eventually executed for his part in a plot to kill Hitler. Rommel and several other German generals felt Hitler was a madman and needed to be stopped. But their plans were discovered before they could be carried out, and Rommel and his co-conspirators were killed instead.

Many stories filtered into camp regarding some of the accidents on maneuvers in the Mojave Desert and around Needles. Tanks driven onto improperly installed pontoon bridges over the Colorado River collapsed trapping and drowning the men inside. Soldiers seeking shelter from the unrelenting desert sun crawled under even the smallest desert shrubs and were accidentally crushed by tanks unaware they were in their path.

On the Arizona side of the Colorado River in Kingman, the Air Force brought in thousands of airmen to train at the newly constructed air base. Both small towns, Needles and Kingman, were bursting at the seams with the sudden influx of so many soldiers, and their military support people.

Many social problems arose, other than those created by the overcrowding of facilities too small to handle this sudden influx of people. But parents were most concerned about their high school daughters dating the servicemen, although most of the soldiers were recent high school graduates themselves. As a high school senior, Shirley Peeples fell into this category. But she chose not to date the servicemen. Her very best friend did, and this was upsetting to Shirley.

Later while she was a freshman at the University of Arizona, Shirley did date a serviceman, but he had attended Kingman High School at the same time she had and lived in Oatman. His name was Bill Ames. He was in the Army Air Corp and was training at Davis-Monthan Air Force Base in Tucson. They had dated a few times while in high school but now renewed their relationship on a serious level. By this time, Goldroad had been

197.

abandoned and all of us were living in New Mexico.

Joe and Ethel Peeples lived next door to us at the USSR&MCo in New Mexico. And the Broughs lived on the other side of them. Bill Ames was a pilot and when he was sent overseas, Shirley came home to live and have their baby, Ricky. The airplane flown by Bill was named *The Shirley Ann.* He had named it after Shirley and the wife of his co-pilot.

When Bill returned to the States after the war ended, he was once again stationed at Davis Monthan Air Force Base. On several of his flights, he flew his bomber low over the Peeples' house, dipped his wings and waved. By the time he made the second flight over the houses, Shirley and Ricky were out on the front porch and waving back. Our family thought it was great he could have this contact with his wife and child, but the Broughs complained and Bill was ordered not to do it anymore. This did not exactly endear the Broughs to the Peeples.

At the beginning of the war, draft boards classified all men. Classification was done by age, marital status, number of children, health, and the priority of their job as it related to the war effort. Gold mining was not considered a high-priority occupation. Because of this, the manganese balls used by the ball mills in Goldroad to crush the gold ore could not be purchased. The mine could not operate without the mill, and the men could not be held on a low priority job without the threat of being drafted into the armed service or being placed by the draft board into a high priority job.

This was the dilemma the USSR&MCo officials faced in 1942—no men and no supplies to operate Goldroad. Because of these factors, the decision was made to develop the lead and zinc property they owned—the Bullfrog shaft—at Vanadium, New Mexico.

During the summer of 1942 while I was away at the Cyclopic, the children remaining in Goldroad participated in the Dig n' Dogie Days Parade held on the Fourth of July. Their float showed the role the Boy Scouts and Girl Scouts could play if a bombing occurred in their area.

War Clouds Gather

Goldroad Scout float in Dig n' Doggie Days Parade July 4 1942. From left in Girl Scout uniform Vella Richards; Anna Marie Heinz; Alma Dean Doolin. Far right on his stomach is Gabrielle, the Mexican boy with the blonde hair and blue eyes.

When I left Goldroad after school was out in May of 1942 to go to the Cyclopic Ranch for the summer, the decision had already been made by the company to close Goldroad and move all of the supervisors and their families to the new property in New Mexico. Little did I realize many of my friends would not be in Goldroad when I returned at the end of the summer to attend school. And Uncle Son and Henny had also moved to Kingman during the summer sometime after Bobby Kay's fifth birthday. That summer on several of our trips to Kingman from the Cyclopic, Uncle Joe took me to their house while he did his business in town. Uncle Tom and Aunt Ruby lived a short distance from them. And I used their phone to call the Standard Station in

War Clouds Gather

Goldroad. They would send a man up our hill to get Mother and I would ask her to meet me in Kingman. One time I did not have the twenty-five cents to give Aunt Ruby to make the call. And when I went back to Henny's house and told her I had not called Mother because of this, she was upset with Aunt Ruby because she had not allowed me to make the call anyway. Also, during one of these visits, I went swimming in the Kingman Public Pool which was a short distance from their houses.

Bobby Kay Massey's 5th birthday party in front of their Goldroad house before their move to Kingman. Back row left to right: Alma Dean Doolin; Madeline Plummer; Vella Richards. Middle row left to right: Billy Richards, Billy Dell Hicks, Tommy Cudney, Fitzpatrick boy. Front row left to right: Fitzpatrick boy, Dale Wright, Bobby Kay Massey

Many did not go to New Mexico—Madeline and her mother, Alice Plummer; Rosie Redding and family; Helen Kristich and family; Roger Williamson and family; Alma Dean Doolin and family; Arlene Phillips and family; Duane Bird and family; William and Johnny Sayer and family. All of them were gone when school started, except Madeline and her mother and the Sayers. Mrs. Plummer was the only teacher in the Goldroad School—for all grades.

War Clouds Gather

Morris and Margaret Bird did not go to New Mexico with USSR&MCo, either. Working in the office so closely with Leo Duriez, Morris saw the closing of Goldroad coming and asked for a transfer to the main office in Salt Lake City, Utah. Their family left Goldroad in early 1942. Later he took a Civil Service exam and took a position at the Las Vegas Gunnery School, which was classified as a high priority job.

Although the Sayer family did not go to New Mexico with us, they were still in Goldroad when we left in early November 1942—Bill Sayer had a job in Louisiana. I did not know why they did not go with us until just a few years ago. At that time, the hardest part of leaving Goldroad was leaving Johnny and William.

The last party at the schoolhouse was our Halloween party—Johnny came as a Marine. Helen Kristich, dressed in a Hawaiian grass skirt, came from her home in Kingman for the party. A few others also came from their new homes in Kingman. I do not even remember what I wore. A deep sadness hung over the party that night—I did not enjoy it, and I believe no one else did, either. All of our other parties had been so much fun! So few of us were left at this time.

In Kingman, Auntie was having her own problems created by the war. The influx of people into Kingman had created a shortage of houses. And individuals could not buy lumber to build new houses. The O.P.A. (Office of Price Administration) was a wartime agency created to ensure the fair treatment of renters by their landlords. This agency had the power to put a ceiling on the rent charged by individual homeowners. Thus, in theory anyway, this ceiling would eliminate excessive rents charged for the few available houses. But as is true in any governmental regulatory agency, misuse of power for payoffs and favoring of friends came into play with the O.P.A.—and Auntie was not pleased with the unfair treatment she received as a landlord. She was neither a friend nor willing to make a payoff.

In the summer of 1942, long convoys of trucks filled with soldiers wound through Goldroad on their way to the training facilities in Needles. At first all of the kids, and many of the adults, gathered along Route 66 to watch and yell encouragement and appreciation to the men as they passed by. Many of the soldiers yelled comments back, such as, "Hell couldn't be any hotter than this place!", or "I think I have died and gone to hell!" But soon there were so many of these troop convoys making their way through camp, no one bothered to interrupt their work or play to notice them anymore.

And night did not stop them. The whine and grinding roar of the truck engines as they labored to negotiate the S curves and steep incline of the highway as it made its way down into Goldroad, added to the chatter of the soldiers, broke the stillness of the night. Because, at this time, all mining and milling operations had ceased in Goldroad. No longer heard was the *heart* of the camp—the constant rhythmic sound of the air compressors as they provided the air supply to the mine day and night. Nor were the sounds from the machine shop heard as the drill bits were sharpened and other equipment maintained. Now, all was quiet.

Daddy had remained behind in Goldroad to electrically prepare all of the heavy equipment for transport to New Mexico and to pull all useable electrical wiring from the operation. All materials and supplies were difficult, if not impossible, to buy even in a high-priority operation such as the lead and zinc mine in New Mexico. The Broughs, Cudneys, Gillespies, Henlines, Duriezs, Peeples, Elgins and Hicks were already settled in Silver City, Bayard or Fierro waiting for the new homes, mine, and mill to be built at the new property in Vanadium.

Bill and Rosie Hicks were friends of our family. Bill worked for Dunton driving truck hauling the ore from Line Road to the Gold Road Shaft where it was dumped into a grizzly and mixed with the ore hoisted from the shaft and carried into the crusher.

But when Goldroad closed, Bill was hired by USSR&MCo to haul the equipment by truck out of Goldroad to the new operation in New Mexico. After this was completed, he worked for the company as a surface worker. And their family lived in one of the smaller houses behind ours. But before this happened, on one of his trips through Silver City on his way to the mine site, he saw Mrs. Duriez on the street. She recognized the company truck and waved to Bill as he went by. And on his next trip to Goldroad to pick up more equipment, he told Daddy about it. This news brought feelings of comfort and security to me.

Not many days after the sad Halloween party at the school, Daddy came home with the news we were leaving for New Mexico in two days. Although all he had planned to do had not been completed, he felt our family needed to leave so we could enroll in our new school in New Mexico. We were already two months into the school year as it was. All of the important equipment had already been prepared and sent. So Daddy left the preparation of the remaining equipment and supplies to Joe Gallegos and others.

While I was spending the summer at the Cyclopic, Mother was busily packing our belongings for the move. Mother had wanted to be certain everything was packed when Daddy made the decision his work was completed in Goldroad. And we *were* ready—all household items had been packed and had been ready to go for several months when Daddy made the

War Clouds Gather

announcement. A moving van was to come and move everything for us except the personal items we packed in our car.

We had one last day at school and then we were off to New Mexico. I am certain there were *good-byes*, because when we arrived in Silver City, I had an address that Johnny had given me my last day of school and where I wrote to him. His family would soon leave Goldroad for their new job in Louisiana. I was so excited to finally be going to New Mexico. At that time I did not comprehend what I was leaving behind—but then by that time, Goldroad was not Goldroad anymore because all of the people there important in my life had gone or soon would be.

That morning of November 7 when we walked out of our back door, we got into our 1937 Nash as if we were making one of our regular family trips to Kingman. Three stops had to be made before Daddy headed our car toward Phoenix where we were to spend the first night of our journey to New Mexico. The first stop was to gas up at Dunton's Standard Station at the bottom of our hill. The second was at the draft board in Kingman where Daddy had to report before leaving the county.

When Daddy entered the draft board office on the second floor and told the man in charge where he was going, he told Daddy that he could not leave the county—they needed him there, and he would not give the clearance for him to leave. Daddy went to the window and pointed down to our car sitting in the parking lot where we were waiting for him and said, "You see that car down there with my family in it? I am going to get in that car, and we are leaving for New Mexico." With that Daddy turned, left the office, got in our car, and we drove away.

Our third stop, the most difficult, was at Auntie and Uncle Joe's home. We were stopping to say good-bye. This was extremely painful to do. Naturally, they did not want us to leave the area. At the time, I did not realize how difficult it was for them. And when we arrived at the house, Uncle Joe was in bed sick. We went into the bedroom where he lay and talked a few minutes about unimportant things—we were anxious to be on our way. Then we gave him and Auntie a hug and left. I realize now their hearts had to have been breaking— they had no children of their own. But Mother had been like a daughter to them, and when I was born I took my special place in their lives. Now we were leaving them alone.

Life would never be the same for me again—the special magic of Goldroad was erased—almost like a Brigadoon—only the mountains and the memories in my mind would remain—memories so poignant and strong they would last for a lifetime.

203.

Epilogue To Chapter 21

War Clouds Gather

Pearl Harbor Vets Still Grieve For Fallen Mates
Painful Memories Make Tough Men Cry

When they remember, tough men sometimes cry.

They were there when World War II began for the United States at 7:55 a.m. Dec 7, 1941, and a never-forgetting few can be found there today.

They left to fight for their country in other places. They held peacetime jobs, they raised families. They got old and returned to be near comrades dead for 55 years.

They are in their 70's now—Richard Fiske, Robert Kinzler, Everett Hyland, Joe Morgan, Warren Berhoff. Almost every day one or another will be at the USS Arizona Memorial to serve as volunteers.

They can tell visitors matter-of-factly what happened that day at Pearl Harbor. Twelve ships sank. Nine others heavily damaged. Fifty men yet entombed in the USS Utah, 1,177 still down on the bottom in the Arizona. The total casualty count on one day of infamy: more than 2,000.

It is not the fighting that gets them. It's a lost friend recalled in the moment, or it's someone else's grief. Then the voices go shaky, and there are long pauses as they struggle for composure. Every one has a different story that is somehow much the same.

Listen to Fiske, 74:

He was only 19 then, and he was so scared. He keeps saying that, sometimes with a laugh, sometimes not.

Fiske, a Marine bugler aboard the USS West Virginia, had risen to sound reveille at 5:30 a.m. He and fellow crew members had finished breakfast, and Fiske was to go off duty in a few minutes.

Suddenly, "I was in a war I never even knew existed. We took nine torpedoes and two bombs. We sank in 11 minutes."

An admiral's inspection was coming up that week, so all the watertight doors aboard the battleship were open to air out the compartments. Only five boilers were lit to provide electricity and it would have taken an hour to fire up the other three. There was no chance of escape.

Epilogue To Chapter 21 –War Clouds Gather

"The only way we moved was straight down. To the bottom. Forty-two feet. Thank God it wasn't deeper."

Fiske's battle station was up on the navigation bridge. He was there when a bomb hit a gun turret on the USS Tennessee anchored nearby. Splintered metal blasted from it killed his captain, Marvin Bennion, who was standing just eight feet away. Then Fiske was really scared. He was scared when he saw the Arizona anchored 60 feet off explode. And he was scared when the USS Oklahoma rolled over.

"I'd never seen that, a battleship, roll over. They lost 418 men, I think." Finally, the executive officer told the men they were useless on the bridge. Fiske ran below to help rescue trapped sailors. He threw sand on injured men to put out the flames on their bodies. He wanted off the ship, he'd wanted off since the first bomb fell, but he stayed until 9:30 when all were given permission to leave.

He was back on duty days later when sailors heard a noise in the hold of the Oklahoma, and they finally got a hole cut through and pulled out 32 sailors still alive. Then they heard a tapping on the West Virginia, his ship. "We couldn't get to those guys. We tried. God, that was a hard part."

It remains hard. Among those killed were his buddies, C.C. Jones and W.W. Finley. He'd gone through boot camp with them. "They are still out there."

So Fiske came back. He'll be there at the sunken Arizona today for the 55th reunion of survivors. In the morning, there will be prayers for the dead. Two Navy divers will swim down to gun turret No. 4 with urns containing the ashes of three men who survived the Arizona, who requested in their wills that they be cremated and entombed in that place. There are seven such urns already there.

Five years ago, while working as a volunteer at the Arizona Memorial, Fiske met one of the Japanese pilots who bombed his ship. Zegii Abe was a lieutenant then. He retired as an admiral.

A strange thing happened. The Marine bugler and the Japanese admiral became friends.

When Abe left for Japan, he asked a favor of the American. He gave Fiske $300 and told him to buy two roses every month, one for each of them, and take them to the Arizona to the shrine room where the names of those killed are listed.

He said to say a prayer and to play taps. "This is my way of saying I'm so sorry," he said.

Once a month ever since, Fiske has taken his bugle to the Arizona and sounded the dirge for the dead. The ceremony is becoming more elaborate.

Epilogue To Chapter 21 —War Clouds Gather

For the 50th anniversary of the end of the war, Abe returned with 350 Japanese veterans to pay respects. He gave Fiske more money and instructions to buy a wreath to take to the memorial when he plays Taps.

Here is where Fiske's voice breaks. "It gets harder and harder. Maybe I'm getting soft. You know she's still leaking oil, the Arizona. She's been leaking oil since 1941. A couple of years ago, I was out there and met a lady. She said, 'Where would the firemen be?' So I went by No. 3 gun turret. She said, 'My three brothers are down there.' About that time some droplets of oil came up to the surface. She grabbed my arm and said, 'The ship is still crying black tears for those boys.'

"I had to walk away from her. I hugged her and I walked away."

Joe, Lena and Flora Onetto taken about 1907
(Courtesy of the descendants of Joe and Flora Onetto)

Some of the information in *Following the Gold—The Onetto Story* was selected from a family history document *Following the Gold: From the Heart of the California Gold Rush to Goldroad Arizona* organized and written by Linda Simpson, a great granddaughter of Joe and Flora Onetto. Words, sentence structure and punctuation are that of the author, Norma Richards Yount.

Chapter 22

Following the Gold—The Onetto Story

When Mrs. Onetto finally moved from Goldroad sometime after 1943 to Needles to make her home, it was the end of the Onettos' trek of following the gold.

After the school year was over the end of May 1943 and the school was closed for good, Flora Onetto was given the key to check on it. Mrs. Plummer, the only teacher remaining for the 1942-1943 school year, and her daughter Madeline, had moved to Kingman. Many times when Mrs. Onetto checked on the schoolhouse, she took her granddaughter Theresa—she loved to play in the building. Also, Mrs. Onetto used the schoolbooks to teach her grandson Jack Connors. Tragically, many years later at age twenty, Jack sustained a traumatic brain injury from a car accident and was then cared for by Mrs. Onetto in her home in Needles for most of his life.

It is not known how long Mrs. Onetto stayed in Goldroad after all USSR&MCo personnel had left. It is doubtful it was for very long—a lone woman in a deserted mining camp would not have been a good thing. Especially with a major highway—Route 66—running through the center of it. At the request of Mr. Duriez, Joe Gallegos a company employee, had only remained in Goldroad with his children after all other company personnel had left in order that the school could remain open until the end of the school year. Perhaps Roy Dunton and his family remained for a time, but all other families would have been gone, or soon would be leaving.

When Mrs. Onetto finally moved from Goldroad sometime after 1943 to Needles to make her home, it was the end of the Onettos' trek of *following the gold*. A trek that had started in the mid 1800s in the Mother Lode region in Sutter Creek, California, where Flora was born and she and Joe Onetto were married. The move to Goldroad was made sometime after 1904 when Joe was offered the job of mine foreman.

After the harsh and primitive living conditions of Goldroad, Mrs. Onetto's move into a lovely three bedroom home in Needles, cooled by a *swamp cooler*, a block from her daughter Irene's house, must have seemed wonderful to her. Or perhaps, she might have thought she had died and gone to heaven! No cooler in Goldroad—only Virginia Creeper vines covering the front porch for cooling, and outside privy! A fitting reward for a woman who had graciously and patiently and kindly endured much—a comfortable home with a few of her children and grandchildren around!

Chapter 23

New Mexico, Here We Come!

Living in Silver City with its paved streets, sidewalks and streetlights was a real cultural shock.

After leaving Auntie and Uncle Joe's house in Kingman, Daddy headed our car for Phoenix by way of Prescott. The wartime speed limit on all highways was 45 miles per hour. After many hours on the road, as we crept along at what seemed to be a snail's pace, we could see the lights of Phoenix in the far distance. It seemed we would never get there! My mother and father would never have considered driving over the speed limit even though no one else was on the highway and the threat of highway patrol was not a factor. It was a matter of integrity.

All motels approaching Phoenix from the west were on Grand Avenue. We chose a motel that looked like one we could afford and would be clean. I do not remember the name, but the motel across from it was called the *Mayfair*. It had a clock on the front of the office with a green neon light around it. But we did not stop there because it looked a little too expensive for us.

Vel and I shared a bed, as we had always done. We climbed in, but I could not go to sleep although I was very tired. I lay for a long time wondering what the problem was—then I realized my sleeping position was not the same as it normally was before falling to sleep. I was on the wrong side of the bed! I visualized our bed in Goldroad and realized I had always slept on the right side of the bed. Vel and I switched places, and I immediately fell asleep. From that time, I have always made certain I have had the right side of the bed no matter where I have slept.

Our next stop was Tucson. The El Rey Motel was chosen for our night's stay. Mother wanted to visit Lorraine Massey, the cousin she had grown up with in Solomonsville. She now lived in Tucson. But because of the suddeness of our departure from Goldroad, Mother had not had time to contact Lorraine regarding our planned stop over in Tucson.

Although Mother had Lorraine's address, we were unable, after much searching, to find her house. We gave up trying, and when we saw a sweet shop in the area, we decided to stop for a soft drink. And as we were waiting for our order to arrive, mother recognized Lorraine sitting at a nearby table with a relative and some friends!

New Mexico, Here We Come!

Lorraine invited us to come to her home, which we did. She prepared dinner for us and for her unmarried aunt. Aunt Josie lived in California but was in Tucson on a short visit with Lorraine.

After leaving Tucson the next morning, we turned north toward Solomonsville to see Mama Bessie, Papa Guy and Dorothy. We visited a short time with them. It was November 9—Billy's eighth birthday.

Our final stop that day was Silver City, New Mexico. Knowing this was to be our new home, how out of place I felt as we drove through the tall oak trees and bear grass in the Burro Mountains—how different the terrain was from what I was used to. And living in Silver City with its paved streets and sidewalks and streetlights was going to be a real cultural shock.

We were to stay with Bill and Rosie Hicks, our friends who had left Goldroad earlier in the year. They had already settled into a home and welcomed us. The Hicks had given us their address. It was on the street directly down the hill from the college. Finding addresses in a town was not a skill any of our family had developed. Our experience had been in finding places by landmarks—large mesquite, green house with oleander in yard. Finally, after much driving, we asked a boy how to get to the address. He told us, and then we went directly to it.

We lived with the Hicks family until after Thanksgiving, which was about a month. They had a family of four and we had a family of five. We got along very well considering the cramped quarters. But all of us were getting tired of living together, and Mother was determined to get us into our own home as soon as possible—definitely by Christmas!

While Daddy was working and we were at school, Mother spent every day looking for a home to rent. All vacant, acceptable housing had been taken by the people who had come into the area earlier. Mother was very particular about where we lived and refused to live in any of the available houses she had seen. Rents had been raised to unreasonable levels due to the large influx of people into the area.

Someway Mother learned of a house located in the newer area of Silver Heights that the owners were willing to rent out for a time. Although the rent was very high, $40, Mother felt we had no other option but to pay it. We rented the house and made plans to move in.

New Mexico, Here We Come!

The house was on Yucca Drive, a block north of the Brough's and a street over from the Duriezs. The Henlines were in an apartment downtown and the Peeples were in the *Walthan Apartments* on College Avenue. The Lees from Oatman lived somewhere in Silver City, and later Lois Lee gave me piano lessons.

When the day came for us to move, Mother was so anxious she loaded our car with all we had brought in it from Goldroad, and we drove to our new home. The Creels, the owners, were still in the process of moving out, but Mother did not falter. She parked our car in the driveway, and we sat there a few hours until the Creel's left—they had told her the house would be available for us on a certain day and she was holding them to it. She was determined we would not live another day with the Hicks.

Our new neighbors were very friendly. The house next door was occupied by a divorced man, his daughter Betty, and a son. The first evening in our new home Betty invited Vel and me over for refreshments. We naturally assumed the woman in the home that night was the mother. But she was not. Much later we learned she had just been living there. At that time, this was a very unusual situation.

Although Betty was a year or two older than I and was extremely overweight, we did a few things together. One night we decided to fix dinner for her dad. We had the meal prepared when he came home and felt excited about having done this for him. But I was surprised and shocked at his reaction when he saw the meal—he was rude and unkind to Betty and did not appreciate our efforts at all. No wonder Betty was overweight.

When I asked her what had happened to the woman who had been in her home the first night we had visited, Betty confided in me. She said the woman was a woman who periodically came to stay with her dad for short periods of time. Betty hated her and the woman hated Betty. I do not know if what Betty said about this woman was true or if Betty resented her relationship with her father and just said those things.

One day we went to a small cafe not far from our home to have a piece of pie. The waitress was very rude to Betty and made snide remarks about Betty's weight and the fact she was eating pie. After we left, Betty told me the waitress was a friend of the woman who sometimes came to stay with her dad. The family who lived on the corner next to Betty had a daughter, Sandra, who was a year younger than I was, and we immediately became close friends. They were a very nice family. Sandra's brother, Harrison Schmidt Jr., "Jackie", would later become the first non-astronaut to go to the moon. He was a geologist like his father, Harrison Schmidt Sr., who was self-employed and later did some work for USSR&MCo.

211.

New Mexico, Here We Come!

They had an unfinished upstairs in their home. Sandra and I spent many hours there playing house. Their backyard sloped down to the front yard. With our skates on, we would get at the top of the slope and roll all the way down to the grass in the front yard—the grass would stop us.

Norma and Sandra Schmidt in front of Creel house on Yucca Drive

Everyday Daddy and the other USSR&MCo men living in Silver City had to make the drive to the new mine site in Vanadium. The road was narrow and curved, and required extra time each morning and evening to make the trip. This was another new experience for our family. Daddy had always walked to work in Goldroad and had eaten his lunch at home.

Another adjustment we made was with the weather. Coming from Goldroad to Silver City in November was very difficult. Our coats were lightweight. And because Daddy had to take the car to work each day and gas and tires were rationed, on numerous occasions we walked with Mother from Silver Heights to the movie theater in downtown Silver City, about a mile. We suffered from the cold until our lightweight coats could be replaced with heavier ones.

But the worst walk we had was to school each morning in the cold. It also was a mile walk. And girls were not allowed to wear long pants. But Mother did all she could do to help us. She bought knee-hi socks for Vel and me to wear. But each morning our legs froze from the top of our knee—hi socks. And our knees would be numb from the cold by the time we arrived at school.

212.

New Mexico, Here We Come!

Our very first Christmas in Silver City was spent alone—when I say *alone*, I mean Auntie and Uncle Joe, Uncle Son and Henny, Bobby Kay and Kenny Guy were not with us. And I do not remember Papa Guy, Mama Bessie and Dorothy being with us, either. We were very homesick. And had it been possible, we would have gone back to Goldroad.

The moving van that brought our furnishings from Goldroad had deposited them in a large warehouse on Bullard Street in downtown Silver City. The Creel house was completely furnished—dishes, everything, but we longed for the comforting feeling a few of our own familiar belongings would bring us. And our family made a trip to the warehouse to retrieve some of those items. All the furniture of the families from Goldroad who were living in Silver City waiting for their homes to be built at the mine, had been stacked closely together. This made it difficult for us to find and retrieve the items we wanted. However, we were able to locate a few things—one was the floor lamp Daddy had given Mother our last Christmas in Goldroad. And the few familiar items we brought home with us to the Creel house did fill the need we had living in a very different environment. Now the Creel house seemed a little more like home. And all of the other differences in our lives since our move were made a little less different when we were surrounded by a few familiar items

Living in a city after having spent five years in a mining camp was a very new experience for me. But I adjusted very well to the changes: the large school where I was surrounded by a*nglos* only (the Mexican children went to a school in a different part of town); sidewalks and paved streets; trees, grass and flowers in most of the yards; two movie theaters and several restaurants; two hotels, several gas stations; many bars; a number of retail stores; a three-story hospital, and a four-year college.

Although I played with Sandra Schmidt a lot, I also made friends with a girl in my class at school—Marilyn Hutchins. We both enjoyed horseback riding and baseball. And we rented horses at the riding stable located about a mile from my house. But just when our relationship had grown into a true friendship, school ended and it was time to make the move to the mine.

Chapter 24

The Move to the Mine

When Vel and I looked back we saw the man picking himself up off the ground!

Bullfrog Mine-Vanadium New Mexico—From right: Mill, Mine, Office (white building) Across the serpentine road, second row, first 5 houses: Leo Duriez, Paris Brough, Joe Peeples, Bill Richards, Walt Elgin. Starting lower right corner, Post Office, Munoz' store. Across the road/railroad in far left corner is the Question Mark Bar (? Bar) and Reynaldo Teran's home.

All of the houses, garages, offices, and mill had been painted Smeltingco Gray with white trim. This was a color of gray also used by USSR&MCo in their other properties. Even the station wagon that was driven from Silver City each morning to bring a few of the office workers to their jobs was painted this color. Fred Ostrom, the warehouseman under Cloyd Henline, lived in Silver City and drove the station wagon. The houses were wood siding construction, and the larger homes the supervisors lived in had hard wood floors.

The Move to the Mine

Our house had been completed before school was out, but Mother refused to change our school before it ended for the summer. And Vel was graduating from eighth grade—a very important event in her life. In fact, by this time Mother and Vel, Billy and I had grown so at home in Silver City and our life there, we were giving Daddy a hard time about moving to the new house at the Bullfrog in Vanadium.

Billy in his burro-riding days.
Uncle Joe called him the Jackass Man.
Kenny Guy with him in the front yard
of our home at the Bullfrog in Vanadium.

Norma in front yard of house at
The Bullfrom in Vavadium

In order to get our support for the move, Daddy promised he would buy a burro for us. That got our attention. I do not know how thrilled Vel was about a burro because she was entering high school in the fall. But Billy and I were *very* excited about owning our own burro.

Daddy had been told about a choice burro available for sale in Hanover, a small town a short distance up the creek from the Bullfrog. The burro belonged to the two McPherson girls who were about Billy's age. And his name was *Jack*. His coat was gray mixed with white. He had never been packed and was trained to ride with a saddle—and he could not bray. We loved him the minute we saw him.

The Move to the Mine

But all the years we owned him he never forgot his former home in the Hanover-Fierro area, and every time he got loose, he would head up that direction. We brought him home many times, but the last time he left, when Billy was too old to ride burros anymore, we did not retrieve him but let him live out his life where he wanted to be.

Uncle Son built a corral and a shed. It was located at the Bullfrog down the hill from his house two rows behind ours. We bought hay and kept Jack there. And Uncle Son had an assortment of horses. One was a black Shetland pony named *Major*. He bought him from a farmer friend of his father who lived on a farm near Solomonsville, Arizona.

Many evenings after school, Billy would hop on Jack and I on Major, and we would ride to Bayard, a mile down the canyon where we went to school and had friends. And some Saturdays we rode with a few of Billy's friends. Their burros were the standard, straight-back, untrained burros that had probably been packed and mistreated.

On one of our outings we were riding along the railroad tracks that went through Bayard. These tracks were used to haul copper ore from the huge open pit at Santa Rita to the smelter in Hurley. Santa Rita was a couple of miles up the canyon from Vanadium. And Hurley was five miles south of Bayard. But I had traded burros before we arrived in Bayard and was riding a burro belonging to one of Billy's friends. All of us were trotting along at a good pace when suddenly I found myself flying over the neck and head of this burro—he had stopped abruptly on all fours when he noticed a half-eaten orange on the ground. I was surprised. Jack would never have done this—he was too well trained.

Although Jack was trained for a saddle, and I still had the one Uncle Joe had bought for me in Kingman, I liked to ride him bareback with just a bridle—I liked the soft, warm feel of the burro beneath me rather than the hard leather saddle.

One morning not long after our move, we were on our front porch and noticed a lot of activity—which included a police car or two—at a small settlement over on the next hill. Rarely does anything exciting happen in a small place like Vanadium. There was no way we could determine what the problem was from our distance away. But we later learned that a murdered man had been found in a half-completed adobe house. To my knowledge, the murderer was never identified and the house was never completed and after many years was destroyed.

The Move to the Mine

Norma age 12 in Seventh grade

Bayard was where Billy and I attended school—me in the 7th grade and him in the 4th. It was a nice little town. Probably began as a railroad town. Rose Hall was our principal. And my 7th grade teacher was a very nice Mrs. Bloodgood. Lots of good families lived there. With the influx of workers at the Bullfrog Mine I'm certain it changed the town somewhat. A new government-built school, where Billy and I attended, and a government housing project, where the Ivan Lee family lived until their home was completed at the USSR&MCo a few years later, were two of those noticeable changes.

As my 7th grade year progressed, Norma Lea Sheppard and I became friends. She lived in Bayard. At lunchtime I would sometimes go to her home and eat my lunch with her. Our friendship lasted into our 8th grade.

On one of the nights I spent at Norma's house, a group of boys and girls were walking near the school when we met a girl who had not lived long in Bayard. She was in the 7th grade, but probably should have been in the 8th, or even possibly freshman in high school. In other words, a large, mature girl. I probably weighed between 90 to 95 pounds.

The Move to the Mine

And I didn't know her other than she had impressed me earlier at school when we had spoken briefly when she had told me her name—Julia Isabella Bonifacia Hair. I had never met anyone with three first names before. But obviously Norma Lea had had some dealings with her before. Because when our group walked up to her, Norma Lea said something to her. And then slapped her across the face! I was surprised by this.

I had just been standing there and had not said a word to Julia. But the next thing I knew I was on top of Julia Isabella Bonifacia Hair and those in the group were shouting *SHE HAS A KNIFE! GET IT FROM HER*! Which I did. I handed her small pocket knife to one of the boys in the group—I have no idea which one. And it was only then that when I realized that when she had attacked ME after Norma Lea slapped her, I had grabbed her by her hair, swung her off her feet, and jumped on top of her without any previous thought of what I was doing. And it wasn't until I let her up that I then noticed that I had a surface cut about 4-inches long on the inside of my right upper leg. Another, a 3-inch surface cut on my chest, and a small puncture wound on my left shoulder where she had first attacked me with her small pocket knife. All three cuts made scars, which I still have. And, sadly to say, the dress I was wearing was ruined. It was a dress Mother had just made for me and I had never worn before. Upon examination the next day, the dress had a hole in the left shoulder. And a hole in the front chest. But my dress must have been up when the cut was made on the inside of my upper leg.

Why she chose to attack me rather than Norma Lea, I have no idea! Maybe I looked like an easier target. My parents nor I told Rose Hall about it. Anyway someone obviously had told her because Julia Isabella Bonifacia Hair spent her recesses for a couple of weeks walking along the school yard fence. I don't remember seeing her at school much after this happened. But it was over and done with as far as I was concerned. Mrs. Betsy Wells was our 8th grade teacher and her explanation of what happened was, *she probably just scratched you with her nails.*

The road from the Bullfrog Mine in Vanadium where we lived, and Santa Rita where the movie theater was located—which we attended two to three times a week—was uphill and one curve after another. No center line. That is where I learned to drive. At age twelve. In our 1937 Nash. With brakes you had to pump in order to get them to stop you. A battery that had to be recharged occasionally by putting your foot on the clutch and revving the motor—this kept the headlights burning. Stick shift. With my mother, my sister, my brother in the car. At age thirteen New Mexico allowed you to get your driver's license—which I did. No written test. No driver's test. Through it all I never scared anyone. I never dented our car or another car.

The Move to the Mine

I never had an accident. Thank you, Mother, for having the confidence in me to allow me to do this!

Vel was attending Hurley High School. A few of her friends attended the weekly Saturday night dances held at the Bayard Lions Club. They wanted her to go and she decided to take them up on it. Although I was in the 7th grade, I felt like I should be able to go as well. I had tagged along on at least one of Vel's friends' parties while we lived in Silver City. I wanted to go badly and was trying to convince Mother I should be able to attend with Vel. Mother disappeared into the bedroom and when she came out she said she and Daddy would take us to the dance—Billy included. That was the great thing about the Lions Club dances—it was a family affair. We attended every week, and as the year progressed, our family, plus boyfriends and girlfriends who came to our house made it one big happy group attending.

In my 7th and 8th grades, jitterbug contests were held and I participated in them—and won! My best partners were Jimmy Rogers and Nat Cordell. A local rancher named Forrest Delk and his *Gully Jumper Band* usually provided the music. A mixture from *Put Your Little Foot* to *In The Mood*. Everyone danced from the youngest to the oldest, and they came from all over Grant County. There was no drinking. They might have come from drinking at some other place, but no drinking happened after arriving.

An intermission was held about 12:00 midnight where soft drinks and sandwiches were sold by the women of the club. Dancing didn't usually end until around 1:00 a.m.

Of course the war was still raging and sugar was rationed, but Mother managed to always have enough sugar to make fudge. Elmo Mitchell, one of the boys who came to our house, loved Mother's fudge more than anyone. In fact, he had his mouth full of it when he had his picture taken with me in my Rainbow Girl formal.

These boys, Elmo, his best friend Harold Cordell, many times arrived on horseback from Santa Rita where they lived. Vel and I would ride Uncle Son's horses with them. Other times Tommy Grogg and Nat Cordell would join them. And we had girlfriends at the house over the weekend, including Ann Johnson. Picnics on the Mimbres River with our family and Uncle Son and Henny and Bobby Kay and Kenny Guy would include all of these boys and girls, plus or minus a few others. Lots of fun times at our home!

The Move to the Mine

Norma, Elmo, Vel ,Tommy Grogg, *Vel on one of Uncle Son's horses*
Bobby Kay
Both pictures showing the Peeples' house

Strange things happen when you put a dried 6-foot yucca stem through the back passenger-side window of a car with a foot or two hanging out. The yucca is the New Mexico state flower. And the area where we lived was full of them. Vel and I found a nice specimen, stuck it through the back seat window and took off for home. I have no idea what we planned to do with it when we got it there. But we were just out of Bayard toodling along in our 1937 Texaco-green Nash, when we passed a small, older Mexican man walking on the 2-3 foot wide shoulder of the road. As we passed him, we heard a noise. When Vel and I looked back we saw the man picking himself up off the ground! The protruding yucca had hit him in the back of the head and knocked him down! We were horrified! We felt badly! But we just kept driving up the road a mile to our house. I have always hoped he didn't think we had deliberately knocked him down. Why didn't we go back to help the man? I don't know. We were sorry, and I guess we assumed he somehow knew we were.

The Move to the Mine

How did two Bayard 8th grade girls influence Hurley High School girls? They get their ears pierced! Auntie had holes in her ears and I had long admired and been intrigued by them. Although she no longer wore earrings and the holes had closed over, I thought it was a great idea. Even though my great-grandmother's ears were pierced and she wore small diamond stud earrings, ear piercing seemed to have passed over my grandmother's and mother's generation. But many of the Mexican mothers were still having their babies ears pierced.

I don't remember who brought up the subject of ear piercing first— Norma Lea or I, but we were in this together. It was something both of us wanted to do. But she was the one who found the Mexican woman who lived in Bayard. She lived just a short distance from the school and she would do it—and for free! Good! Because neither one of us had the money to pay the woman to do it. Norma Lea made arrangements for us to go to her house the following day after school. This was my regular night to spend at Norma Lea's so I would not need to ride the Wysong school bus home as I normally did. When I approached Mother and asked if I could have my ears pierced her answer was *No*. I went ahead anyway. That is the first time I had ever done something Mother had told me directly I couldn't do. But when I came home with looped red strings—yes, I said looped *red* strings—in my ears, surprisingly, she was not angry.

The instructions given to us by the woman were simple—put salt water on our ears several times a day and pull the strings through. Every time I did this, I would *dance* through the house. Salt water on raw flesh stings! Later as the healing progressed, the pus would be released. I attended—in a formal—my induction into the Rainbow Girls with these red strings in my ears.

How did the red strings get looped through holes in my ears—with a sewing needle threaded with red sewing thread! Just a little rub of the ear lobe between the woman's fingers, and the needle was pushed through and then the red string was pulled through and tied in a small loop. No pain, really! Just later when pulling the salted strings through the hole began.

How did we influence the girls at Hurley High? Vel attended Hurley High. She decided to have her ears pierced by the same Bayard woman. When she went to school with red strings in her ears, the girls all wanted to have their ears pierced. But, and this is important, they went to a doctor to have theirs done. Earrings were inserted immediately and the instructions were to use alcohol to heal them. There were many infected ears and trips to the doctor to have them lanced and many finally just gave up and let the holes grow back together. But a few made it through.

222.

The Move to the Mine

Norma in Rainbow Girls induction formal and red strings through her ears.
Elmo Mitchell with a piece of Mother's fudge sticking out of his mouth.
Taken against the wall of the Peeples' house next door.

Vi's Drive Inn in Bayard New Mexico—White Building on Right

223.

The Move to the Mine

Vi's Drive Inn! What a wonderful place! After a high school game or dance, Robert Neel and I, and Ann Johnson and Milton Bryant, and sometimes Bill Anderson and Bill (Hambone) Hamilton, and others, would stop by Vi's Drive Inn. Our order was always a hamburger—25 cents. And a drink—5 cents—chosen from the many flavors in the Barq's soft drink refrigerated cooler. Cheeseburgers were 30 cents—good, but too expensive. No fountain drinks. Everyone met there! It was a rocking place on Friday and Saturday nights. Jukebox with loud music piped outside and lots of people having a good time. Sometimes even the drunks from the Manhattan Bar next door would stagger down for a hamburger or two! But the police were never called for any problem while I was there. Families also ate at Vi's.

A few years later when I was working as the payroll clerk at USR&MCo, Mother took a two year lease on the drive inn—it was then owned by Polly Cross and had been enlarged and renamed Polly's Drive Inn. Before taking the lease Mother had worked days there for a couple of years. Our family moved into the three bedroom-living room-bath apartment built onto the back of the drive inn. But we still had our house at the Bullfrog in Vanadium. When the lease expired we moved back there. Daddy still worked for the company during this tine, which he would continue doing for many, many more years.

Over our high school and college years, both Vel and I worked occasionally on weekends at Polly's. Can you imagine carhopping on sloped uneven dirt and rocks? Thank goodness most people came inside.

Back then people minded their own business. Most everyone knew each other. And there were no *experts* around to tell you what and how you should live your life, or how you should raise your kids! Imagine that! How did we manage to get along without the *experts*? The speed limit was as fast as you felt it was safe for you to drive. If you wrecked your car, you had to pay to get it repaired, or drive it that way—no car insurance. No restrictions on teenage drinking. Just the consequences if a parent found out, or a wreck. And some parents didn't care if their kids drank. Mine did. And I am grateful for that. (Thank you Mother and Daddy for caring.)

You could go to a dance at Casa Loma or Chino and order a beer or a mixed drink without questions asked.

I find it incredibly interesting that people who had the freedom to make their own choices without government restrictions, and suffer the consequences for those choices, either good or bad, raised the *Greatest generation this country has ever known.*

When the USSR&MCo pulled out of Goldroad, it was with the idea that it would be reopened when the war was over and all of us would return.

224.

The Move to the Mine

But sometime after the war had ended Daddy came home from work one day and asked Mother if she would be willing to return to Goldroad. Leo Duriez had asked him, and maybe the other supervisors as well, this question. Mother thought for a minute and then replied. She told Daddy she had not wanted to leave Goldroad when we were forced to leave in 1942. And there had been a time when she had wanted to go back. But she did not want to go back now. She felt Goldroad would not be the same as it had been before we left. Many of the same people would not be there.

Nothing more was said about it. Perhaps, Leo Duriez was trying to get a feel how the men, those who would be returning to Goldroad if it reopened, felt about going back. Especially Daddy because he would be the person in charge of re-installing all of the large mine and mill equipment and keeping it working. In a letter written to me in 1974, Mrs. Duriez corroborates this statement: *We love all your family. Leo always speaks of your father and how much he helped him around the mine.*

Sometime later Daddy returned home from work saying the company had decided to take everything out of Goldroad. The decision had been made not to reopen Goldroad anytime in the near future. This was upsetting to me. Because as long as Goldroad remained as we had left it — houses, all mine and mill buildings and businesses intact, except the equipment — there was always the possibility of our returning and sliding back into our old homes and lives as before. Now there was no hope of that happening. However, at that time in my life I did not realize you can never go back.

Mining is an up and down business. The operation at Bullfrog was no exception. When Mexico forced all foreign mining companies to leave their country, the USSR&MCo pulled a large group of staff out of their property there and brought them to the Bullfrog, including the Manager. And he became sort of a co-manager with Mr. Duriez. But these added salaried staff put a heavy burden on our operation to support them. The operation faltered a little and in late 1948 or early 1949 the decision was made to curtail operations at Bullfrog for a short time and no ore was produced. However, Leo Duriez, Paris Brough, Bert Rindlisbach, Daddy, Gale Cudney, Joe Peeples, Cloyd Henline, Ivan Lee, Stearns Cook and Skip Clark were kept at the Bullfrog on salary. This was also an opportunity to rid the company of a few trouble-making union men.

But in the spring of 1950, the decision was made to reopen and resume mining operations on a much smaller scale. At this time Mr. Duriez was replaced as Manager and J.T. Lewis, Jr., one of the men from the Mexico operation, was made Manager. Mr. Duriez remained for a few months as Consultant and then retired to California to be near his children.

225.

The Move to the Mine

At this same time, my freshman year at college was nearing an end and I was hired as the Payroll Clerk for the company. And for two years I was a part of this new opening and had the opportunity of working with men I had known as family friends in Goldroad and the Bullfrog. Joe Peeples was sent to the oil operation that was opening in Midland, Texas—a new area for USSR&MCo, which later proved to be a financial disaster.

A Canadian, Mr. Smith, was transferred from the Salt Lake Office to fill the Cashier spot left open by Mr. Peeples.

A new union was formed by a group of loyal company workers who did not want to be a part of the radical CIO-Mine-Mine Union that had caused so much trouble in the county. The president of this new union was Tommy Putnam, a hoistman who had worked for the company in Goldroad but had lived in Oatman.

During my two years in the office, Mr. Duriez made several trips from his home in California, stopping in Goldroad to do token work to satisfy the demands for retaining claim on the mining property. He would always come into the office and offer to pay me for the postage I had used to send his mail to him in California. Although it was the company's stamps I used, I refused to accept his money. I told him I felt the company owed him that much for all he had done for them. That seemed to please him.

This operation under Mr. Lewis, who was a good man, limped along on a shoestring for a couple more years after I left and married. But in 1954 the operation was really shut down and the only salaried staff left on the property were Daddy and Gale Cudney. It was during this time that Daddy and Gale were responsible for the company property and made the decision to diamond drill at their Continental property up the canyon from the Bullfrog in Fierro. In this drilling, large copper ore deposits were found that brought USSR&MCo back into operation on a grand scale

The new manager for this operation was Dick Gerwells who had been on the engineering staff at the Bullfrog before the curtailment in 1948-1949, and who left the company at that time. This is the only man I know of that my father ever disliked and never got over disliking.

After the decision had been made by USSR&MCo to develop the Continental property, a mill had to be built to process the ore. Daddy had wired and installed all of the equipment when the mill at the Bullfrog Mine was built back in 1942-1943. But a contractor was hired to do this work at the new Continental mill. What reason? Daddy too old? Daddy with no degree to show? Who knows.

The Move to the Mine

Anyway, he was left totally out of the construction of this mill and remained at the Bullfrog property in Vanadium—the Continental was in Fierro a few miles up the canyon.

But when the construction of the mill was completed and the day came for the contractors to start it up—guess what? The contractors couldn't get it started! No matter what they did, it wouldn't start. They worked and made changes and worked some more—but no start. The USSR&MCo had hired all the degreed *experts* to build it. And there sat on the side of a mountain a huge expensive mill that wouldn't start. What do they do now? The only thing they could do at this point—they hold a conference. Gail Cudney was in that conference. He told them, "I know an old man down at the Bullfrog who can get this mill started—Bill Richards." Of course these men all knew Daddy. And Daddy was approached. But when he agreed to do it, this is what he told them, "I want you to get the hell out of my way! No one else will be in the mill. Only me and Richard (Burcham). I'll either start the damn thing up, or I'll blow it off the side of the hill!" Well—he didn't blow it off the side of the hill—he started it!

I don't know how long it took him and Richard to make the changes to the mill, or what the changes were, but whatever they were, they worked. Started by a man who had never had any formal schooling in electricity, no degree. Just a lifetime of experience! Gained by always doing the best job he could on everything he did.

Daddy worked for a few more years and retired. But at this time, the men he had hired fresh out of high school who had worked under him and he had trained for years, stepped into positions that were instrumental in keeping the equipment running and this operation a success. One of these men was Richard Burcham who took Daddy's position. And Daddy took a great deal of satisfaction in knowing those he had trained and taught and left behind were responsible for the successful operation of this property. With this legacy of men, Daddy's expertise, abilities and skills lived on in the company, although he was not there.

But United States Smelting, Refining and Mining Co. is no more. After the Continental operation opened, through the years the company took on several different names.

■■

The photograph shown on the next page was taken in 1948. At that time a few men not from the Goldroad operation had been added to the staff, and Walt Elgin had left the company. Those men from the Goldroad Operation are in italics.

1st Row left to right: 1. *Leo H. Duriez, Manager* 2. *J.V. Neuman, Jr. Asst to Manager* 3. *Joe B. Peeples, Cashier* 4. *Paris V. Brough, Mill Superintendent* 5. *Gale Cudney, Gen. Mine Foreman* 6. *R.T. Schultz, Safety Engineer* 7. *Skip Clark, Assistant Mine Superintendent* 8. *Bill Richards, Chief Electrician* 9. *Bert Rindlisbach, Master Mechanic*

2nd Row left to right: 1. *Ivan Lee, Chief Chemist* 2. **R.P. Gerwels, Mine Engineer** 3. **J.T. Lewis, Jr. Mine Superintendent** 4. **T.E. Harrington, Diamond Drill Foreman** 5. *Cloyd Henline, Purchasing Agent* 6. **I. Gladstone, Geologist** 7. **R.L. Luelf, Asst. diamond drill foreman** 8. **O.L. Sanders, Carpenter Foreman** 9. *Kenny Gillespie, Asst. Mill Superintendent*

Concluding Comments

As I have reflected back on the day-to-day happenings that I lived and witnessed as a young child in Goldroad, I realize how those experiences have affected the way I raised my three daughters. And it also instilled in me the values I wanted for them, as well as for my grandchildren.

Although many years have passed, I still have the desire to return to Goldroad, and I do it often. But each time I return I know it will never be the same—and that is all right—the memories are still vivid in my mind and that brings me peace and happiness.

Returning with my family various times has been a choice experience for them and for me. Sharing my life in Goldroad with them through these visits and this book, has been a source of much joy.

The legacy of Goldroad lies not in the gold they dug from the mountains, nor the springtime poppies that covered them. The real gold in Goldroad lives on still in the vivid memories of those good people who lived there.

The author Norma Jean Richards in a field of golden poppies in Goldroad

229.

Concluding Comments

The AddWest Operation in 1990s

Grease Rack at Dunton's Garage

Concluding Comments

What was left of the Walt Elgin Home

A grave in the Goldroad Cemetery

Concluding Comments

Family reunion in Goldroad—Norma with daughters: Chris, left; Lisa,center; Nancy, left with head turned and dark glasses. Also, three grandchildren—Seth, Becky and Adam. They were tasting the desert tea bush in the foreground.

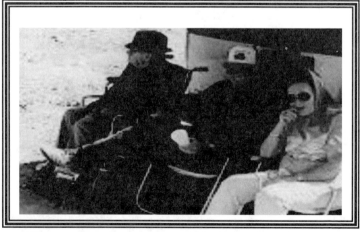

Bill Richards, Billy Richards, Lillian Richards at Goldroad

Concluding Comments

Family Reunion in Goldroad. Chris, Henny Massey telling one of her famous stories, Bill Richards, Lisa, Norma Jean

Family Reunion in Goldroad. Nancy with daughter Jessica, Becky, Larry, Bill Richards, Lillian Richards, Norma Jean, Darlene

Concluding Comments

The Onetto Spring today

Cool Springs today--- a popular must see stop

Concluding Comments

Family reunion in 2004 walking down Historic Route 66 in Oatman. Billy Richards pushing Lillian Richards in wheelchair.

Norma Jean and husband Richard in canyon north over Saddleback Mountain at the spring where she played as a child.

235.

At this writing

The Bill Richards Family:

Bill died 23 January 1992 at the age of 91 in Chandler, Arizona. Lillian died 16 February 2011 at the age of 99 in San Tan Valley, Arizona in the home of her daughter Norma Yount.

Vel and her husband Ralph Harshbarger were both teachers and live in Bayard, New Mexico. They have one daughter Michelle, three grandchildren and four great grandchildren.

Billy graduated from Arizona State University, married Carol Delancey, and retired from the U. S. Air Force as a Colonel. They live in Riverside, California and have two children Lance and Robyn and five grandchildren.

Norma married Richard Yount and has three daughters, Chris, Nancy, and Lisa, ten grandchildren and eight great grandchildren.

The Son Massey Family:

Uncle Son became a welder for Kennecott Mining Company in Hurley, New Mexico, about 10 miles from the USSR&MCO operation. He died in September 1987 in Silver City, New Mexico. His wife Henny died December 2000 in Silver City, New Mexico. They had two children Bobby and Kenny Guy still living—Bobby in Cliff, New Mexico, and Kenny Guy in Las Cruces, New Mexico.

The Leo H. Duriez Family:

Leo died in September 1976. They were living in California. Mrs. Duriez died in May 1991, also in California. Phillip, their second son, died in December 1989.

The Bill Sayer Family:

Bill died sometime in the 1970s near Tucson, Arizona. Monte died in 1972 in Arizona. John died in April 2006 at his daughter's home in Murfreesboro, Tennessee. Alice, their daughter, died 29 June 1960 in California.

The Cloyd Henline Family:

Cloyd died 15 January, 2008 in Payson, Arizona, and his wife June died in Payson in May 1998.

The Alice Plummer Family:

Alice died in Kingman, Arizona, in June 1987. Madeline married and worked in the Education field. She died in Kingman in October 2006.

At this writing

The George Marich Family:
George and Ella lived most of their married life in California where he was in the education field. They retired to Sedona, Arizona, where Ella died in March 1989. George died in Flagstaff, Arizona, in May 2008. His father, Sam, died in April 1970 in Globe, Arizona.

The Walt Elgin Family:
After leaving the USSR&MCO, he and Effie moved to Silver City, New Mexico, where he established a successful cement block company. Effie died in Silver City in December 1948. Walt died in July 1975 in California.

The Paris Valentine Brough Family:
Paris died in Arizona in September 1986. Inez died in April 1982 in Arizona. Bobby died in California in May 1970.

The Lamar Bird Family:
Lamar died in Utah in Jan 1979, and Fern died in August 1986, also in Utah. Joan is still living in Utah. Her cousin Duane Bird died in Feb 2001.

The Morris Bird Family:
Morris and Margaret retired to Green Valley, Arizona. He died in Nov 1993 in Arizona, and Margaret died in Jan 1994. Their son Terry who was born in Goldroad is now also dead.

The Gale Cudney Family:
Gale and Babe divorced after Tommy and Sharon were married. Gale remarried and retired with his wife to Silver City, New Mexico, where he died in August 1992. Tommy lives in Tucson, Arizona. I do not know about Sharon. She lives somewhere on the east coast. Babe was living with her, and I don't know if she is living.

The Bill Hicks Family:
When Bill and Rosie left the USSR&MCO, they moved back to Texas where both were born. Bill died sometime after 1981 in Texas. Rosie died in Odessa, Texas, in March 1994. Billy Dell died in October 1981 in Midland, Texas, where they were living at the time.

At this writing

Flora Onetto:
Flora died 15 November 1962 in Needles California.

Auntie and Uncle Joe:
A few years after we left Goldroad, they moved to Tucson, Arizona. Uncle Joe died at our home at the Bullfrog Mine in New Mexico in January 1948. After his death, Auntie lived in Tucson, Arizona, until shortly before her death in Silver City, New Mexico, in September 1961.

Uncle Joe and Auntie not long before he was told in April 1947 that he had inoperable pancreatic cancer. He would die at our home at the Bullfrog Mine from this cancer nine months later on 27 January 1948.